WRITER: Fred Van Lente
ARTIST: Kev Walker
COLORIST: Jean-François Beaulieu
LETTERER: VC's Rus Wooton
ASSISTANT EDITORS: Lauren Sankovitch, Lauren Henry
& Michael Horwitz
EDITOR: Bill Rosemann
SENIOR EDITOR: Ralph Macchio

COVER ARTISTS: Greg Land & Justin Ponsor and Arthur Suydam

COLLECTION EDITOR: Mark D. Beazley
ASSISTANT EDITORS: John Denning & Alex Starbuck
EDITOR, SPECIAL PROJECTS: Jennifer Grünwald
SENIOR EDITOR, SPECIAL PROJECTS: Jeff Youngquist
SENIOR VICE PRESIDENT OF SALES: David Gabriel
PRODUCTION: Jerry Kalinowski

EDITOR IN CHIEF: Joe Quesada
PUBLISHER: Dan Buckley
EXECUTIVE PRODUCER: Alan Fine

IT STARTED WITH A FLASH IN THE SKY, THE ARC OF A ROCKET RIPPING THROUGH THE HEAVENS. WHEN IT FELL BACK TO EARTH, WITH THE FOUR ASTRONAUTS INSIDE IT FOREVER CHANGED, THE ENTIRE WORLD CHANGED AS WELL...

IT IS A WORLD OF INFINITE WONDERS AND BOTTOMLESS HORRORS, A WORLD WHERE HUMANITY'S HIGHEST ASPIRATIONS AND DARKEST PASSIONS WAGE DAILY BATTLE WITH EVERY POWER IMAGINABLE.

THIS IS NO WORLD OF MARVEL ZOMBIES.

THIS IS THE MARVEL UNIVERSE.

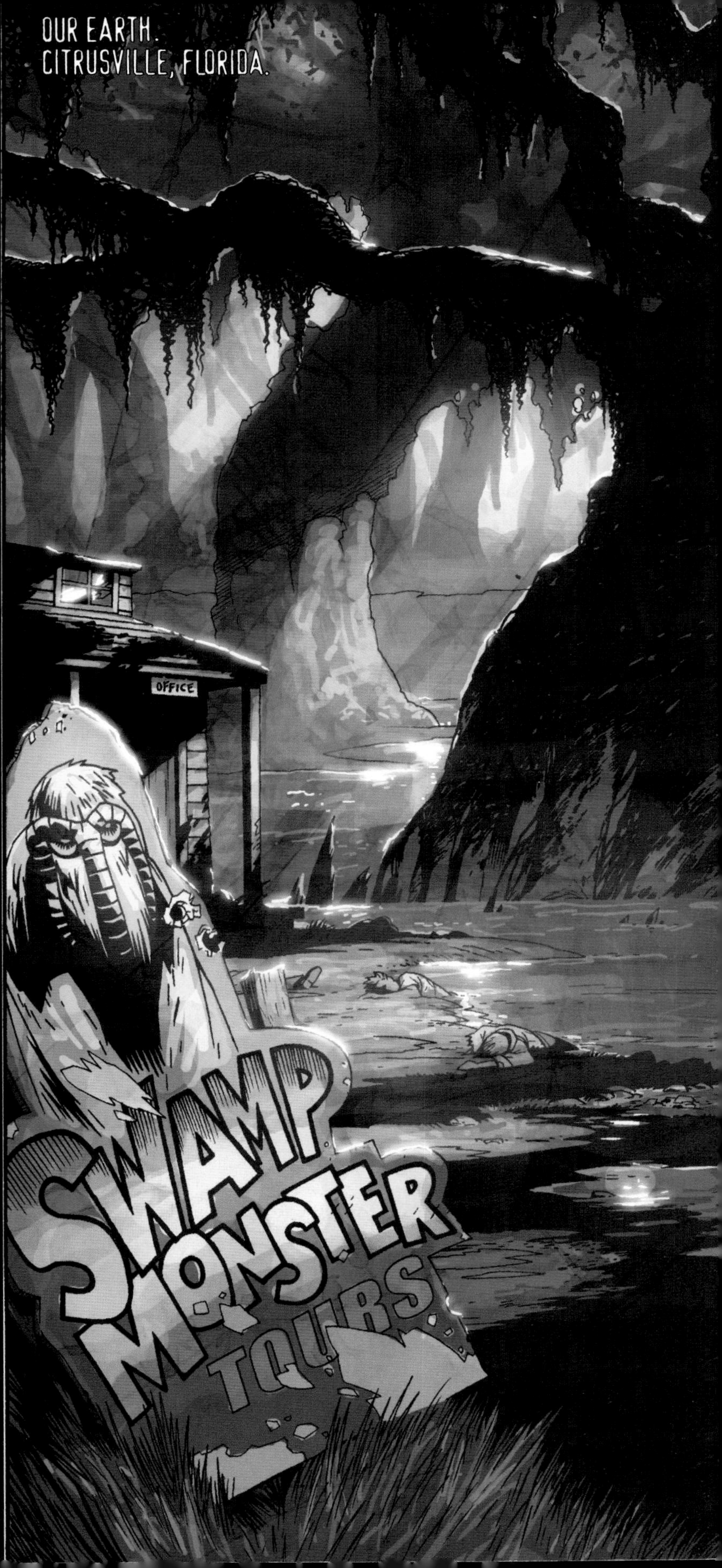
OUR EARTH.
CITRUSVILLE, FLORIDA.
OFFICE
SWAMP MONSTER TOURS

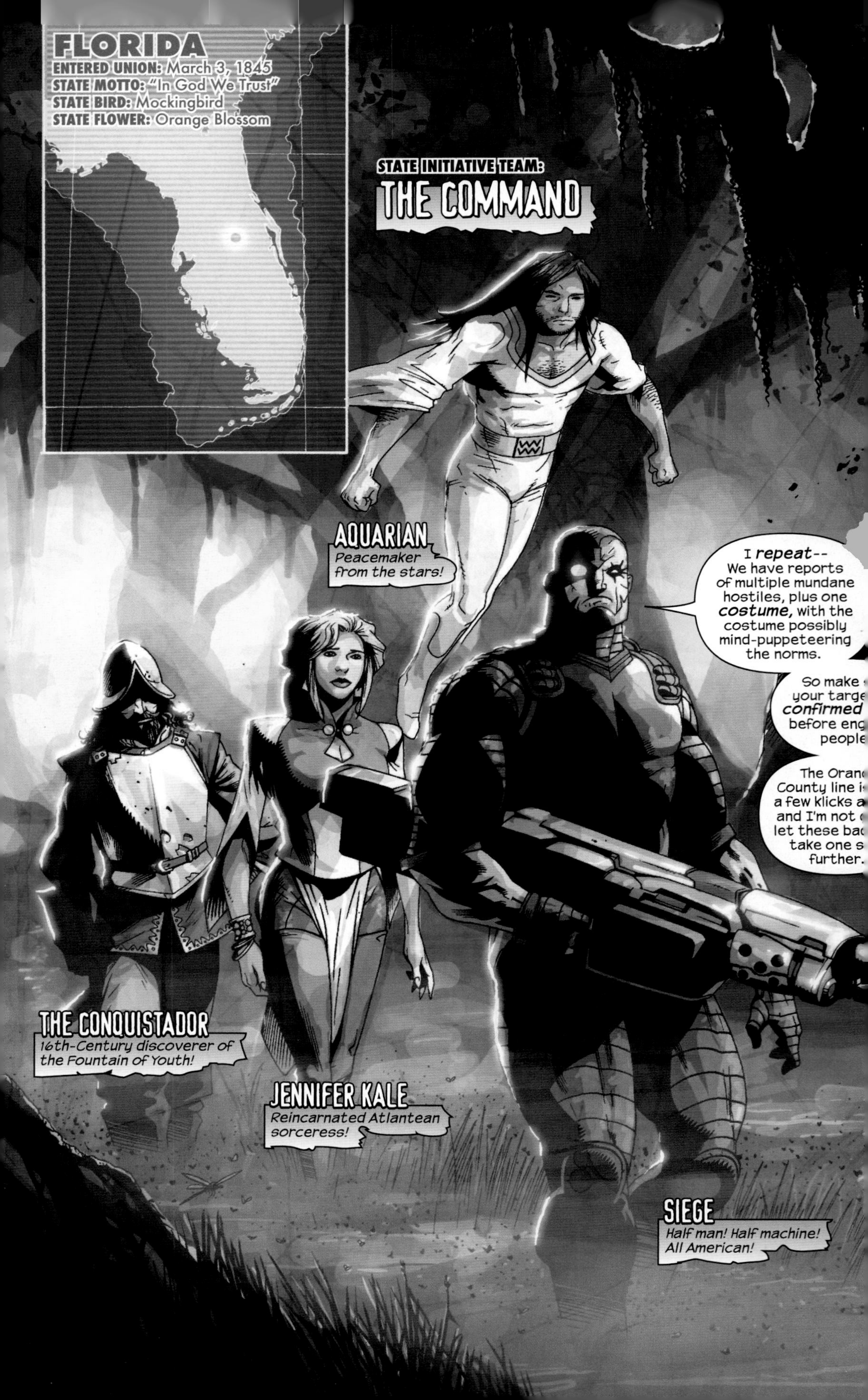

FLORIDA
ENTERED UNION: March 3, 1845
STATE MOTTO: "In God We Trust"
STATE BIRD: Mockingbird
STATE FLOWER: Orange Blossom
STATE INITIATIVE TEAM:
THE COMMAND
AQUARIAN
Peacemaker from the stars!
I repeat-- We have reports of multiple mundane hostiles, plus one costume, with the costume possibly mind-puppeteering the norms.
So make your targe confirmed before eng people
The Oran County line i a few klicks a and I'm not let these ba take one s further.
THE CONQUISTADOR
16th-Century discoverer of the Fountain of Youth!
JENNIFER KALE
Reincarnated Atlantean sorceress!
SIEGE
Half man! Half machine! All American!

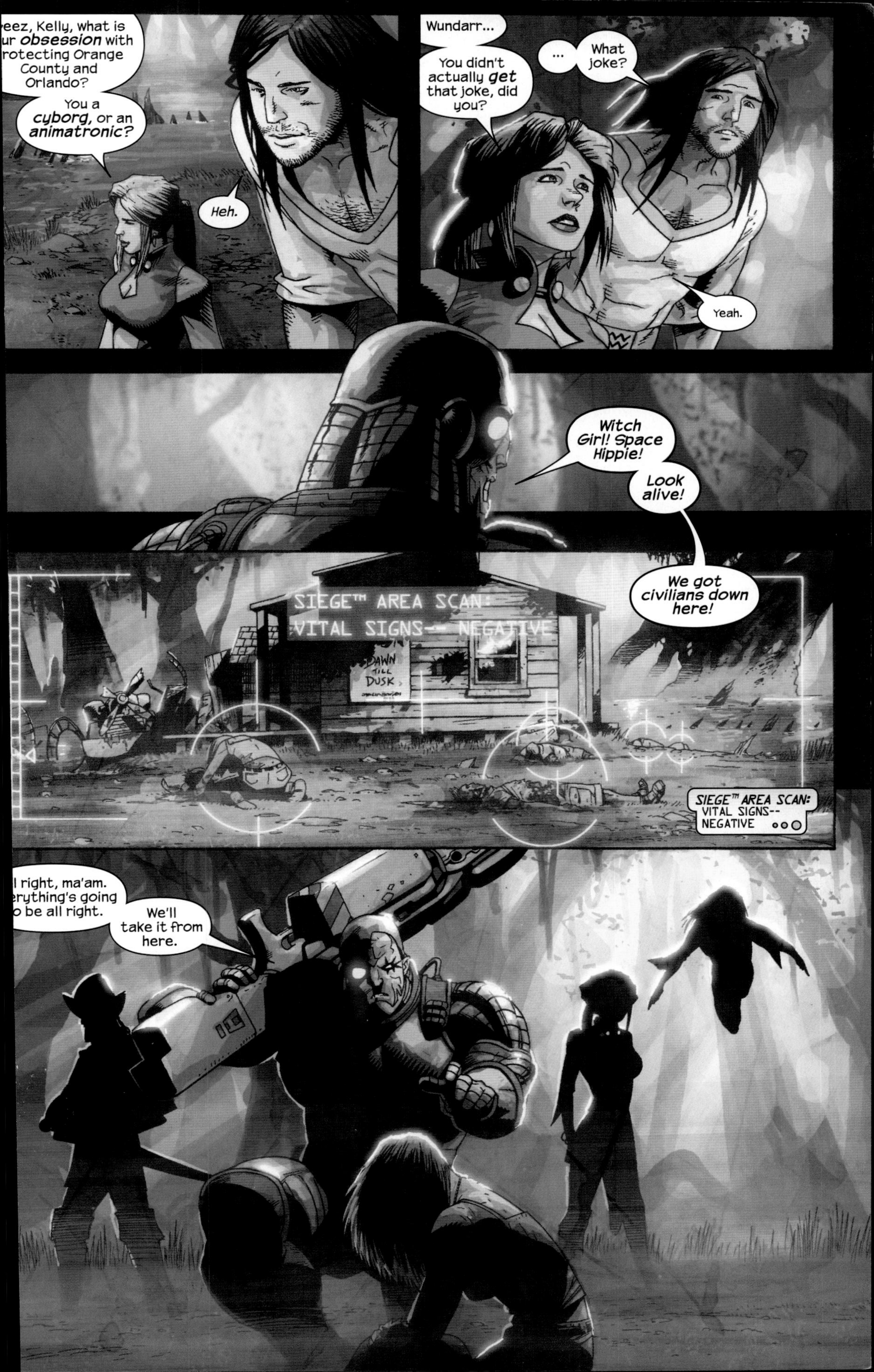
eez, Kelly, what is ur obsession with rotecting Orange County and Orlando?
You a cyborg, or an animatronic?
Heh.
Wundarr...
You didn't actually get that joke, did you?
...
What joke?
Yeah.
Witch Girl! Space Hippie!
Look alive!
We got civilians down here!
SIEGE™ AREA SCAN:
VITAL SIGNS-- NEGATIVE
DAWN TILL DUSK
SIEGE™ AREA SCAN: VITAL SIGNS-- NEGATIVE
l right, ma'am. erything's going o be all right.
We'll take it from here.

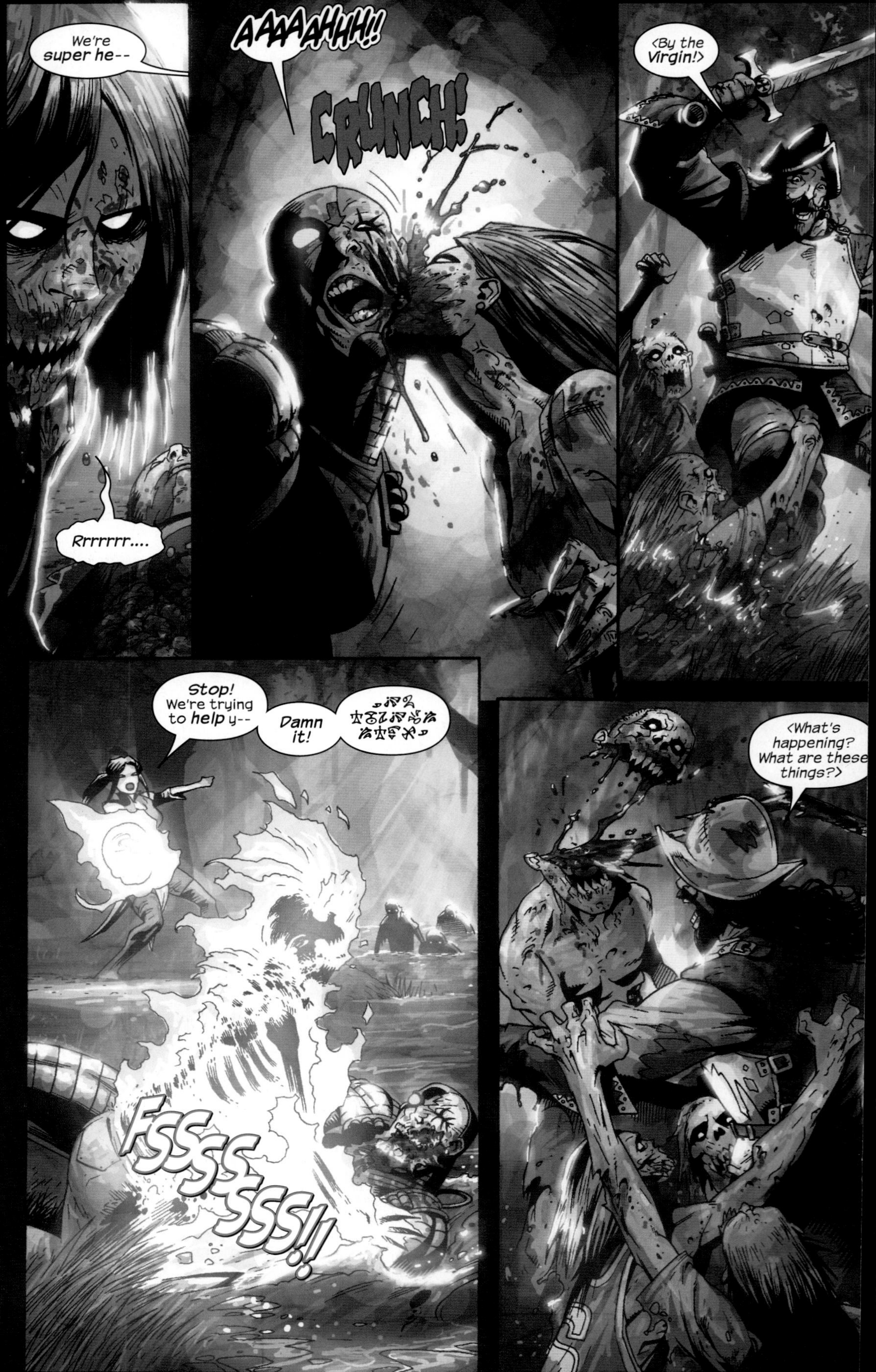
We're super he--
Rrrrrrr....
AAAAAHHH!!
CRUNCH!
<By the Virgin!>
Stop! We're trying to help y--
Damn it!
FSSSSSSS!!
<What's happening? What are these things?>

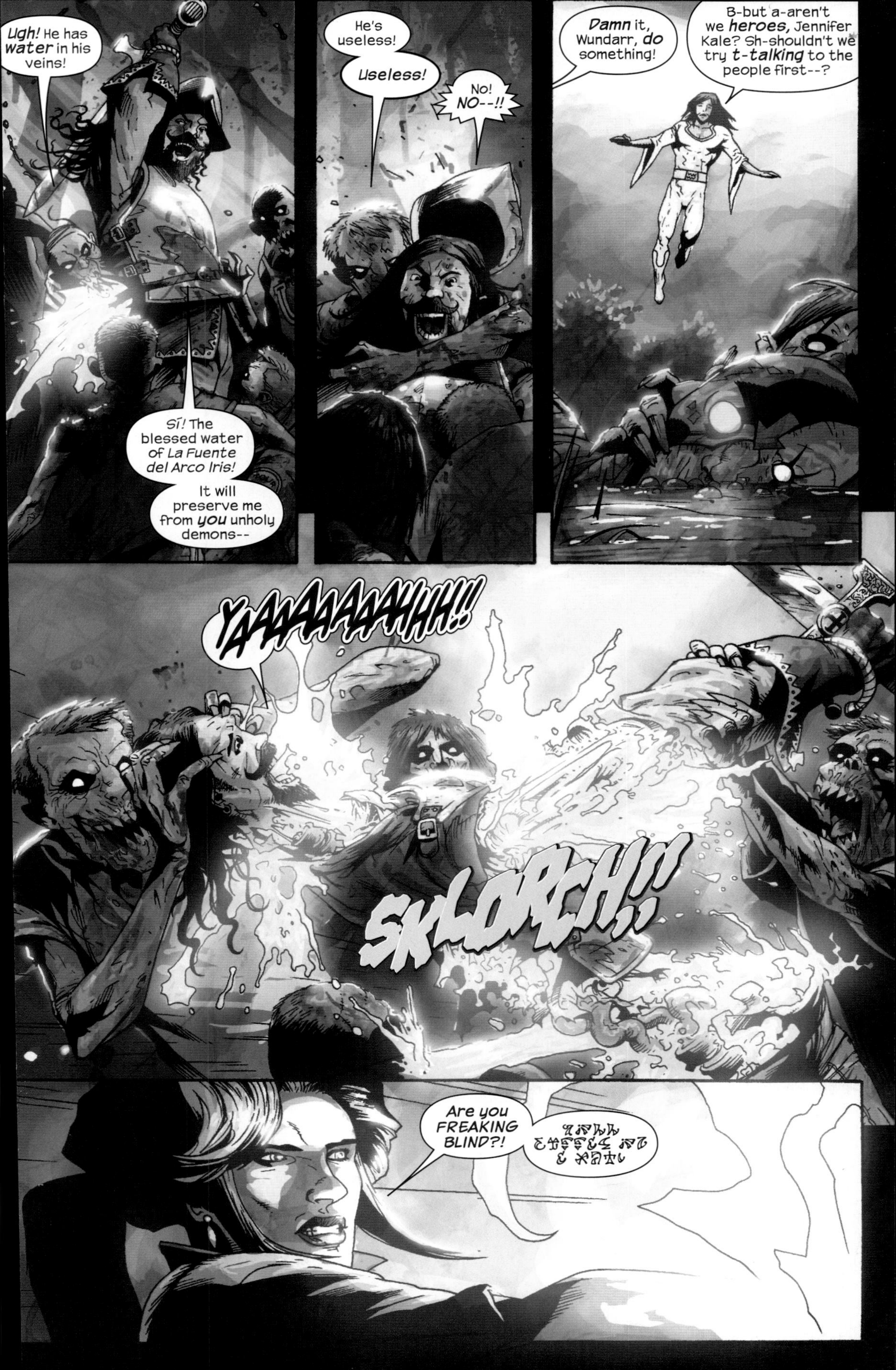

Ugh! He has water in his veins!
Sí! The blessed water of La Fuente del Arco Iris!
It will preserve me from you unholy demons--
He's useless!
Useless!
No! NO--!!
Damn it, Wundarr, do something!
B-but a-aren't we heroes, Jennifer Kale? Sh-shouldn't we try t-talking to the people first--?
YAAAAAAAAHHH!!
SKLORCH!!
Are you FREAKING BLIND?!

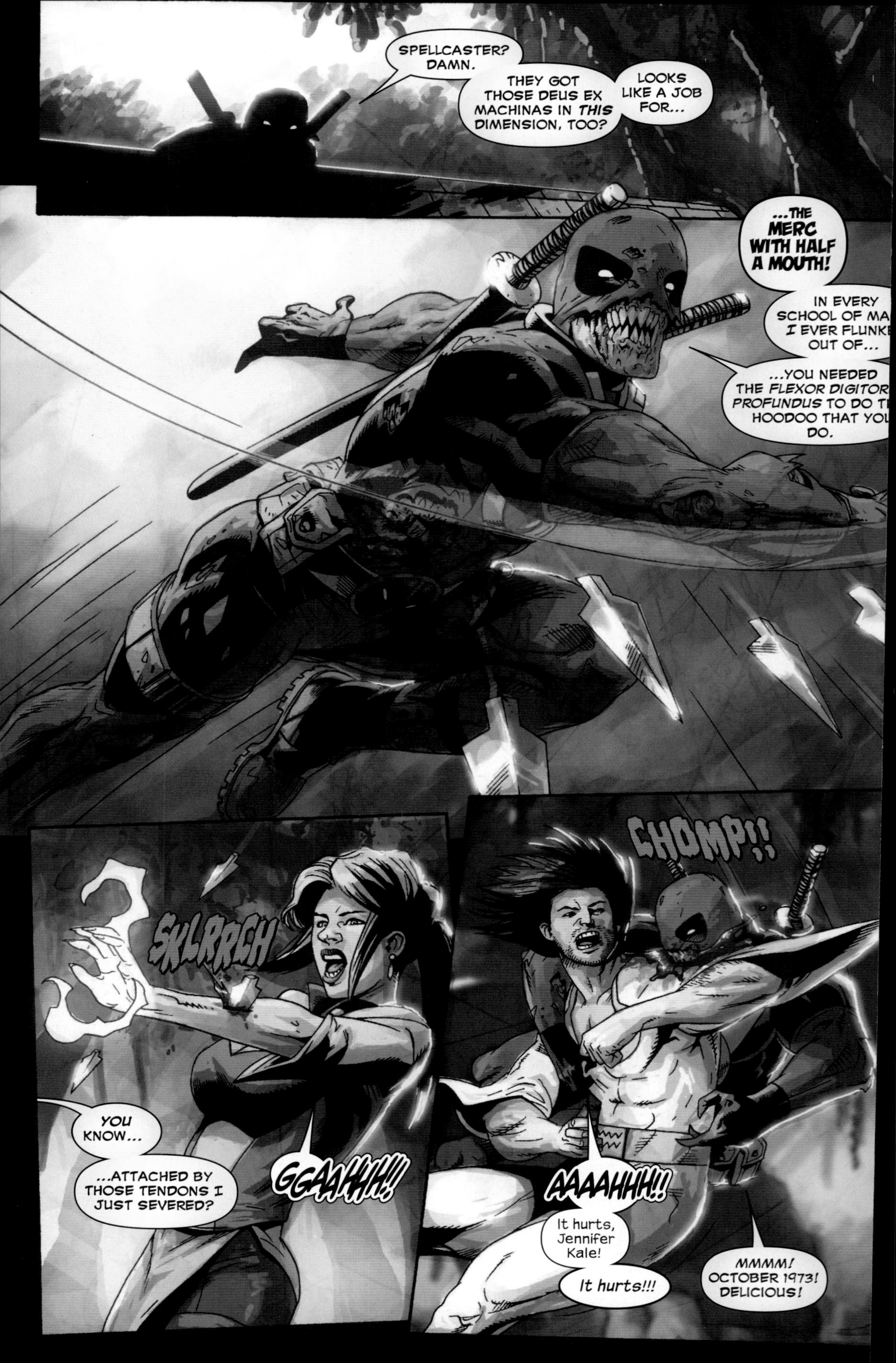

SPELLCASTER? DAMN.
THEY GOT THOSE DEUS EX MACHINAS IN *THIS* DIMENSION, TOO?
LOOKS LIKE A JOB FOR...
...THE **MERC WITH HALF A MOUTH!**
IN EVERY SCHOOL OF MA
I EVER FLUNKE
OUT OF...
...YOU NEEDED THE *FLEXOR DIGITOR*
PROFUNDUS TO DO T
HOODOO THAT YOU
DO.
SKLRRCH
YOU KNOW...
...ATTACHED BY THOSE TENDONS I JUST SEVERED?
GGAAHHH!!
CHOMP!!
AAAAHHH!!
It hurts, Jennifer Kale!
It hurts!!!
MMMM! OCTOBER 1973! DELICIOUS!

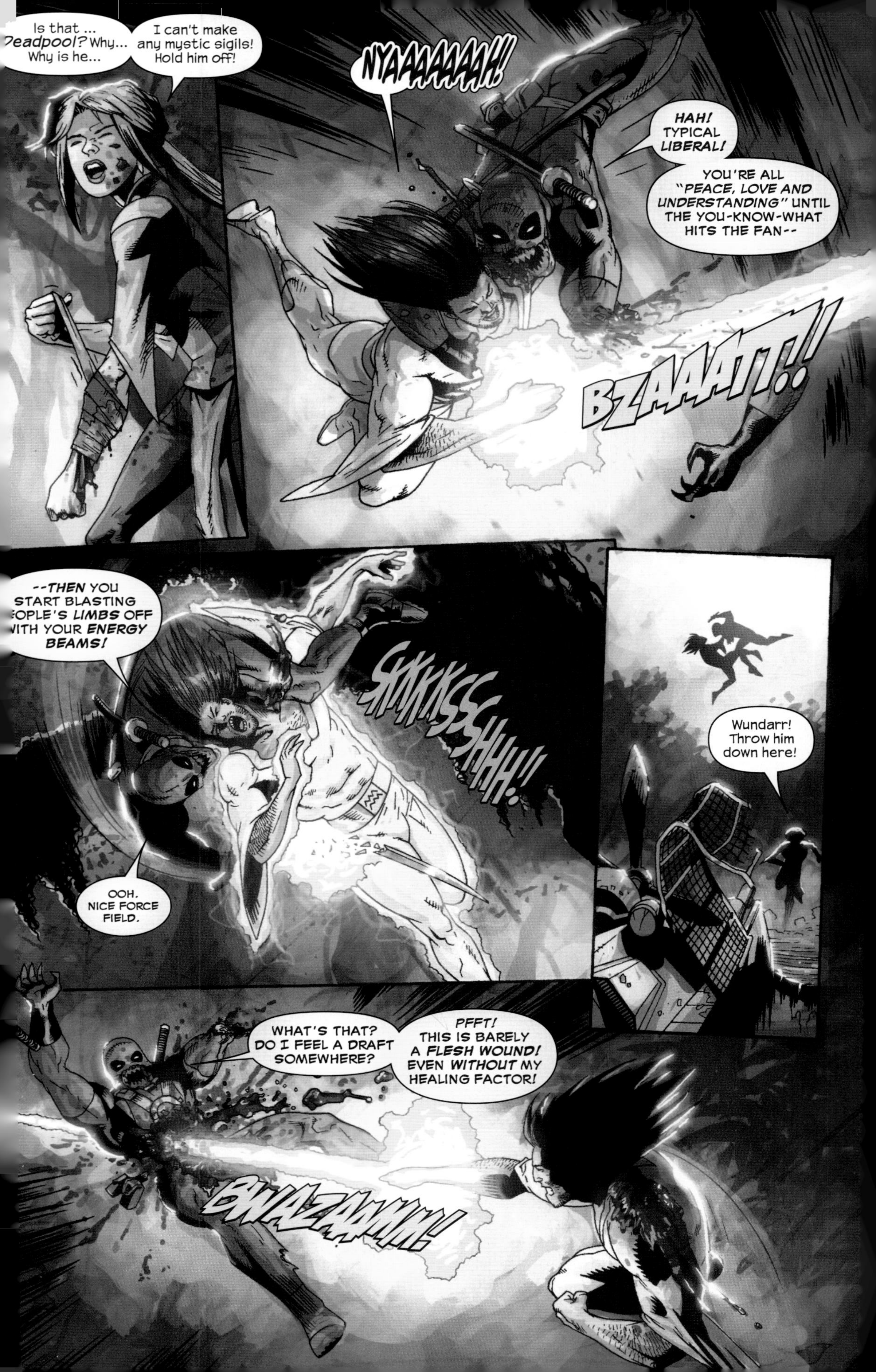
Is that ... Deadpool? Why... Why is he...
I can't make any mystic sigils! Hold him off!
NYAAAAAAH!!
HAH! TYPICAL LIBERAL!
YOU'RE ALL "PEACE, LOVE AND UNDERSTANDING" UNTIL THE YOU-KNOW-WHAT HITS THE FAN--
BZAAATT!!
--THEN YOU START BLASTING PEOPLE'S LIMBS OFF WITH YOUR ENERGY BEAMS!
SKKKSSHHH!!
OOH. NICE FORCE FIELD.
Wundarr! Throw him down here!
WHAT'S THAT? DO I FEEL A DRAFT SOMEWHERE?
PFFT! THIS IS BARELY A FLESH WOUND! EVEN WITHOUT MY HEALING FACTOR!
BWAZAMM!

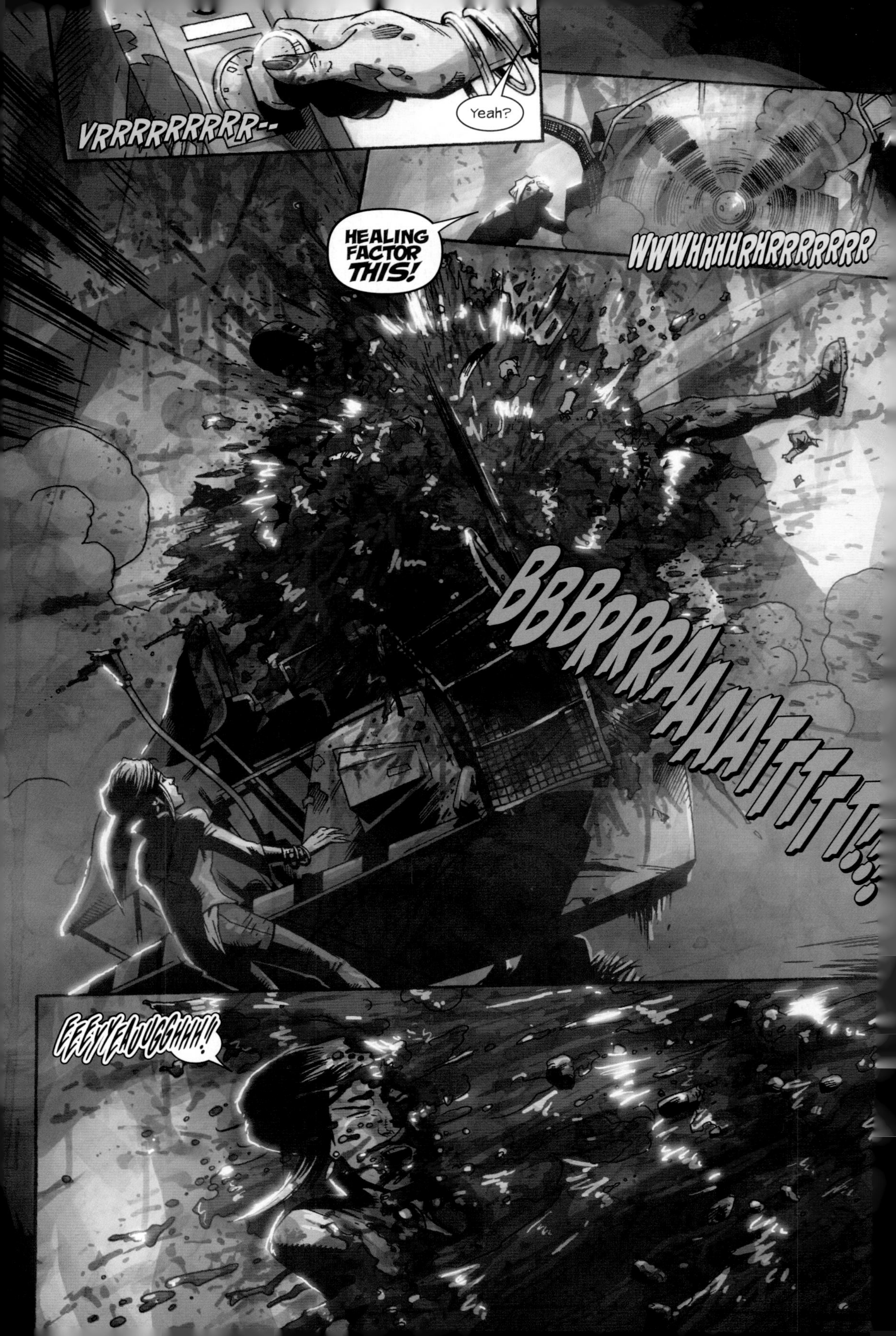
VRRRRRRRR--
Yeah?
HEALING FACTOR THIS!
WWWHHHHRHRRRRRRR
BBBRRRAAAATTTT!!...
EEEYYEAUUGGHHH!

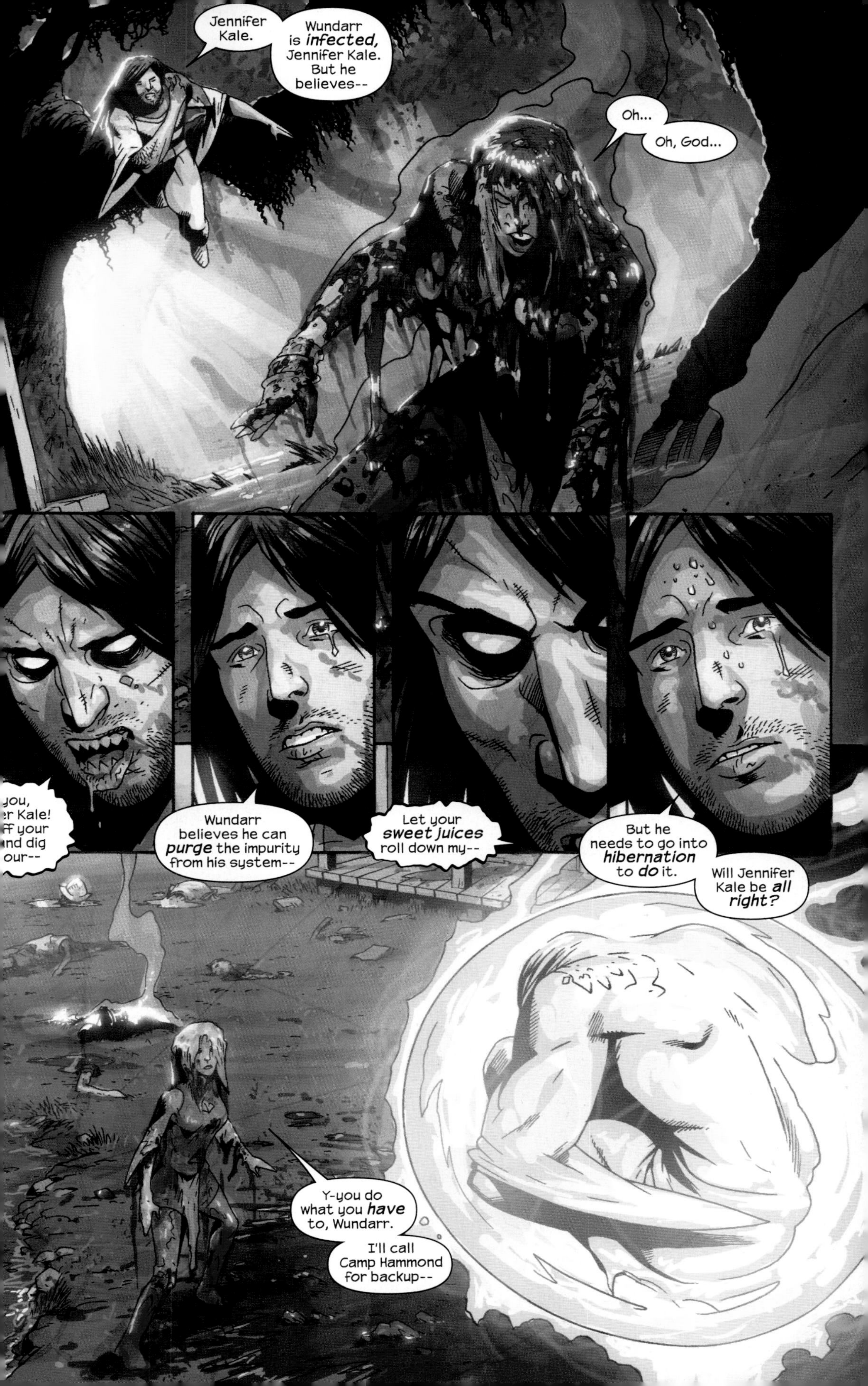
Jennifer Kale.
Wundarr is *infected,* Jennifer Kale. But he believes--
Oh...
Oh, God...
Wundarr believes he can *purge* the impurity from his system--
Let your *sweet juices* roll down my--
But he needs to go into *hibernation* to *do* it.
Will Jennifer Kale be *all right?*
Y-you do what you *have* to, Wundarr.
I'll call Camp Hammond for backup--

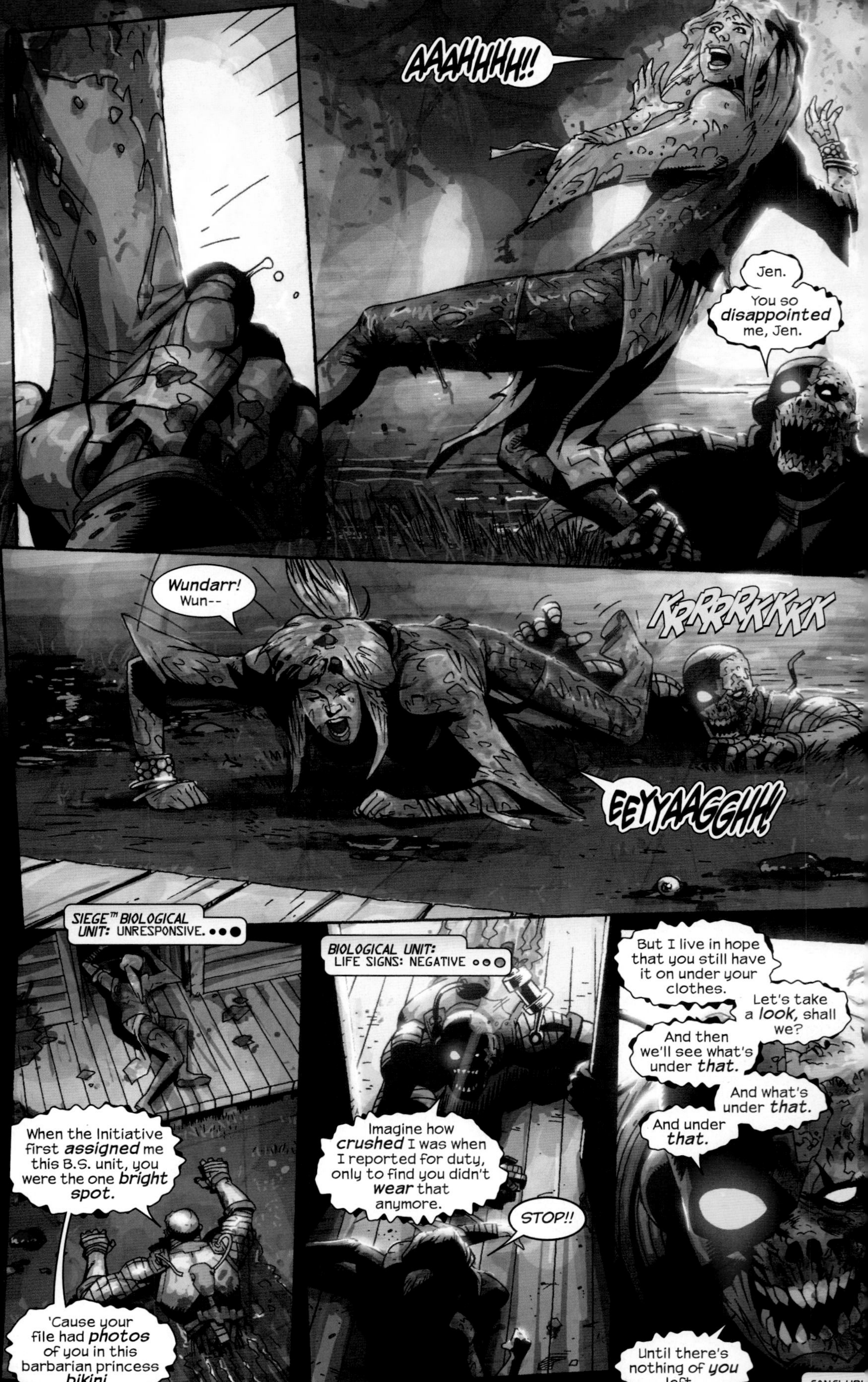
AAAHHHH!!
Jen.
You so *disappointed* me, Jen.
Wundarr! Wun--
KRRRKKKK
EEYYAAGGHH!
SIEGE™ BIOLOGICAL UNIT: UNRESPONSIVE.
When the Initiative first *assigned* me this B.S. unit, you were the one *bright spot.*
'Cause your file had *photos* of you in this barbarian princess *bikini.*
BIOLOGICAL UNIT: LIFE SIGNS: NEGATIVE
Imagine how *crushed* I was when I reported for duty, only to find you didn't *wear* that anymore.
STOP!!
But I live in hope that you still have it on under your clothes.
Let's take a *look,* shall we?
And then we'll see what's under *that.*
And what's under *that.*
And under *that.*
Until there's nothing of *you* left.
CONCLUSI

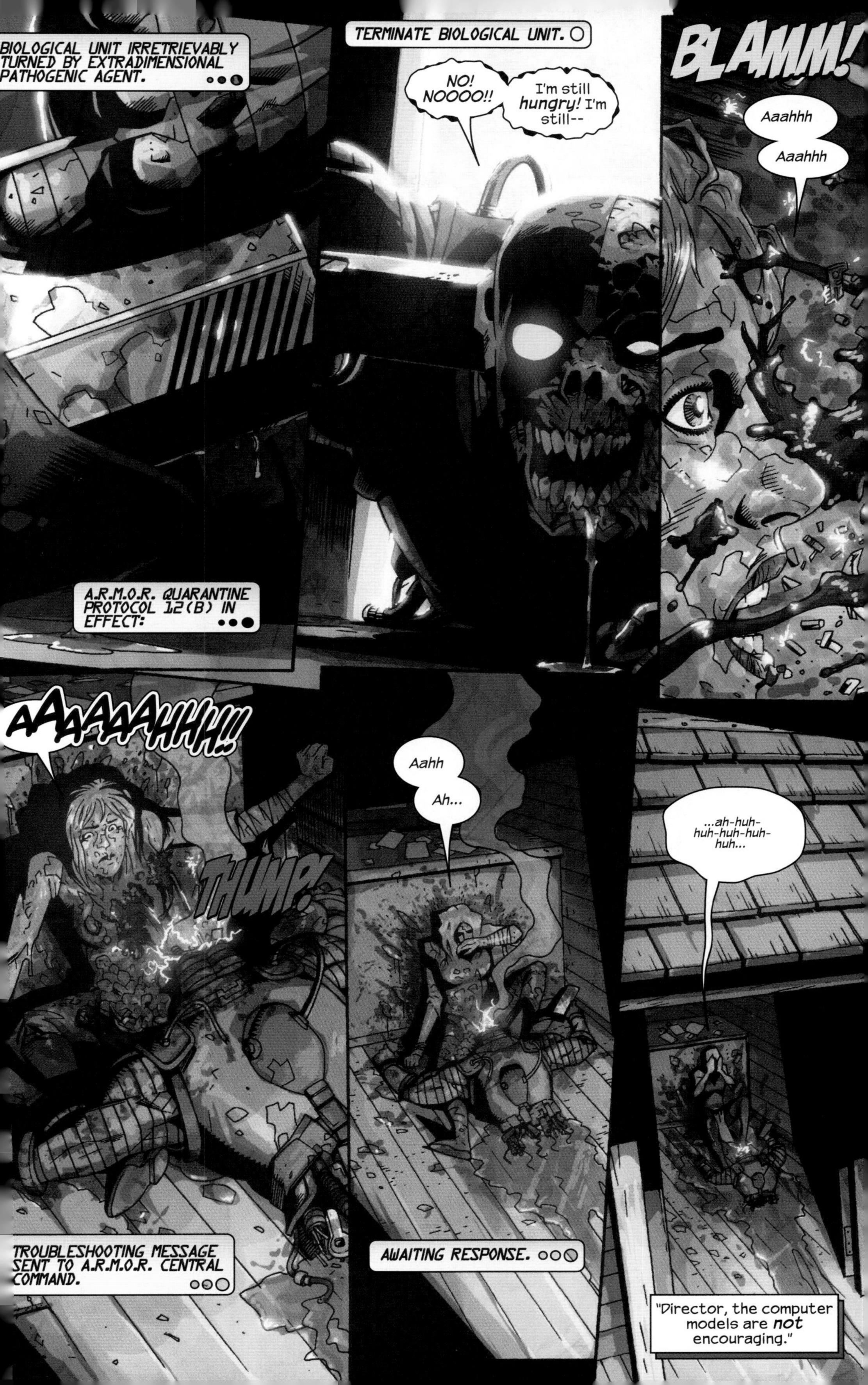
BIOLOGICAL UNIT IRRETRIEVABLY TURNED BY EXTRADIMENSIONAL PATHOGENIC AGENT.
A.R.M.O.R. QUARANTINE PROTOCOL 12(B) IN EFFECT:
TERMINATE BIOLOGICAL UNIT.
NO! NOOOO!!
I'm still hungry! I'm still--
BLAMM!
Aaahhh
Aaahhh
AAAAAAAHHH!!
THUMP!
TROUBLESHOOTING MESSAGE SENT TO A.R.M.O.R. CENTRAL COMMAND.
Aahh
Ah...
AWAITING RESPONSE.
...ah-huh-huh-huh-huh-huh...
"Director, the computer models are not encouraging."

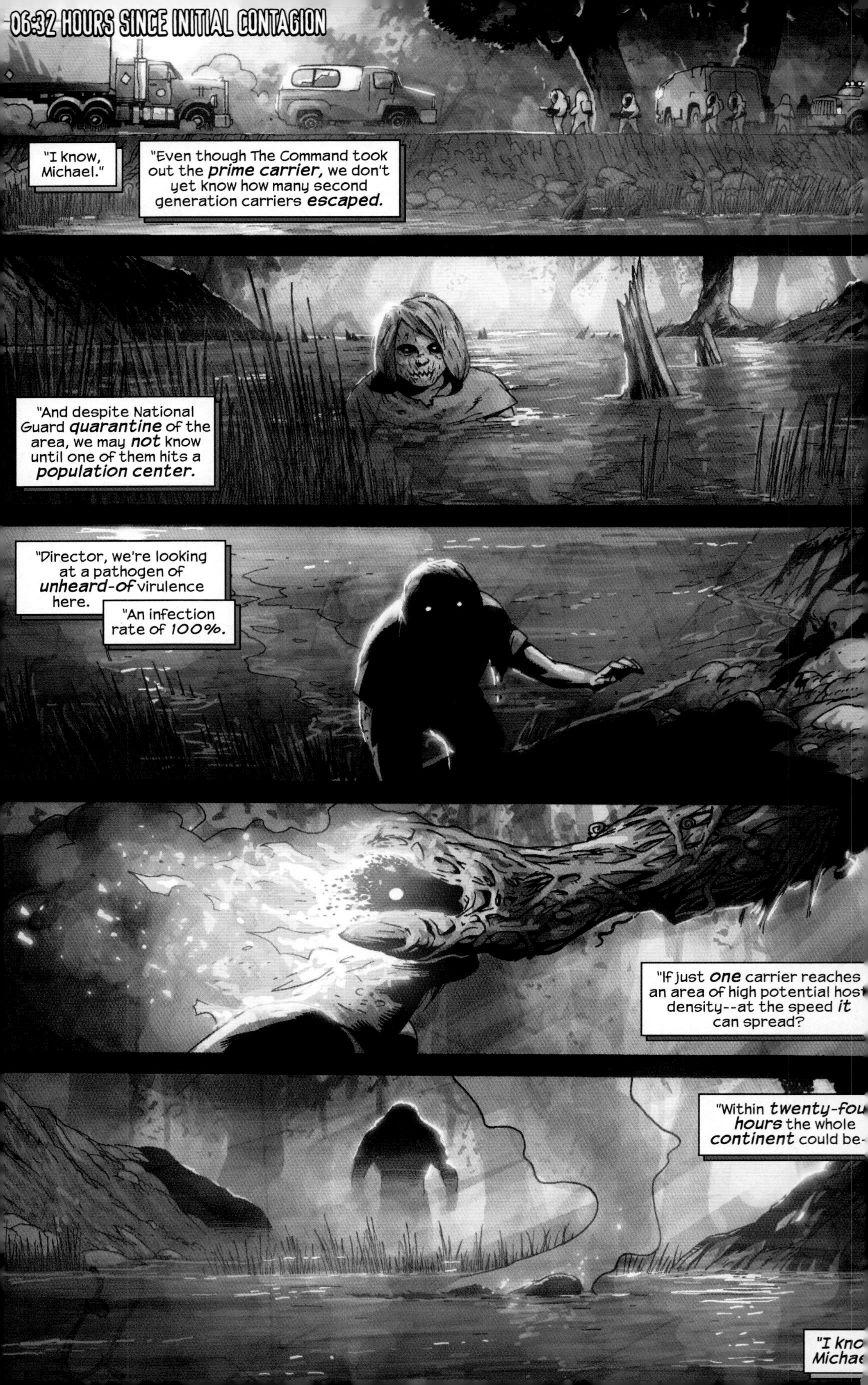
06:32 HOURS SINCE INITIAL CONTAGION
"I know, Michael."
"Even though The Command took out the *prime carrier,* we don't yet know how many second generation carriers *escaped.*
"And despite National Guard *quarantine* of the area, we may *not* know until one of them hits a *population center.*
"Director, we're looking at a pathogen of *unheard-of* virulence here.
"An infection rate of *100%.*
"If just *one* carrier reaches an area of high potential hos density--at the speed *it* can spread?
"Within *twenty-fou* *hours* the whole *continent* could be-
"*I kno* *Michae*

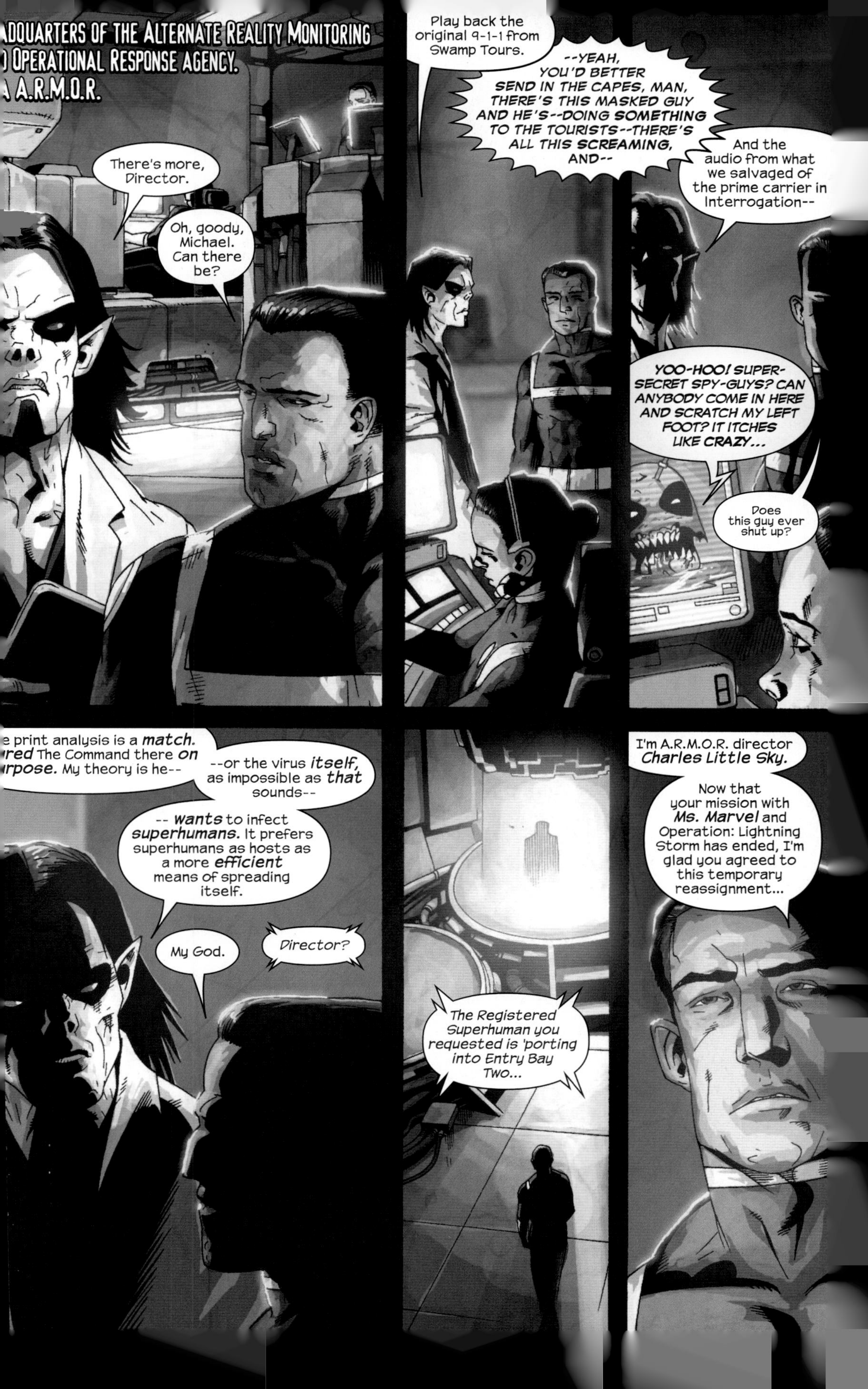

ADQUARTERS OF THE ALTERNATE REALITY MONITORING
D OPERATIONAL RESPONSE AGENCY.
A A.R.M.O.R.
There's more, Director.
Oh, goody, Michael. Can there be?
Play back the original 9-1-1 from Swamp Tours.
--YEAH, YOU'D BETTER SEND IN THE CAPES, MAN, THERE'S THIS MASKED GUY AND HE'S--DOING SOMETHING TO THE TOURISTS--THERE'S ALL THIS SCREAMING, AND--
And the audio from what we salvaged of the prime carrier in Interrogation--
YOO-HOO! SUPER-SECRET SPY-GUYS? CAN ANYBODY COME IN HERE AND SCRATCH MY LEFT FOOT? IT ITCHES LIKE CRAZY...
Does this guy ever shut up?
e print analysis is a match.
red The Command there on
rpose. My theory is he--
--or the virus itself, as impossible as that sounds--
-- wants to infect superhumans. It prefers superhumans as hosts as a more efficient means of spreading itself.
My God.
Director?
The Registered Superhuman you requested is 'porting into Entry Bay Two...
I'm A.R.M.O.R. director Charles Little Sky.
Now that your mission with Ms. Marvel and Operation: Lightning Storm has ended, I'm glad you agreed to this temporary reassignment...

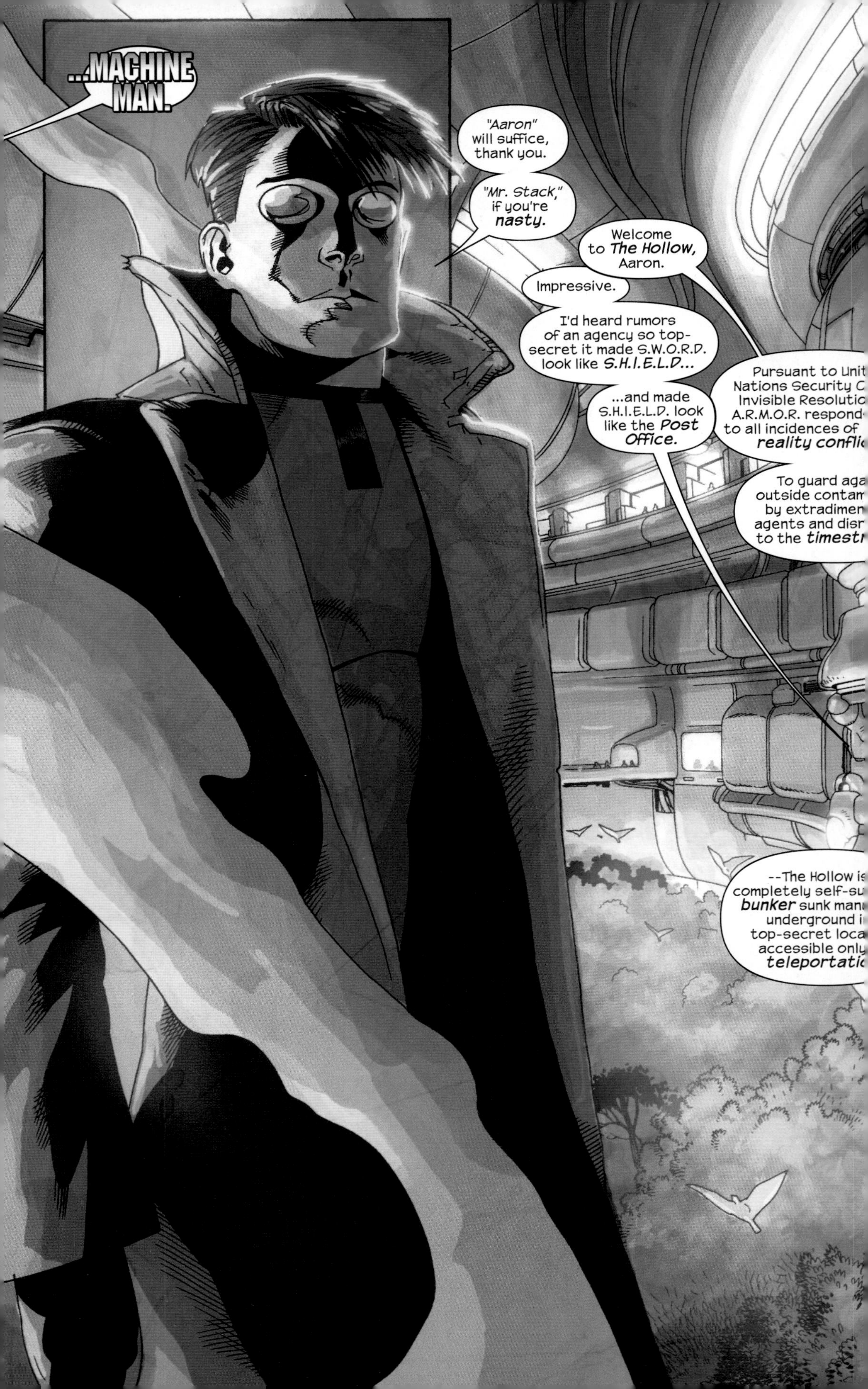
...MACHINE MAN.
"Aaron" will suffice, thank you.
"Mr. Stack," if you're nasty.
Welcome to The Hollow, Aaron.
Impressive.
I'd heard rumors of an agency so top-secret it made S.W.O.R.D. look like S.H.I.E.L.D...
...and made S.H.I.E.L.D. look like the Post Office.
Pursuant to Unit Nations Security Invisible Resolutio A.R.M.O.R. respond to all incidences of reality confli
To guard aga outside contam by extradimen agents and disr to the timestr
--The Hollow is completely self-su bunker sunk man underground i top-secret loca accessible only teleportati

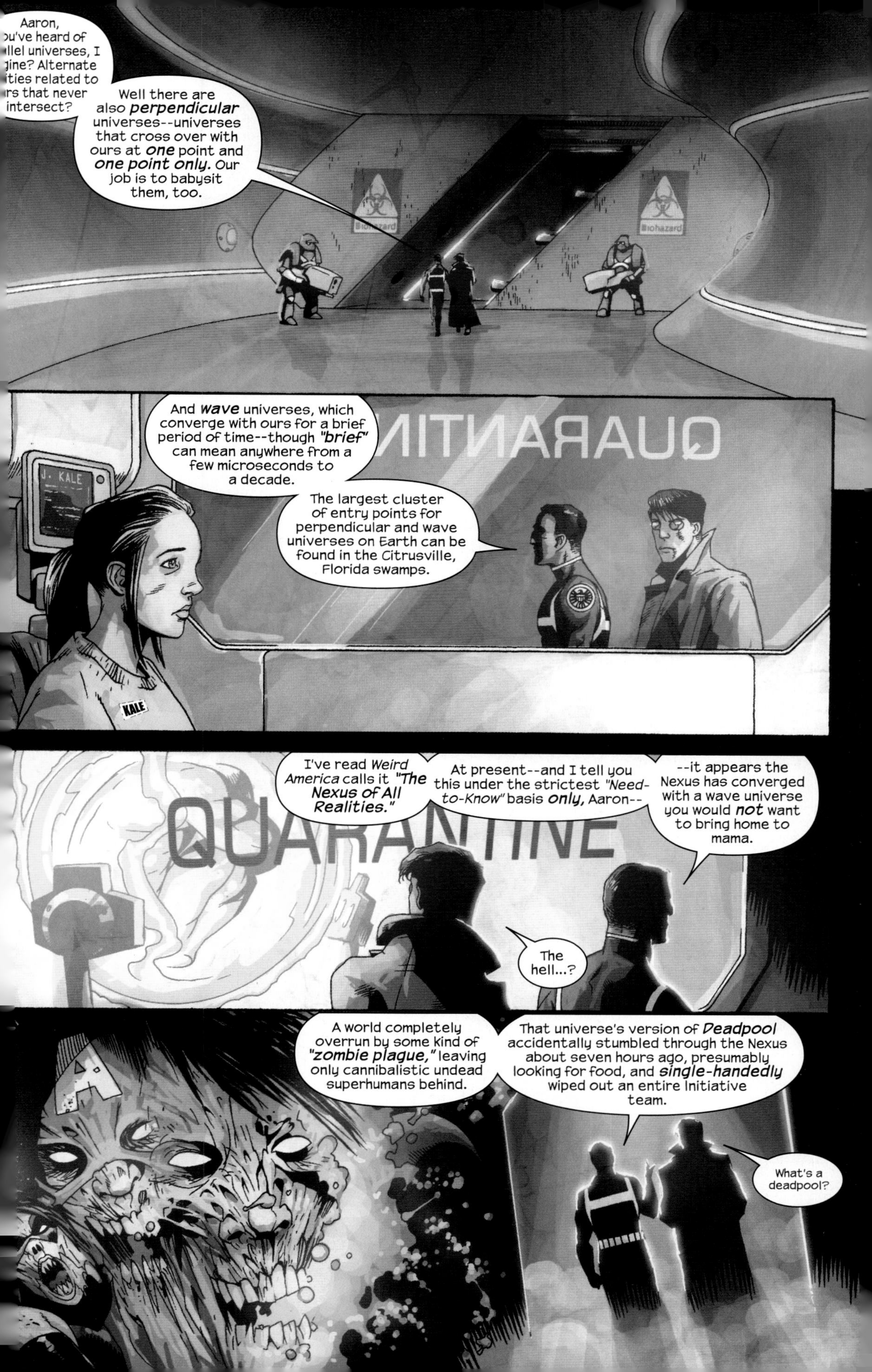

Aaron, ɔu've heard of ıllel universes, I gine? Alternate ities related to rs that never intersect?
Well there are also **perpendicular** universes--universes that cross over with ours at **one** point and **one point only.** Our job is to babysit them, too.
Biohazard
Biohazard
And **wave** universes, which converge with ours for a brief period of time--though *"brief"* can mean anywhere from a few microseconds to a decade.
QUARANTIN
J. KALE
The largest cluster of entry points for perpendicular and wave universes on Earth can be found in the Citrusville, Florida swamps.
KALE
I've read *Weird America* calls it ***"The Nexus of All Realities."***
At present--and I tell you this under the strictest *"Need-to-Know"* basis **only,** Aaron--
--it appears the Nexus has converged with a wave universe you would **not** want to bring home to mama.
QUARANTINE
The hell...?
A world completely overrun by some kind of ***"zombie plague,"*** leaving only cannibalistic undead superhumans behind.
That universe's version of ***Deadpool*** accidentally stumbled through the Nexus about seven hours ago, presumably looking for food, and ***single-handedly*** wiped out an entire Initiative team.
What's a deadpool?

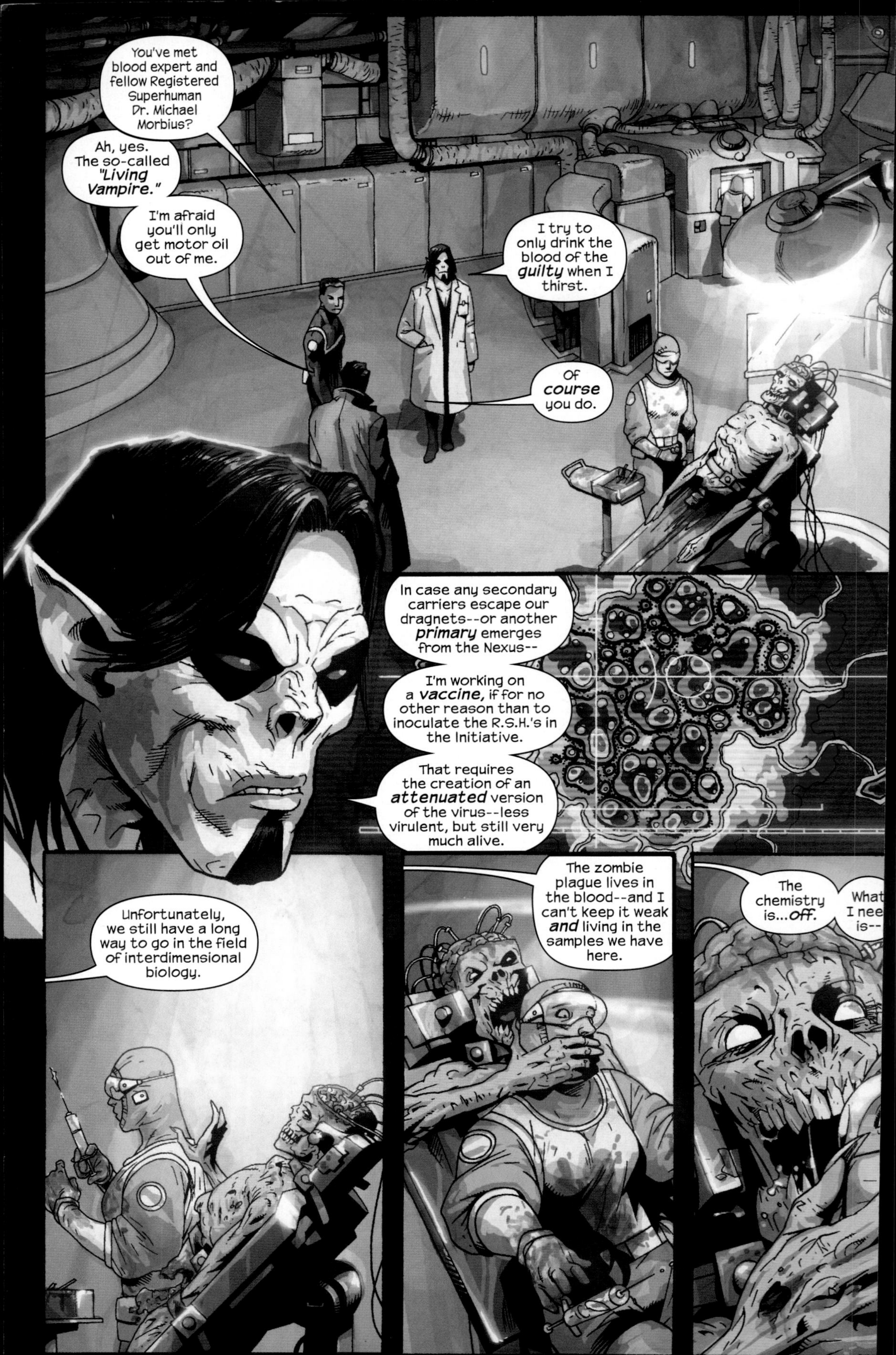

You've met blood expert and fellow Registered Superhuman Dr. Michael Morbius?
Ah, yes. The so-called "Living Vampire."
I'm afraid you'll only get motor oil out of me.
I try to only drink the blood of the guilty when I thirst.
Of course you do.
In case any secondary carriers escape our dragnets--or another primary emerges from the Nexus--
I'm working on a vaccine, if for no other reason than to inoculate the R.S.H.'s in the Initiative.
That requires the creation of an attenuated version of the virus--less virulent, but still very much alive.
Unfortunately, we still have a long way to go in the field of interdimensional biology.
The zombie plague lives in the blood--and I can't keep it weak and living in the samples we have here.
The chemistry is...off.

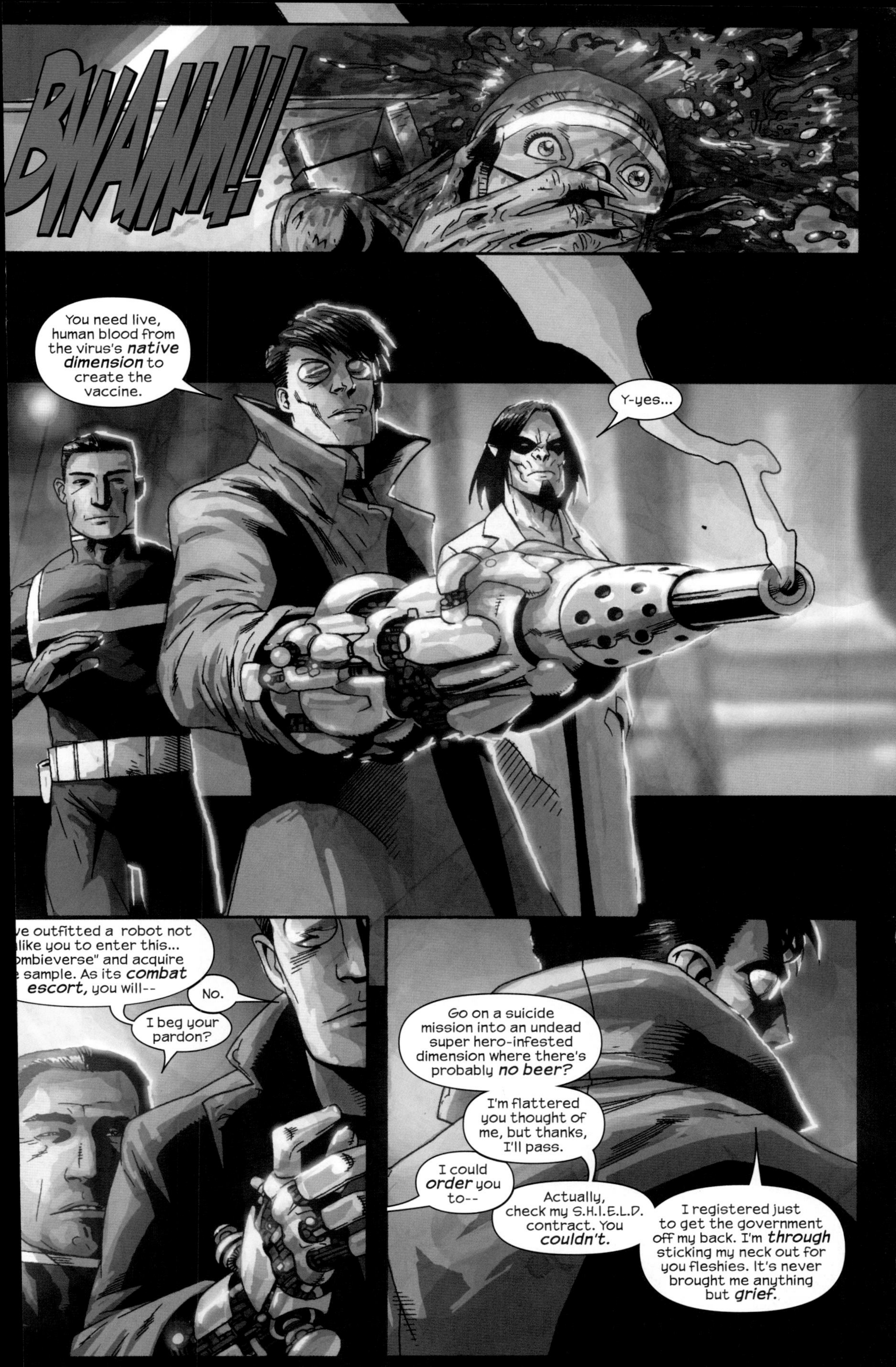
BWAMM!!
You need live, human blood from the virus's *native dimension* to create the vaccine.
Y-yes...
ve outfitted a robot not like you to enter this... ombieverse" and acquire sample. As its *combat escort,* you will--
No.
I beg your pardon?
Go on a suicide mission into an undead super hero-infested dimension where there's probably *no beer?*
I'm flattered you thought of me, but thanks, I'll pass.
I could *order* you to--
Actually, check my S.H.I.E.L.D. contract. You *couldn't.*
I registered just to get the government off my back. I'm *through* sticking my neck out for you fleshies. It's never brought me anything but *grief.*

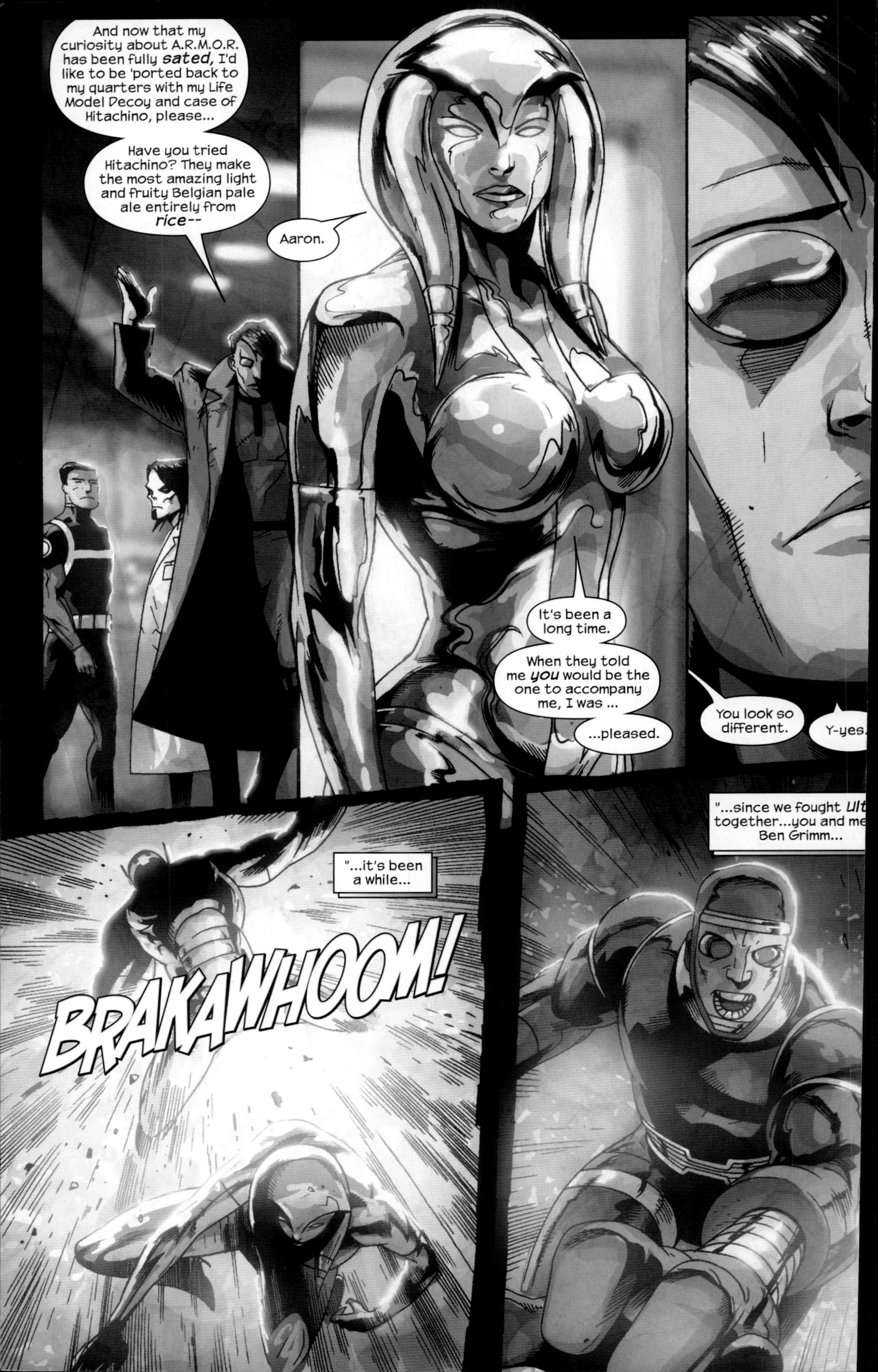
And now that my curiosity about A.R.M.O.R. has been fully *sated,* I'd like to be 'ported back to my quarters with my Life Model Decoy and case of Hitachino, please...
Have you tried Hitachino? They make the most amazing light and fruity Belgian pale ale entirely from *rice*--
Aaron.
It's been a long time.
When they told me *you* would be the one to accompany me, I was ...
...pleased.
You look so different.
Y-yes.
"...it's been a while...
BRAKAWHOOM!
"...since we fought *Ult*
together...you and me
Ben Grimm...

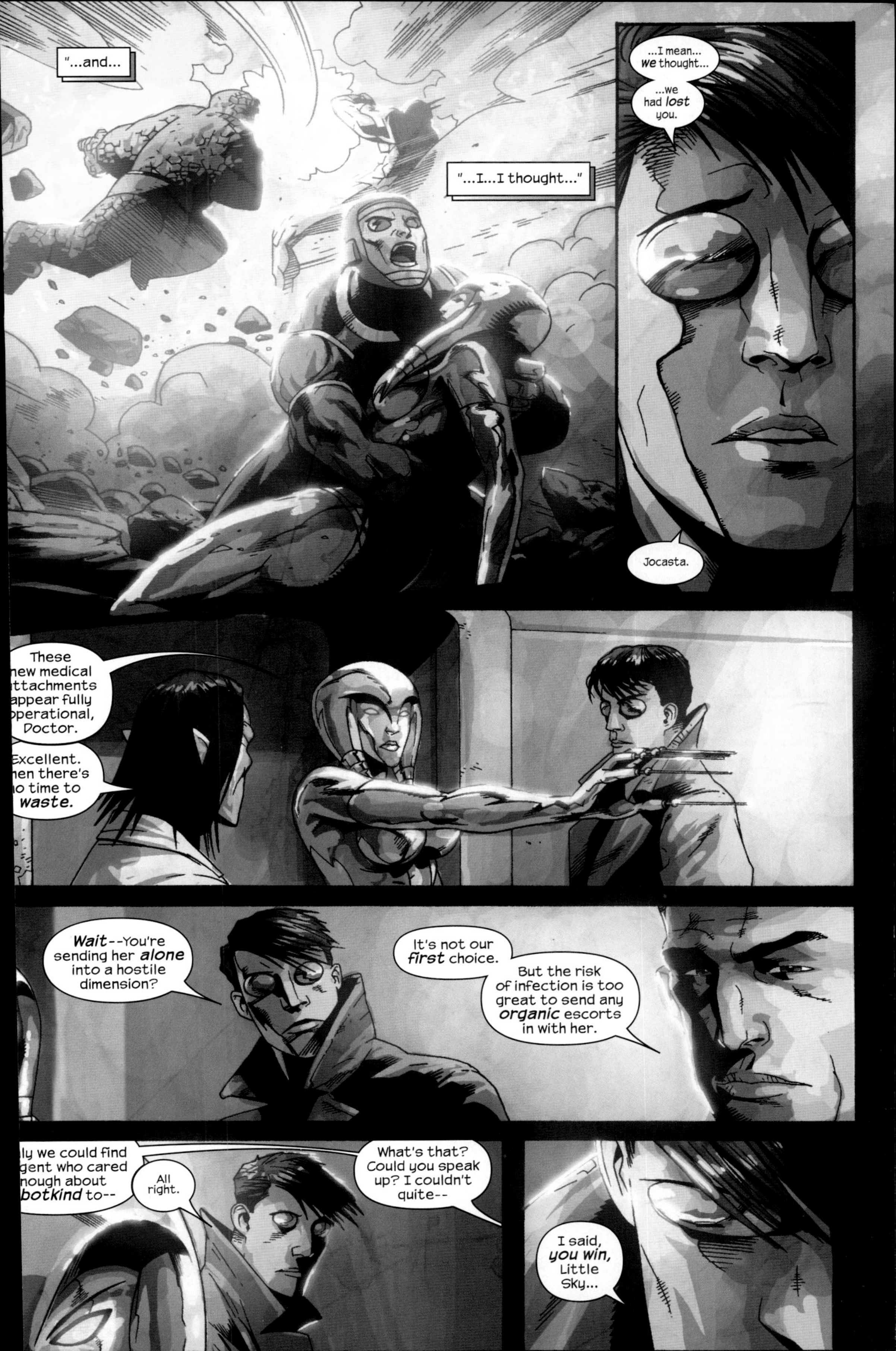
"...and...
"...I...I thought..."
...I mean... we thought...
...we had lost you.
Jocasta.
These new medical attachments appear fully operational, Doctor.
Excellent. Then there's no time to waste.
Wait--You're sending her alone into a hostile dimension?
It's not our first choice.
But the risk of infection is too great to send any organic escorts in with her.
ly we could find gent who cared nough about botkind to--
All right.
What's that? Could you speak up? I couldn't quite--
I said, you win, Little Sky...

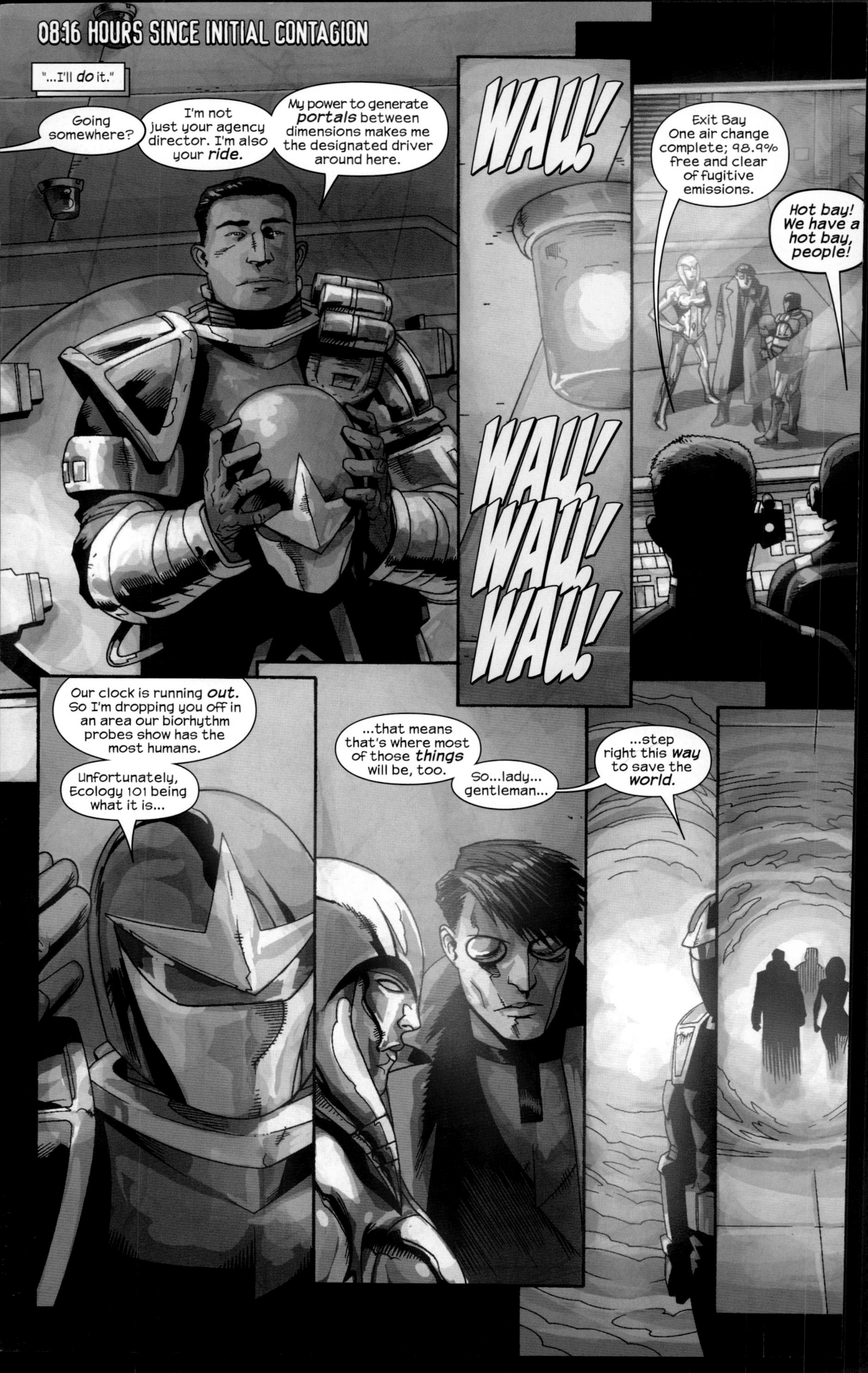
08:16 HOURS SINCE INITIAL CONTAGION
"...I'll do it."
Going somewhere?
I'm not just your agency director. I'm also your ride.
My power to generate portals between dimensions makes me the designated driver around here.
WAU!
WAU! WAU! WAU!
Exit Bay One air change complete; 98.9% free and clear of fugitive emissions.
Hot bay! We have a hot bay, people!
Our clock is running out. So I'm dropping you off in an area our biorhythm probes show has the most humans.
Unfortunately, Ecology 101 being what it is...
...that means that's where most of those things will be, too.
So...lady... gentleman...
...step right this way to save the world.

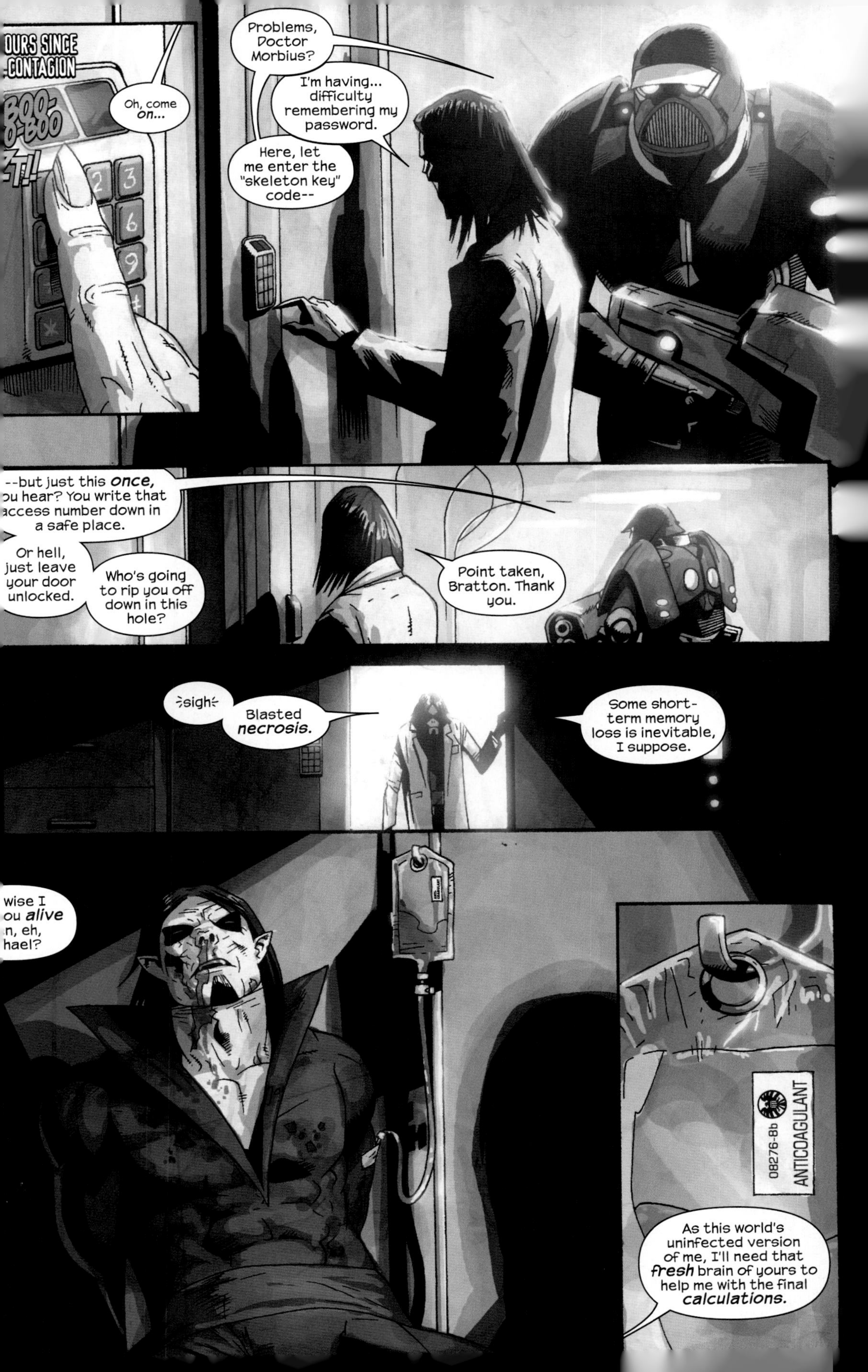
OURS SINCE CONTAGION
BOO-O-BOO
ZT!!
Oh, come on...
Problems, Doctor Morbius?
I'm having... difficulty remembering my password.
Here, let me enter the "skeleton key" code--
--but just this once, ou hear? You write that access number down in a safe place.
Or hell, just leave your door unlocked.
Who's going to rip you off down in this hole?
Point taken, Bratton. Thank you.
sigh
Blasted necrosis.
Some short-term memory loss is inevitable, I suppose.
wise I ou alive n, eh, hael?
08276-8b
ANTICOAGULANT
As this world's uninfected version of me, I'll need that fresh brain of yours to help me with the final calculations.

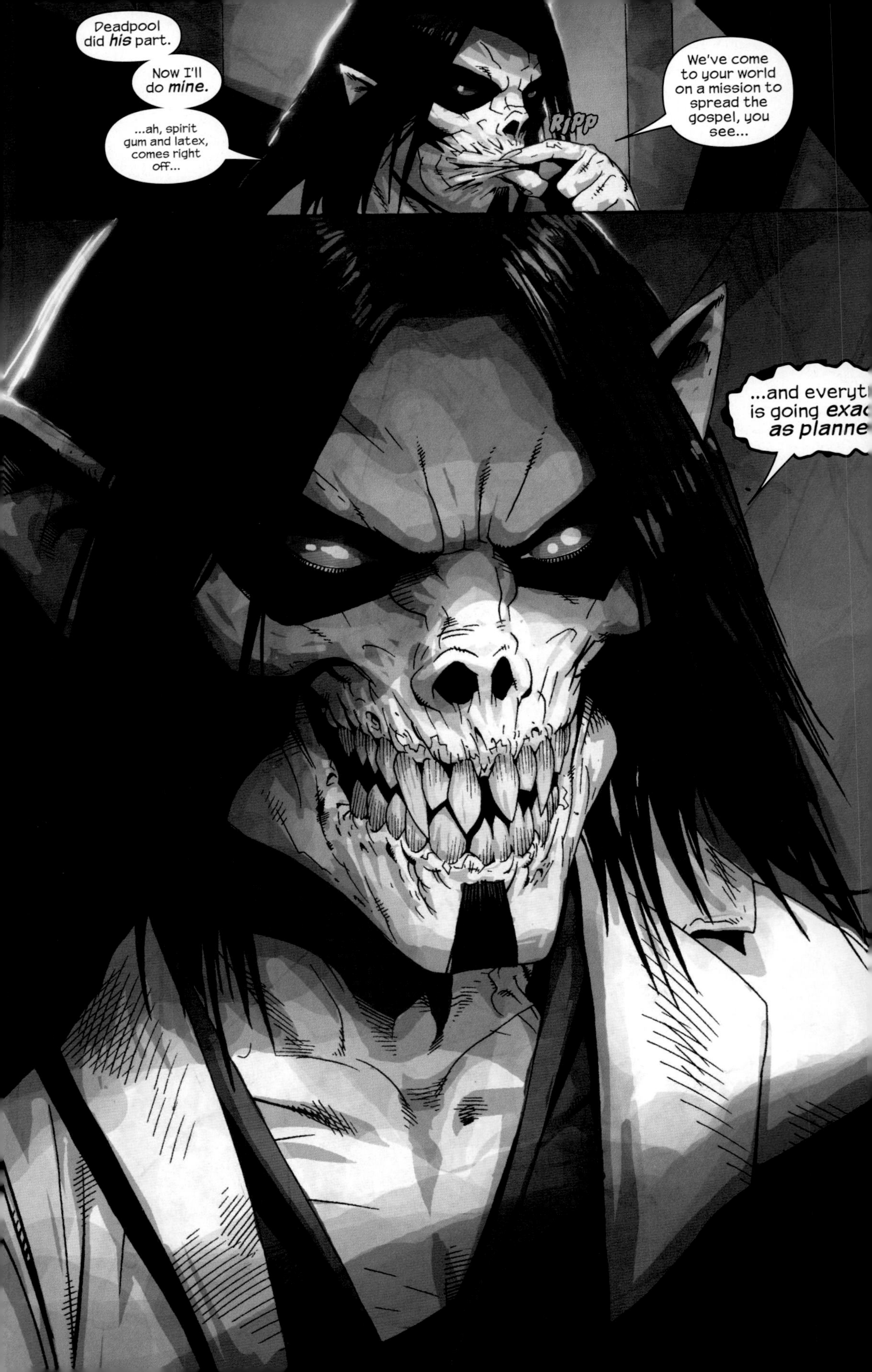
Deadpool did *his* part.
Now I'll do *mine.*
...ah, spirit gum and latex, comes right off...
RIPP
We've come to your world on a mission to spread the gospel, you see...
...and everyt
is going *exac*
as planne

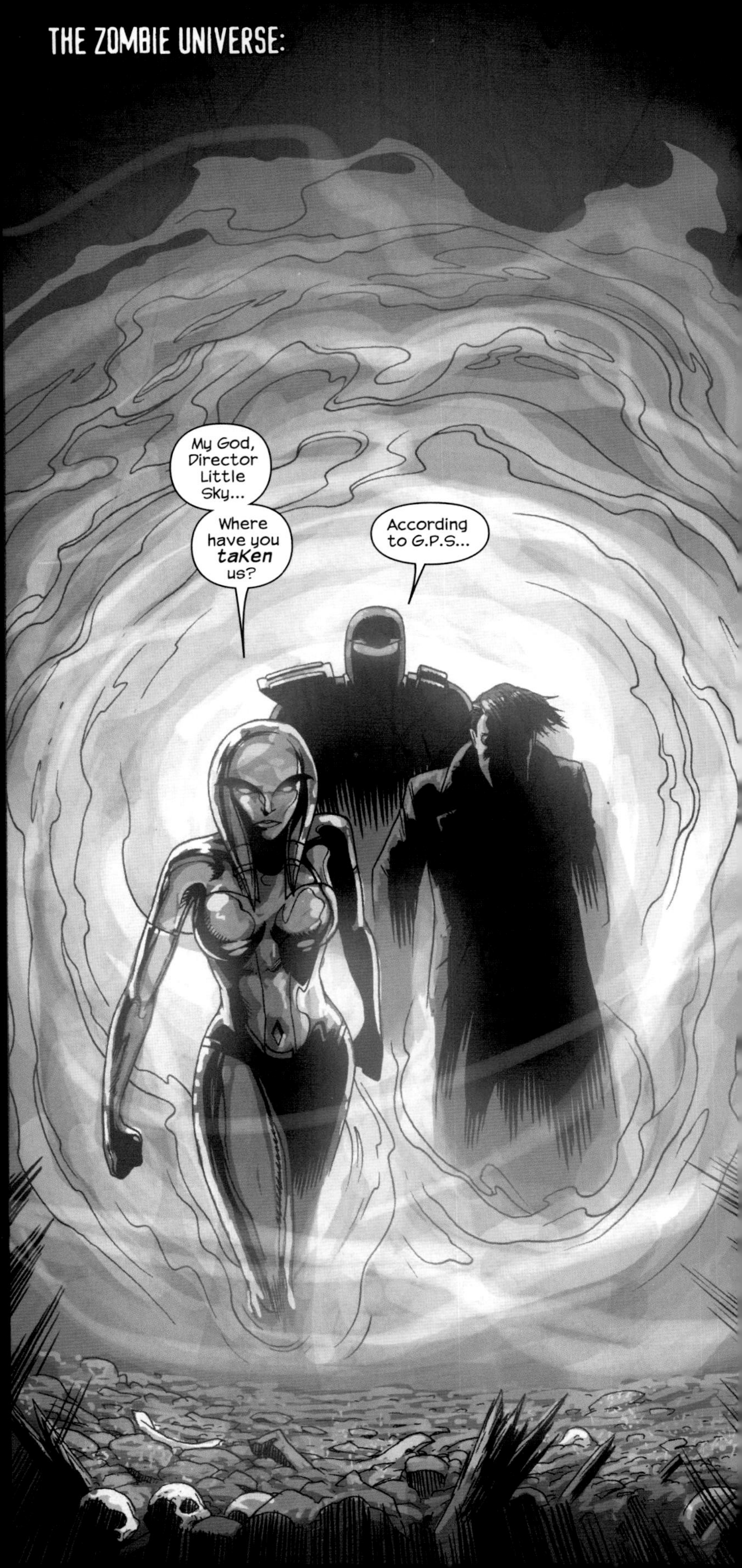
THE ZOMBIE UNIVERSE:
My God, Director Little Sky...
Where have you taken us?
According to G.P.S...

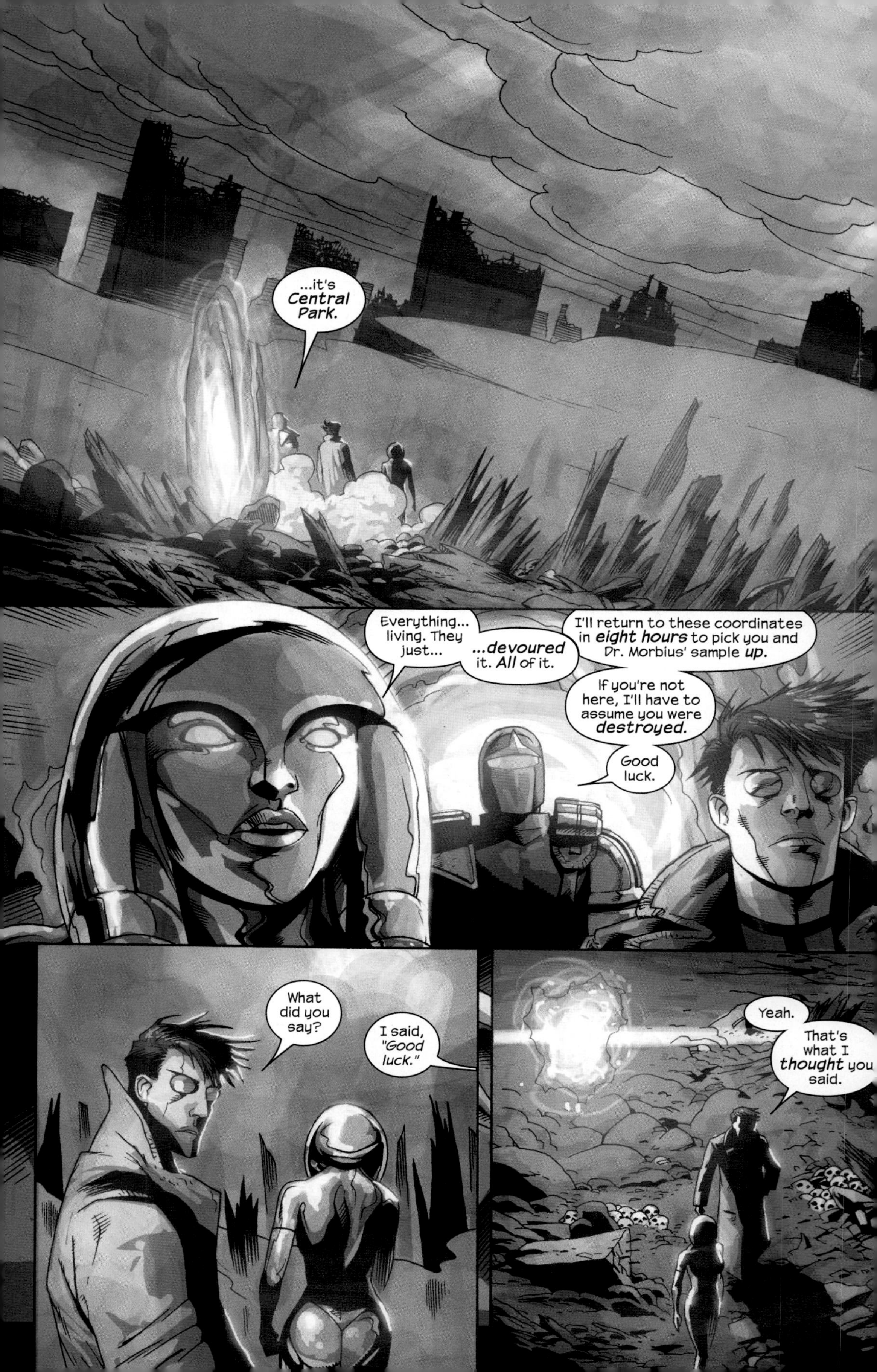
...it's *Central Park.*
Everything... living. They just...
...devoured it. *All* of it.
I'll return to these coordinates in *eight hours* to pick you and Dr. Morbius' sample *up.*
If you're not here, I'll have to assume you were *destroyed.*
Good luck.
What did you say?
I said, *"Good luck."*
Yeah.
That's what I *thought* you said.

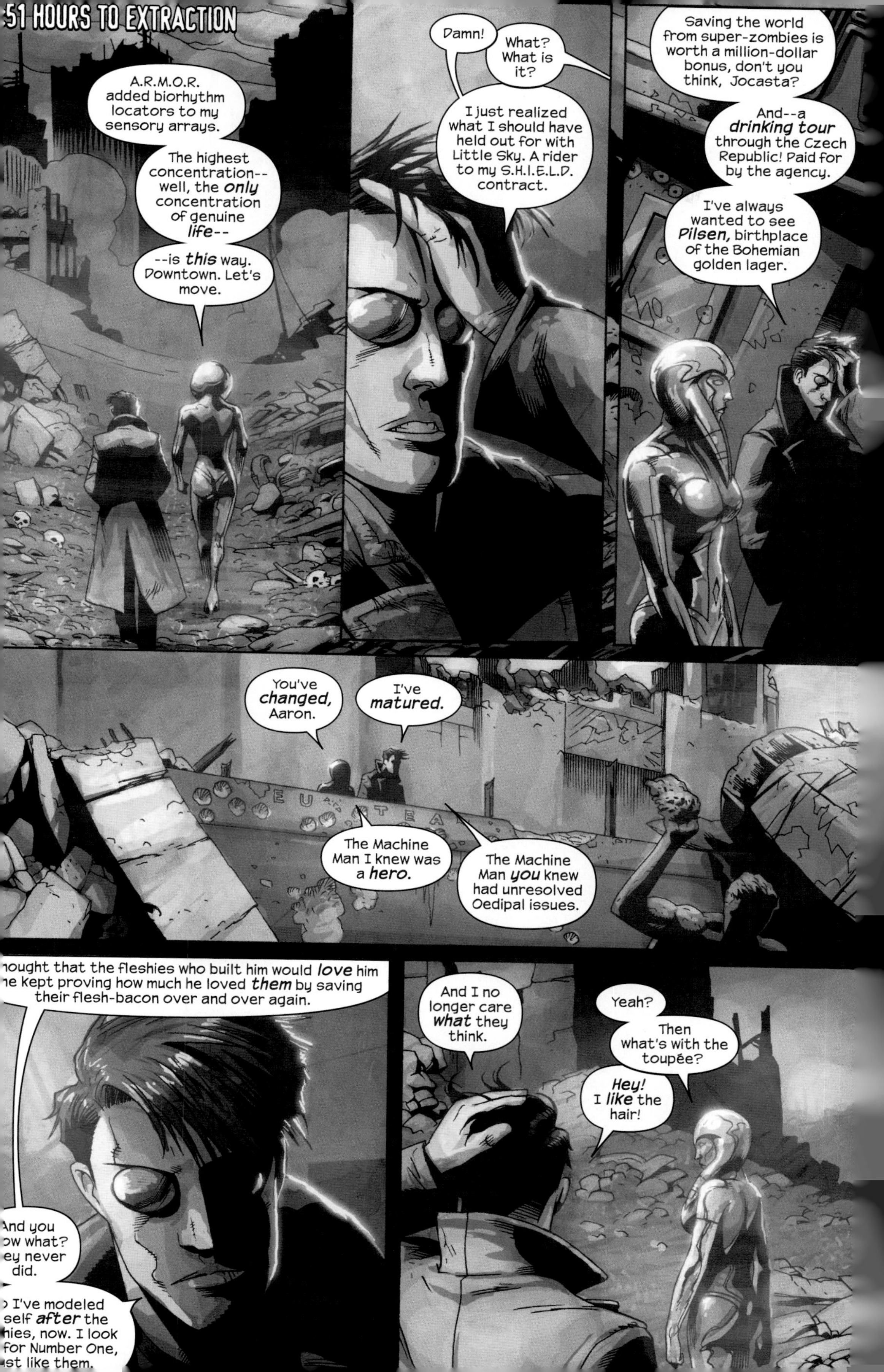
51 HOURS TO EXTRACTION
A.R.M.O.R. added biorhythm locators to my sensory arrays.
The highest concentration-- well, the only concentration of genuine life--
--is this way. Downtown. Let's move.
Damn!
What? What is it?
I just realized what I should have held out for with Little Sky. A rider to my S.H.I.E.L.D. contract.
Saving the world from super-zombies is worth a million-dollar bonus, don't you think, Jocasta?
And--a drinking tour through the Czech Republic! Paid for by the agency.
I've always wanted to see Pilsen, birthplace of the Bohemian golden lager.
You've changed, Aaron.
I've matured.
The Machine Man I knew was a hero.
The Machine Man you knew had unresolved Oedipal issues.
hought that the fleshies who built him would love him he kept proving how much he loved them by saving their flesh-bacon over and over again.
And you ow what? ey never did.
I've modeled self after the hies, now. I look for Number One, st like them.
And I no longer care what they think.
Yeah?
Then what's with the toupée?
Hey! I like the hair!

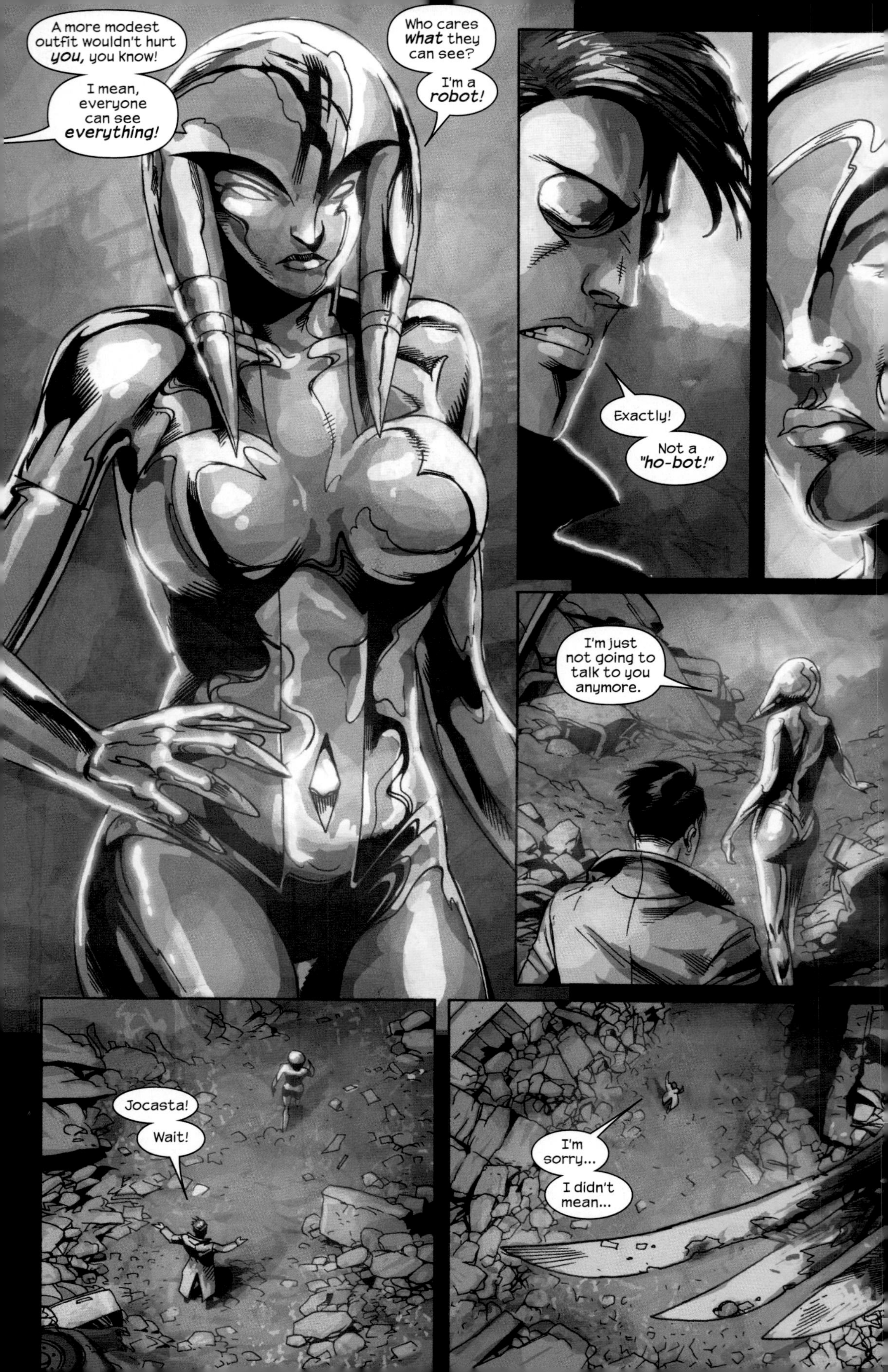
A more modest outfit wouldn't hurt *you,* you know!
I mean, everyone can see *everything!*
Who cares *what* they can see?
I'm a *robot!*
Exactly!
Not a *"ho-bot!"*
I'm just not going to talk to you anymore.
Jocasta!
Wait!
I'm sorry...
I didn't mean...

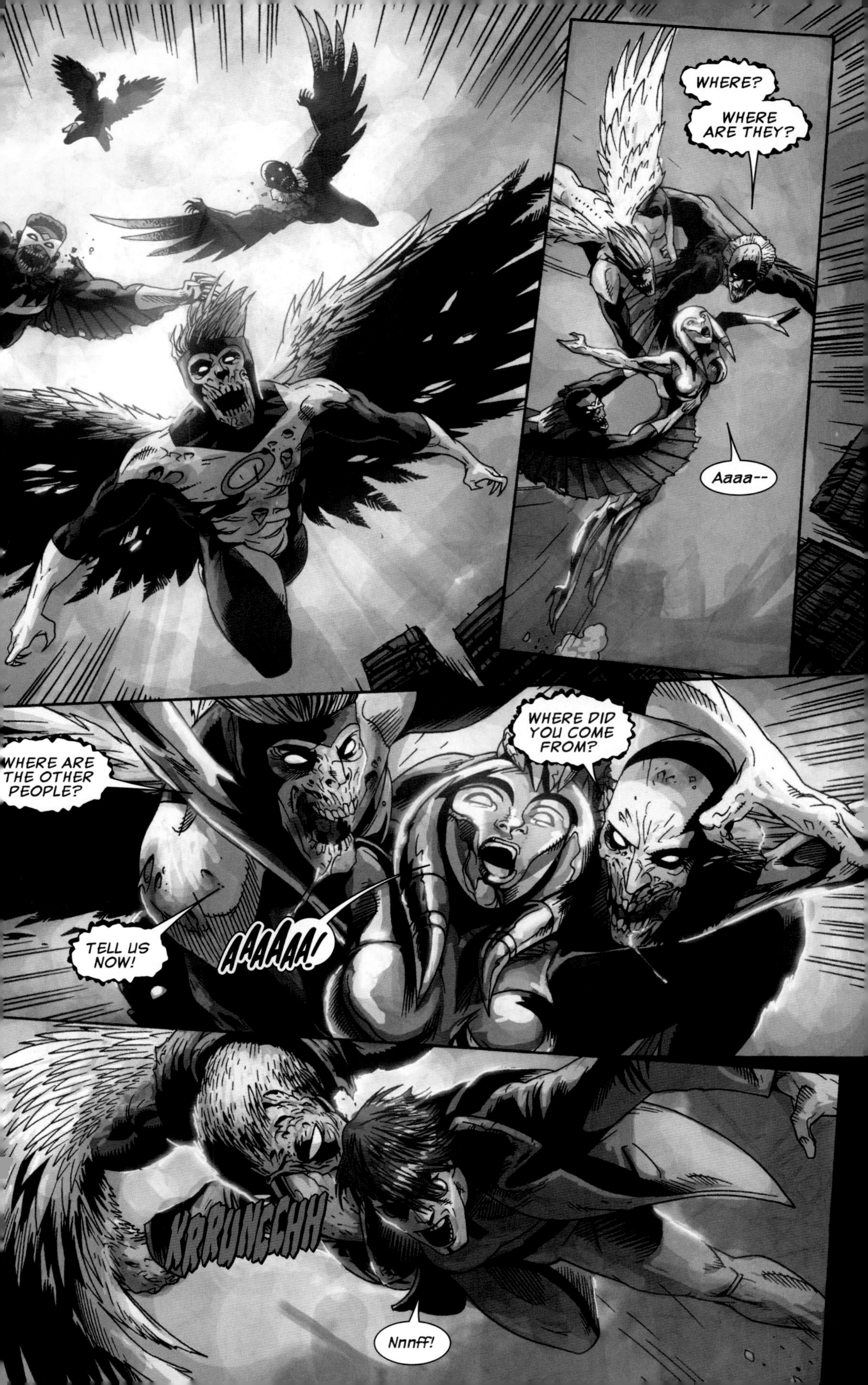

WHERE?
WHERE ARE THEY?
Aaaa--
WHERE ARE THE OTHER PEOPLE?
WHERE DID YOU COME FROM?
TELL US NOW!
AAAAAA!
KRRUNCHH
Nnnff!

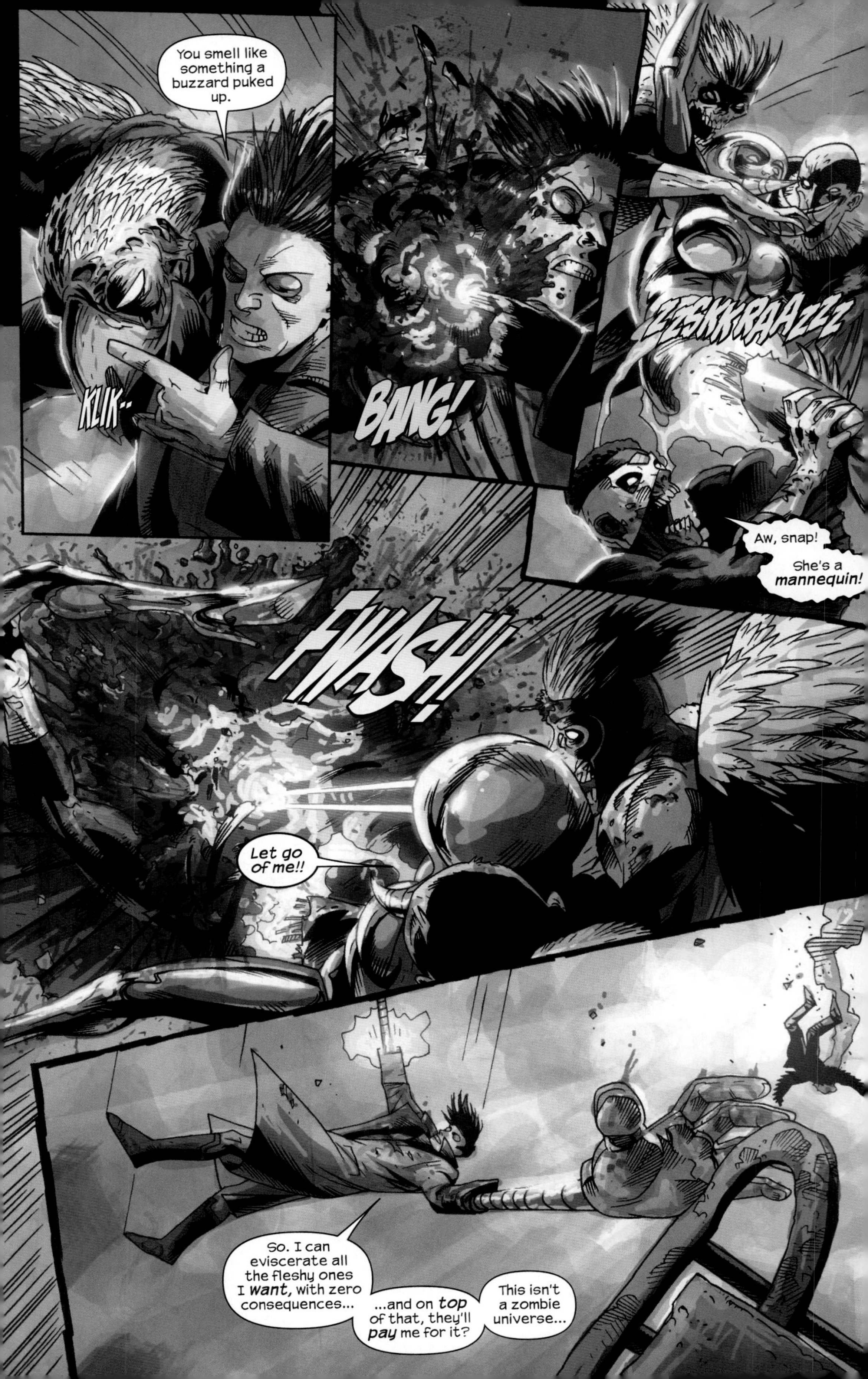
You smell like something a buzzard puked up.
KLIK-
BANG!
ZZSKKRAAZZZ
Aw, snap! She's a *mannequin!*
FWASH!!
Let go of me!!
So. I can eviscerate all the fleshy ones I *want,* with zero consequences...
...and on *top* of that, they'll *pay* me for it?
This isn't a zombie universe...

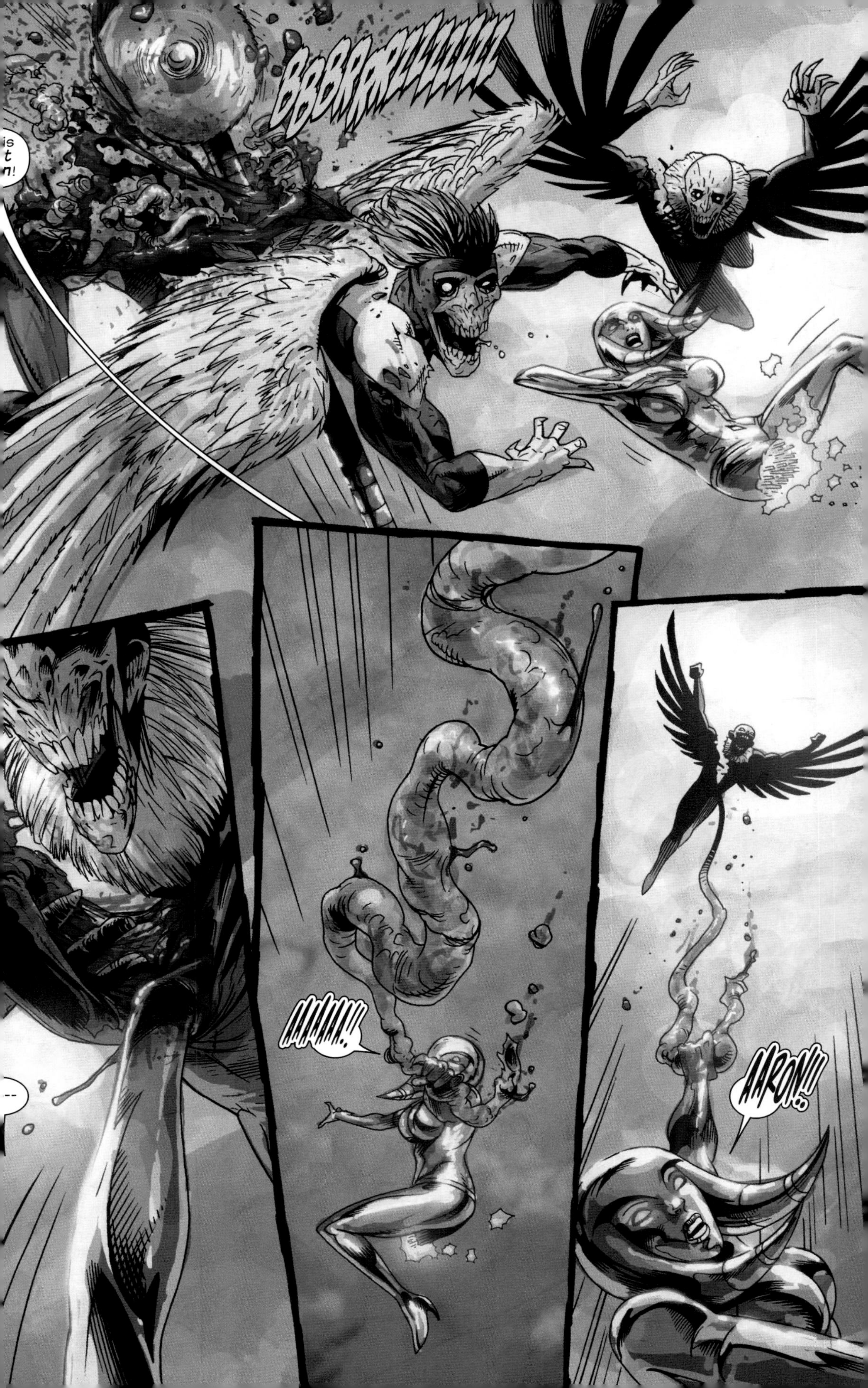
BBBRRRZZZZZZZ!
AAAHHH!!
AARON!!

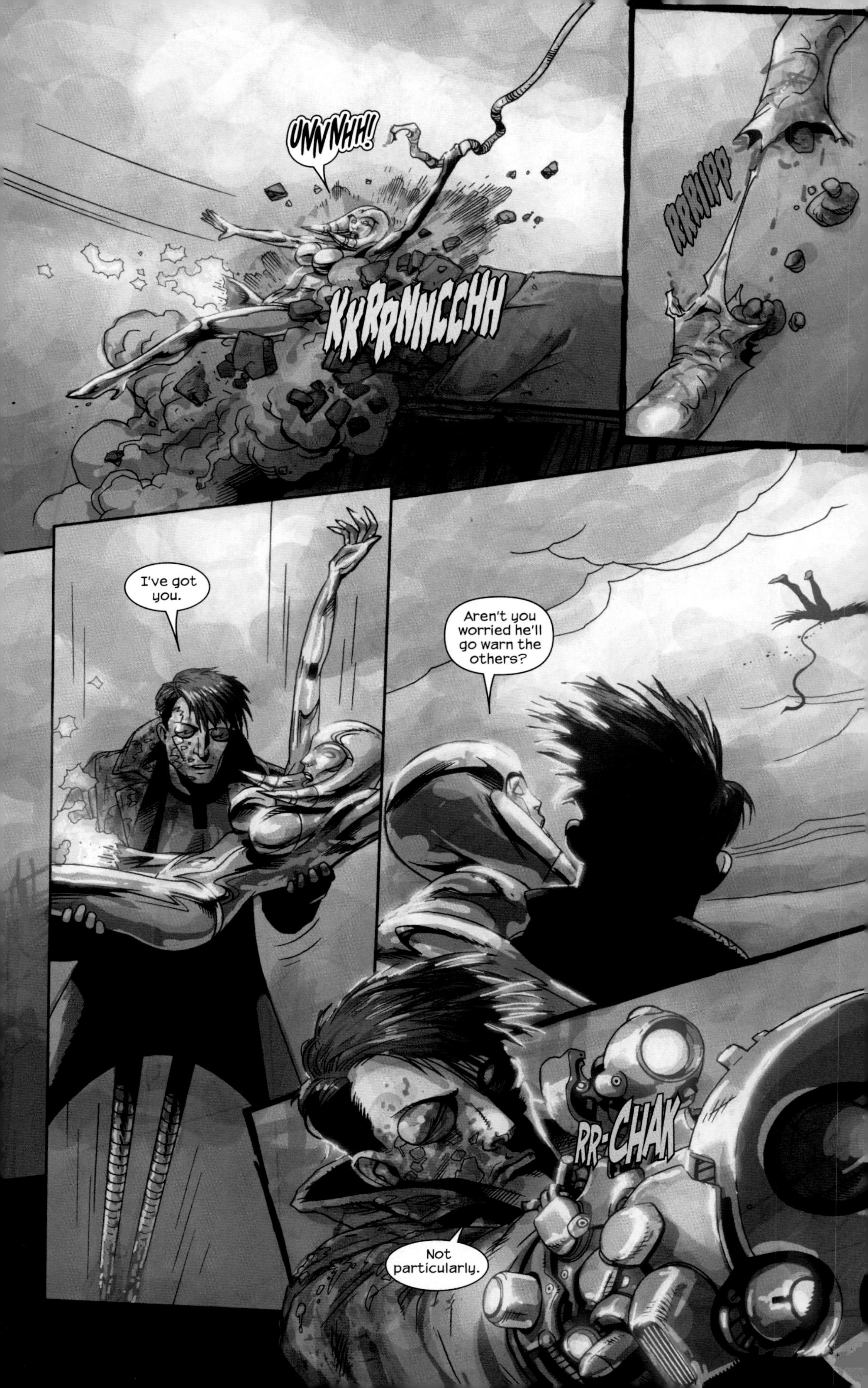
UNNHH!
KKRRNNCCHH
RRRIPP
I've got you.
Aren't you worried he'll go warn the others?
RR-CHAK
Not particularly.

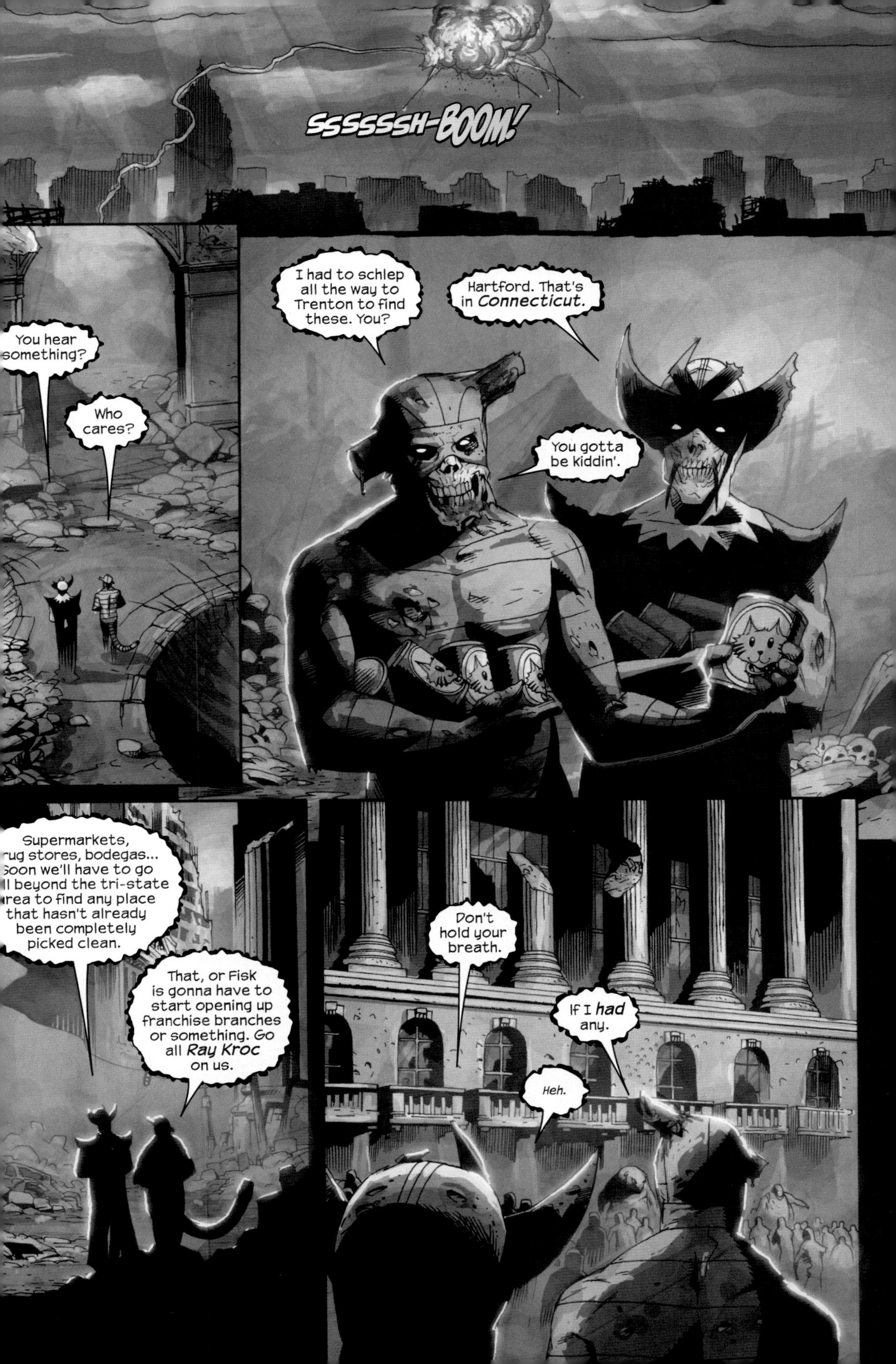
SSSSSSH-BOOM!
You hear something?
Who cares?
I had to schlep all the way to Trenton to find these. You?
Hartford. That's in *Connecticut.*
You gotta be kiddin'.
Supermarkets, rug stores, bodegas... Soon we'll have to go ll beyond the tri-state rea to find any place that hasn't already been completely picked clean.
That, or Fisk is gonna have to start opening up franchise branches or something. Go all *Ray Kroc* on us.
Don't hold your breath.
If I *had* any.
Heh.

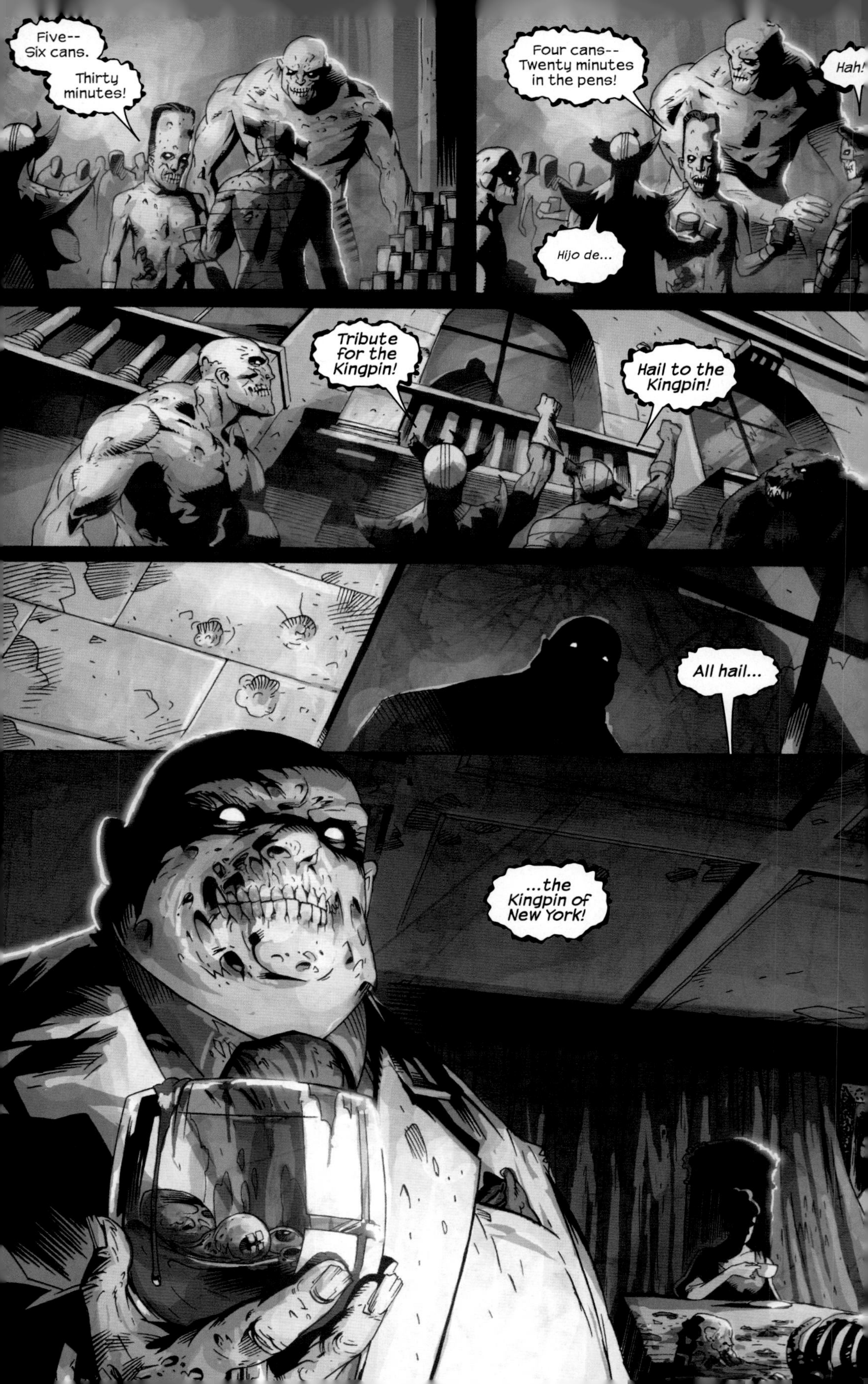
Five--
Six cans.
Thirty minutes!
Four cans--
Twenty minutes
in the pens!
Hah!
Hijo de...
Tribute for the Kingpin!
Hail to the Kingpin!
All hail...
...the Kingpin of New York!

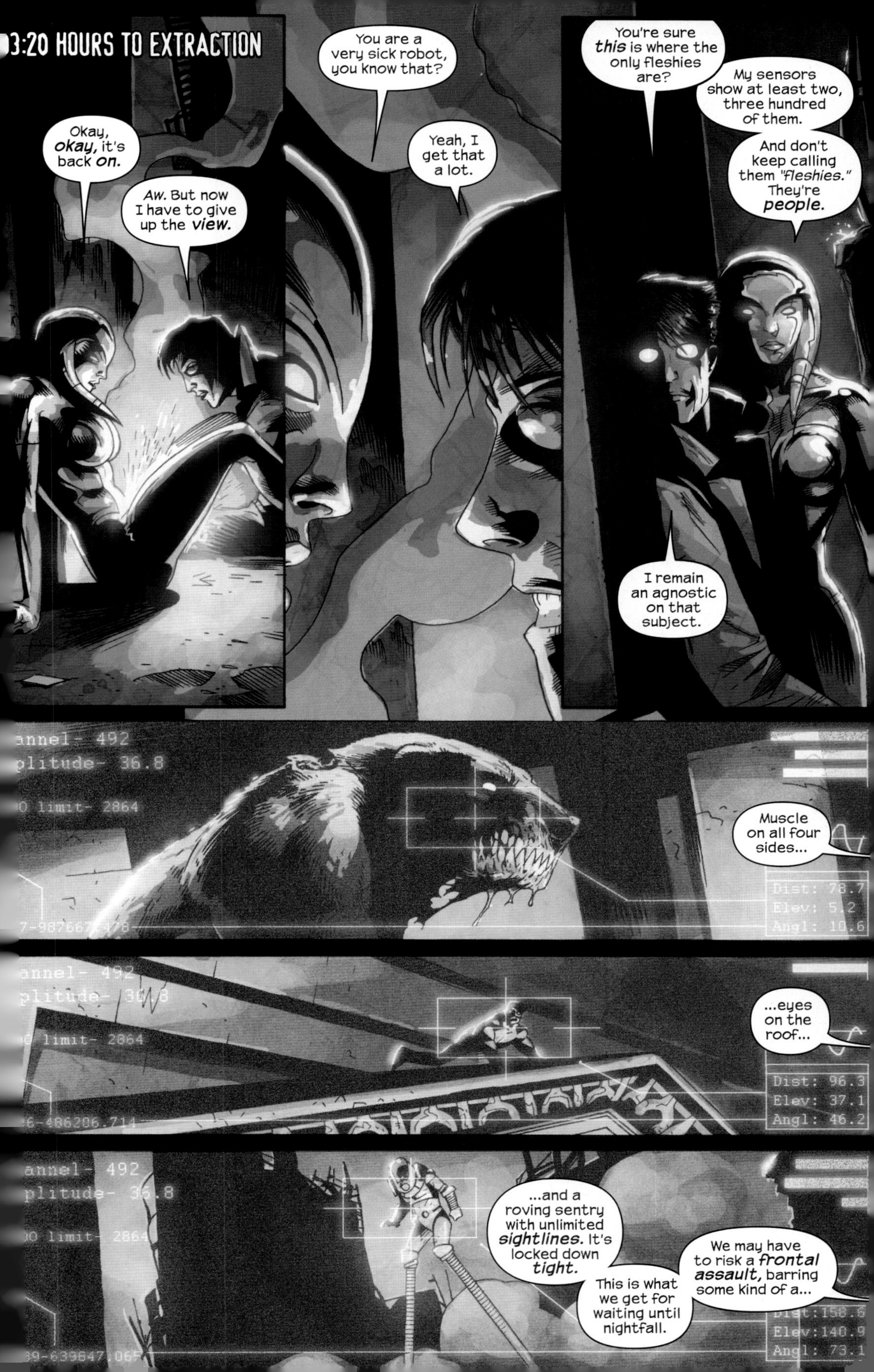
3:20 HOURS TO EXTRACTION
Okay, *okay,* it's back *on.*
Aw. But now I have to give up the *view.*
You are a very sick robot, you know that?
Yeah, I get that a lot.
You're sure *this* is where the only fleshies are?
My sensors show at least two, three hundred of them.
And don't keep calling them "fleshies." They're *people.*
I remain an agnostic on that subject.
Muscle on all four sides...
Dist: 78.7
Elev: 5.2
Angl: 10.6
...eyes on the roof...
Dist: 96.3
Elev: 37.1
Angl: 46.2
...and a roving sentry with unlimited *sightlines.* It's locked down *tight.*
This is what we get for waiting until nightfall.
We may have to risk a *frontal assault,* barring some kind of a...
Elev: 140.9
Angl: 73.1

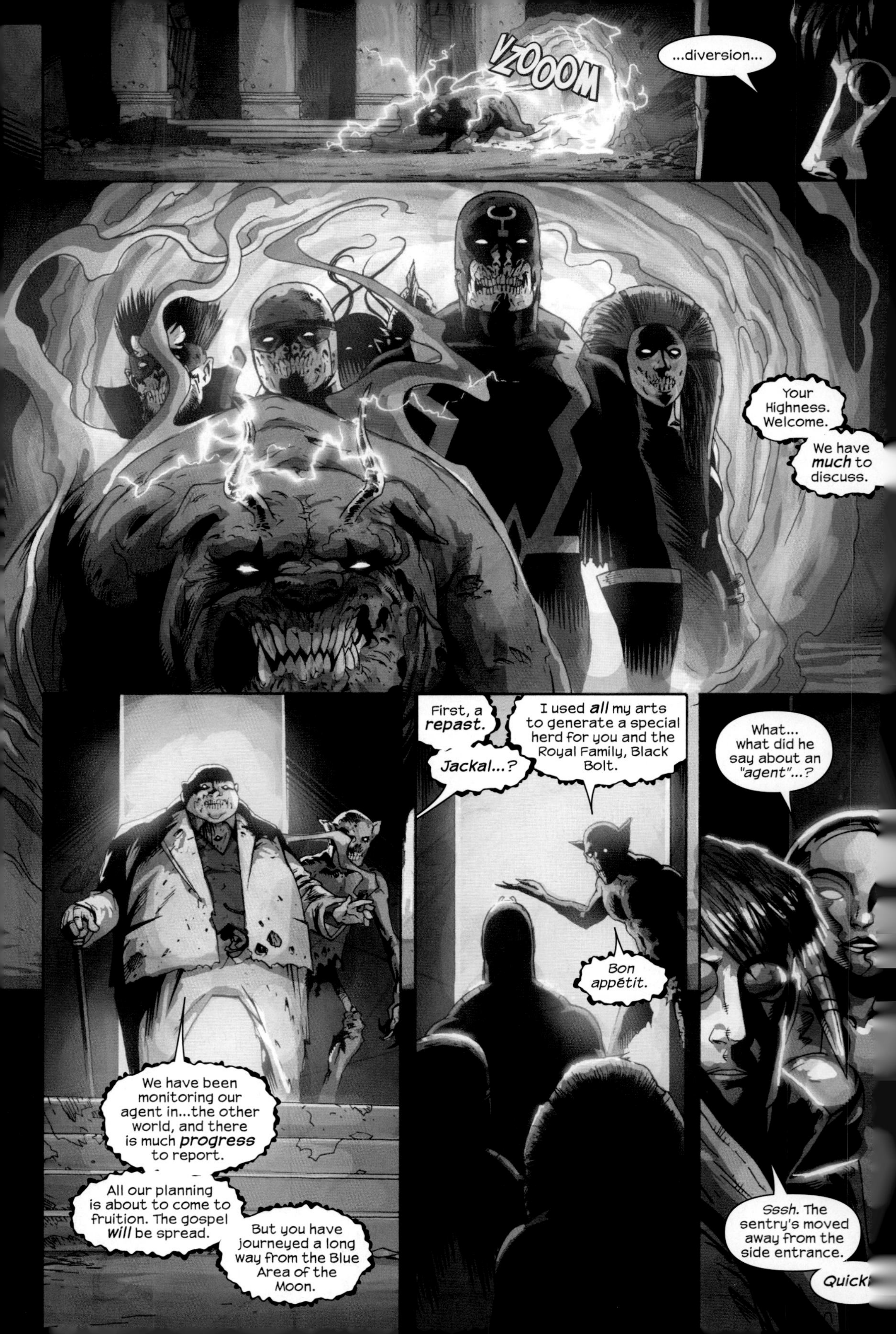

VZOOOM
...diversion...
Your Highness. Welcome.
We have *much* to discuss.
We have been monitoring our agent in...the other world, and there is much *progress* to report.
All our planning is about to come to fruition. The gospel *will* be spread.
But you have journeyed a long way from the Blue Area of the Moon.
First, a *repast.*
Jackal...?
I used *all* my arts to generate a special herd for you and the Royal Family, Black Bolt.
Bon appétit.
What... what did he say about an *"agent"...?*
Sssh. The sentry's moved away from the side entrance.
Quick!

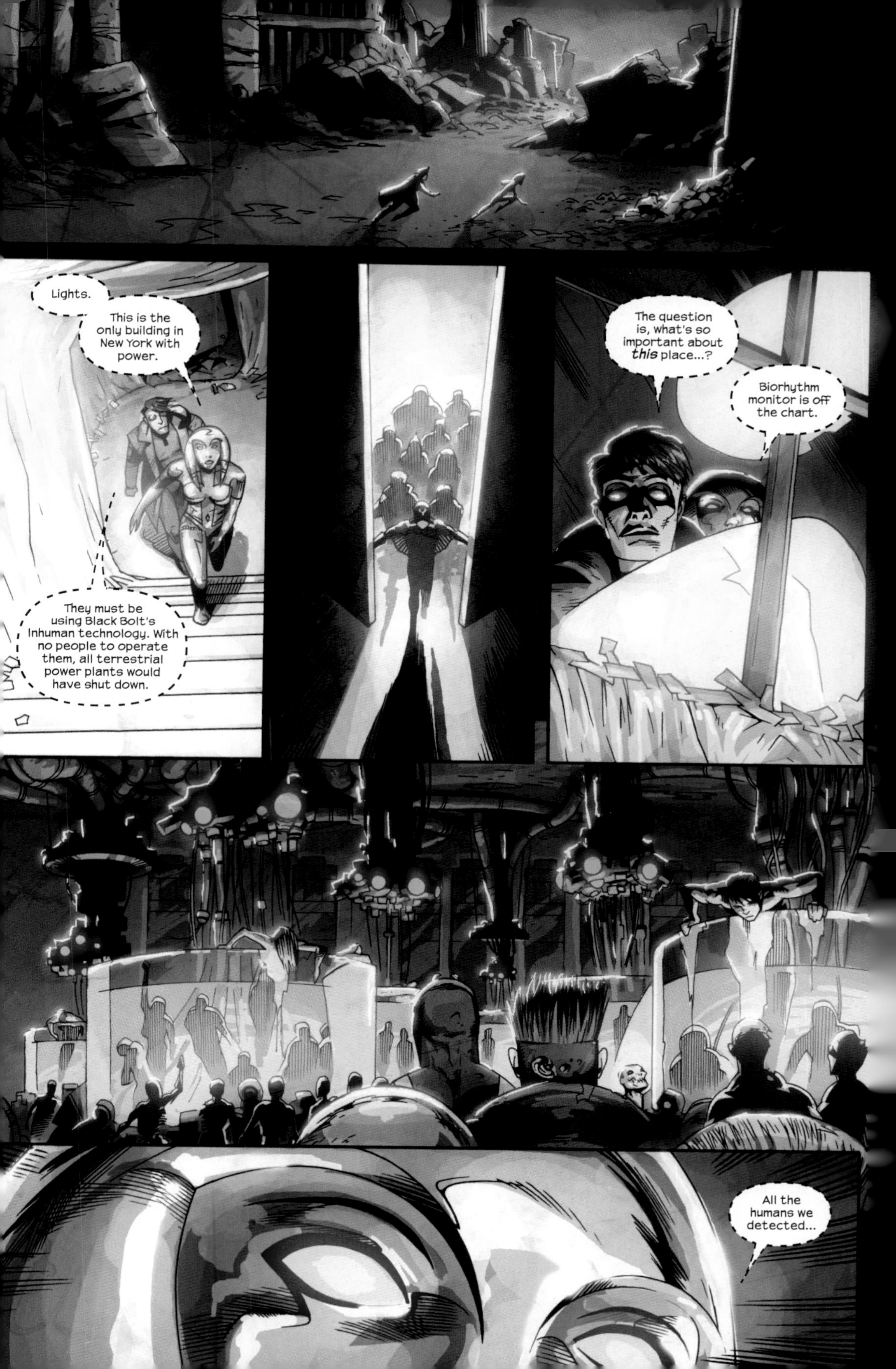
Lights.
This is the only building in New York with power.
They must be using Black Bolt's Inhuman technology. With no people to operate them, all terrestrial power plants would have shut down.
The question is, what's so important about *this* place...?
Biorhythm monitor is off the chart.
All the humans we detected...

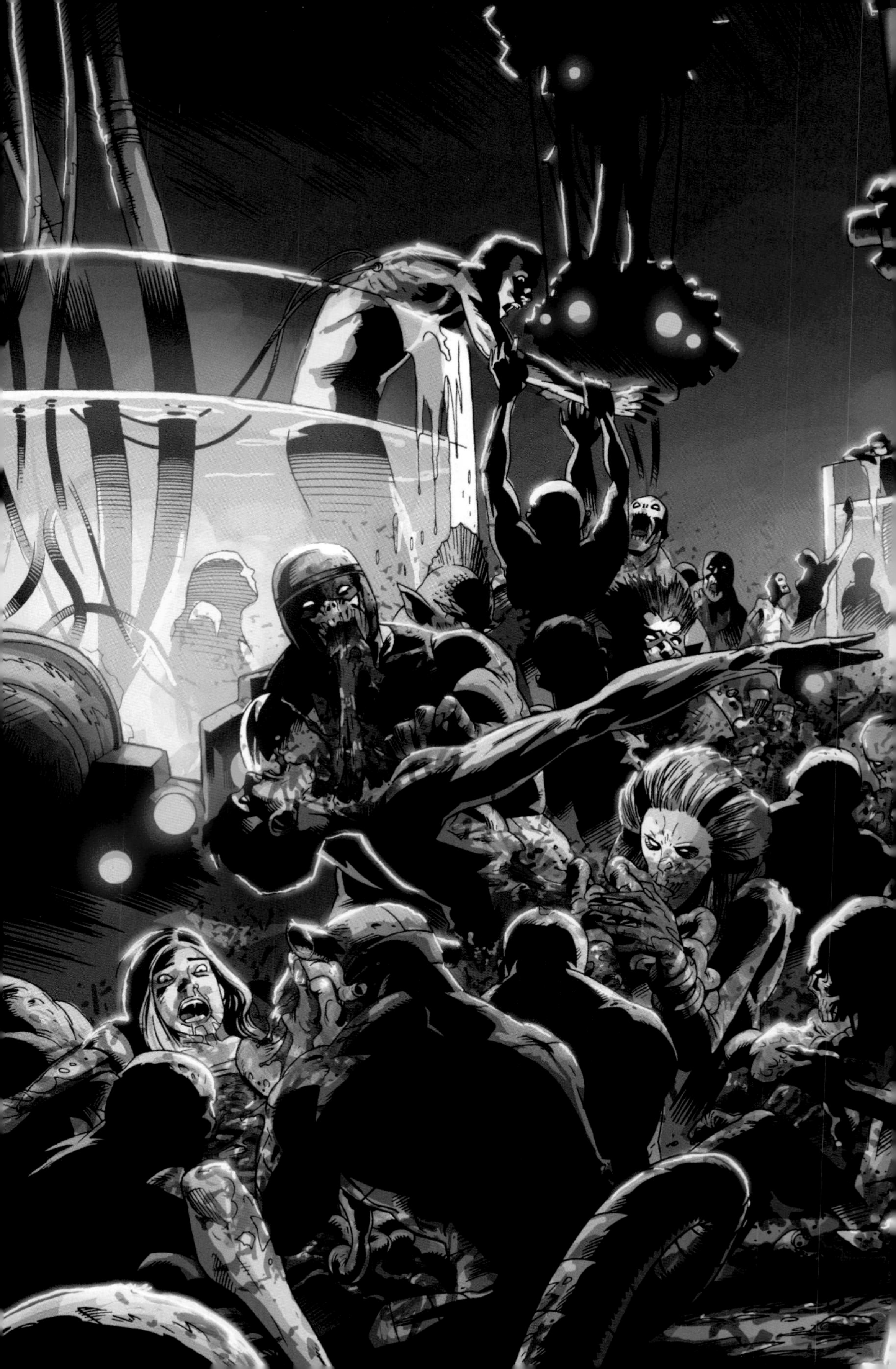

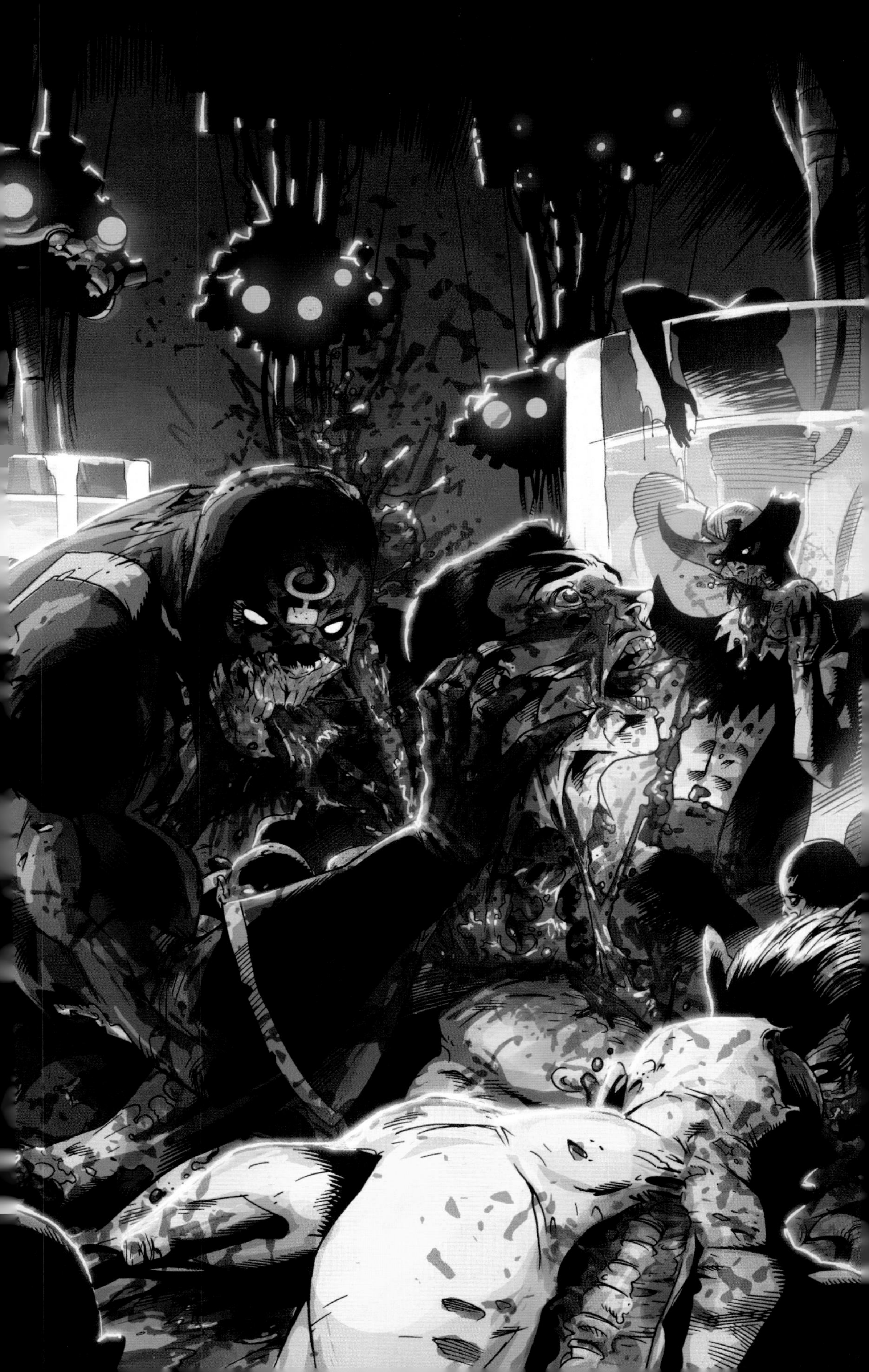

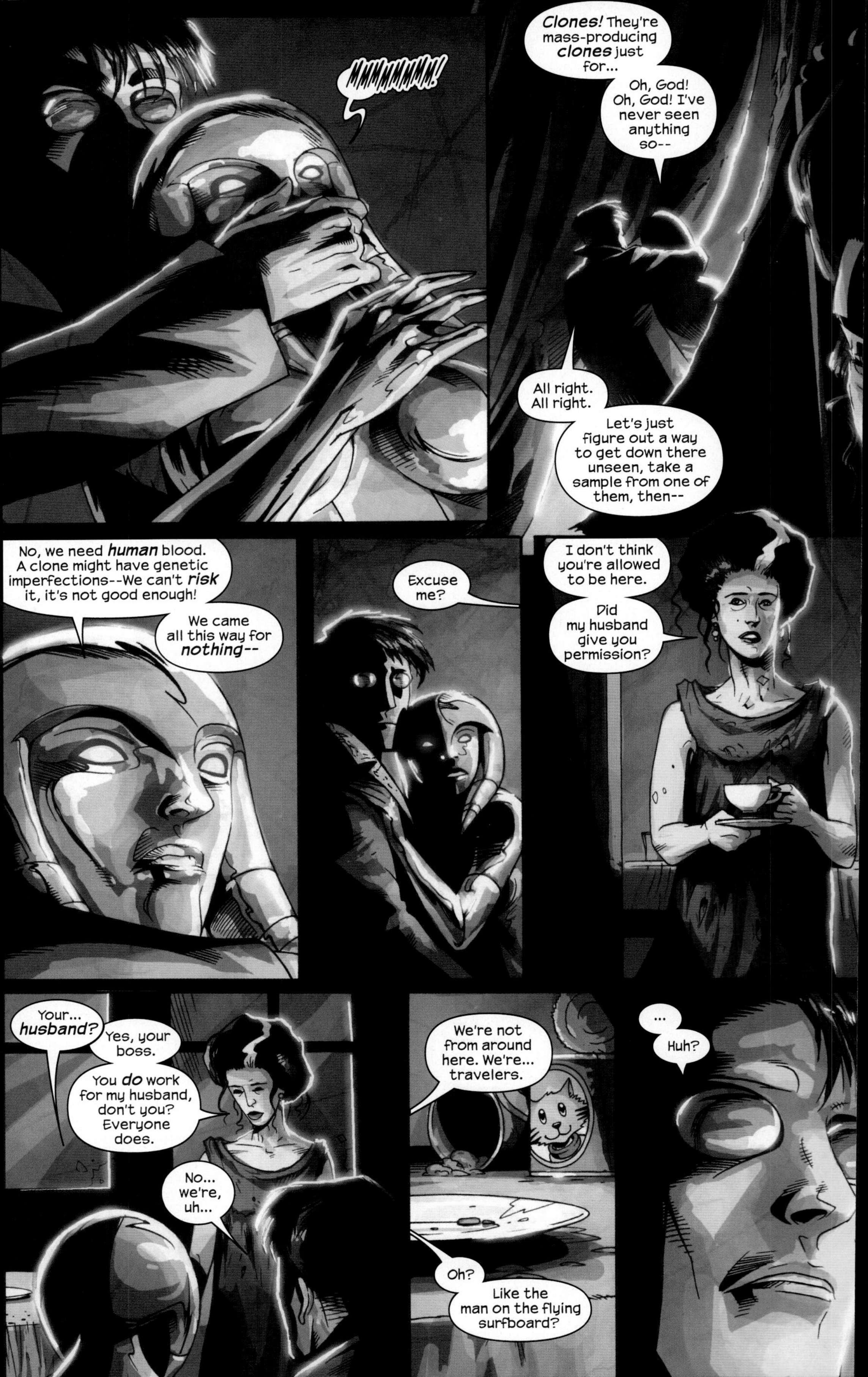
MMMMMMM!
Clones! They're mass-producing clones just for...
Oh, God! Oh, God! I've never seen anything so--
All right. All right.
Let's just figure out a way to get down there unseen, take a sample from one of them, then--
No, we need human blood. A clone might have genetic imperfections--We can't risk it, it's not good enough!
We came all this way for nothing--
Excuse me?
I don't think you're allowed to be here.
Did my husband give you permission?
Your... husband?
Yes, your boss.
You do work for my husband, don't you? Everyone does.
No... we're, uh...
We're not from around here. We're... travelers.
Oh?
Like the man on the flying surfboard?
...
Huh?

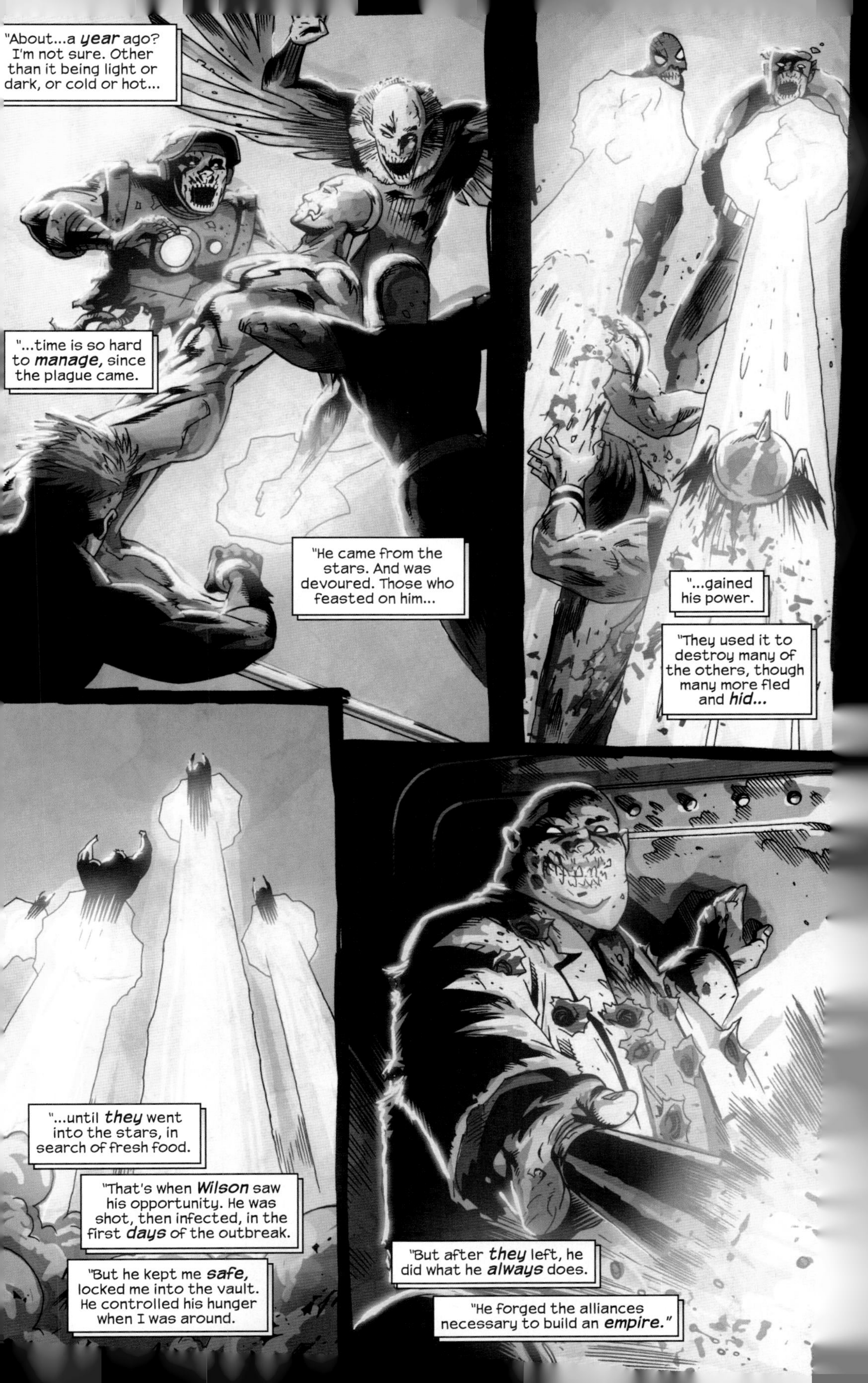
"About...a year ago? I'm not sure. Other than it being light or dark, or cold or hot...
"...time is so hard to manage, since the plague came.
"He came from the stars. And was devoured. Those who feasted on him...
"...gained his power.
"They used it to destroy many of the others, though many more fled and hid...
"...until they went into the stars, in search of fresh food.
"That's when Wilson saw his opportunity. He was shot, then infected, in the first days of the outbreak.
"But he kept me safe, locked me into the vault. He controlled his hunger when I was around.
"But after they left, he did what he always does.
"He forged the alliances necessary to build an empire."

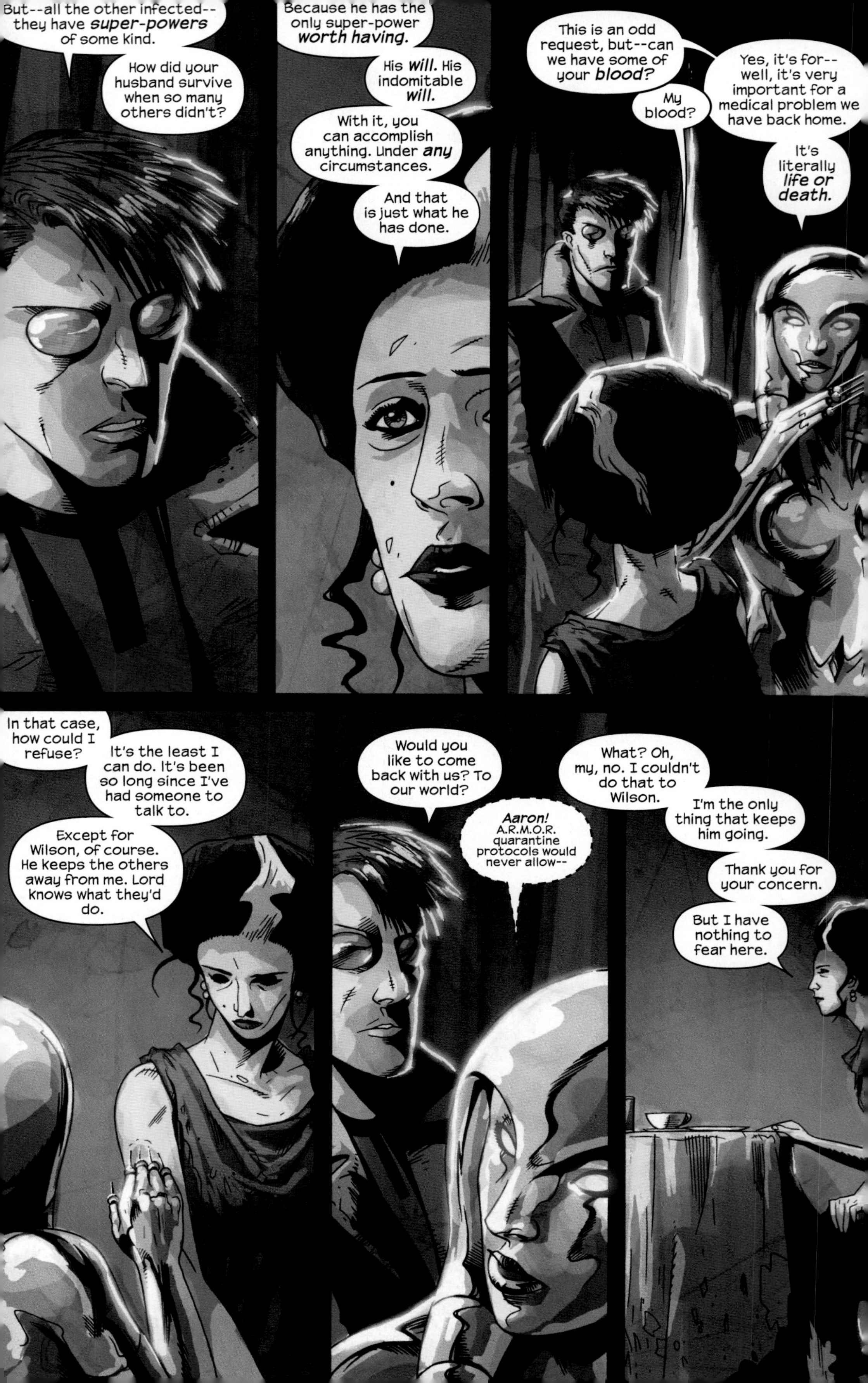
But--all the other infected--they have *super-powers* of some kind.
How did your husband survive when so many others didn't?
Because he has the only super-power *worth having.*
His *will.* His indomitable *will.*
With it, you can accomplish anything. Under *any* circumstances.
And that is just what he has done.
This is an odd request, but--can we have some of your *blood?*
My blood?
Yes, it's for--well, it's very important for a medical problem we have back home.
It's literally *life or death.*
In that case, how could I refuse?
It's the least I can do. It's been so long since I've had someone to talk to.
Except for Wilson, of course. He keeps the others away from me. Lord knows what they'd do.
Would you like to come back with us? To our world?
Aaron! A.R.M.O.R. quarantine protocols would never allow--
What? Oh, my, no. I couldn't do that to Wilson.
I'm the only thing that keeps him going.
Thank you for your concern.
But I have nothing to fear here.

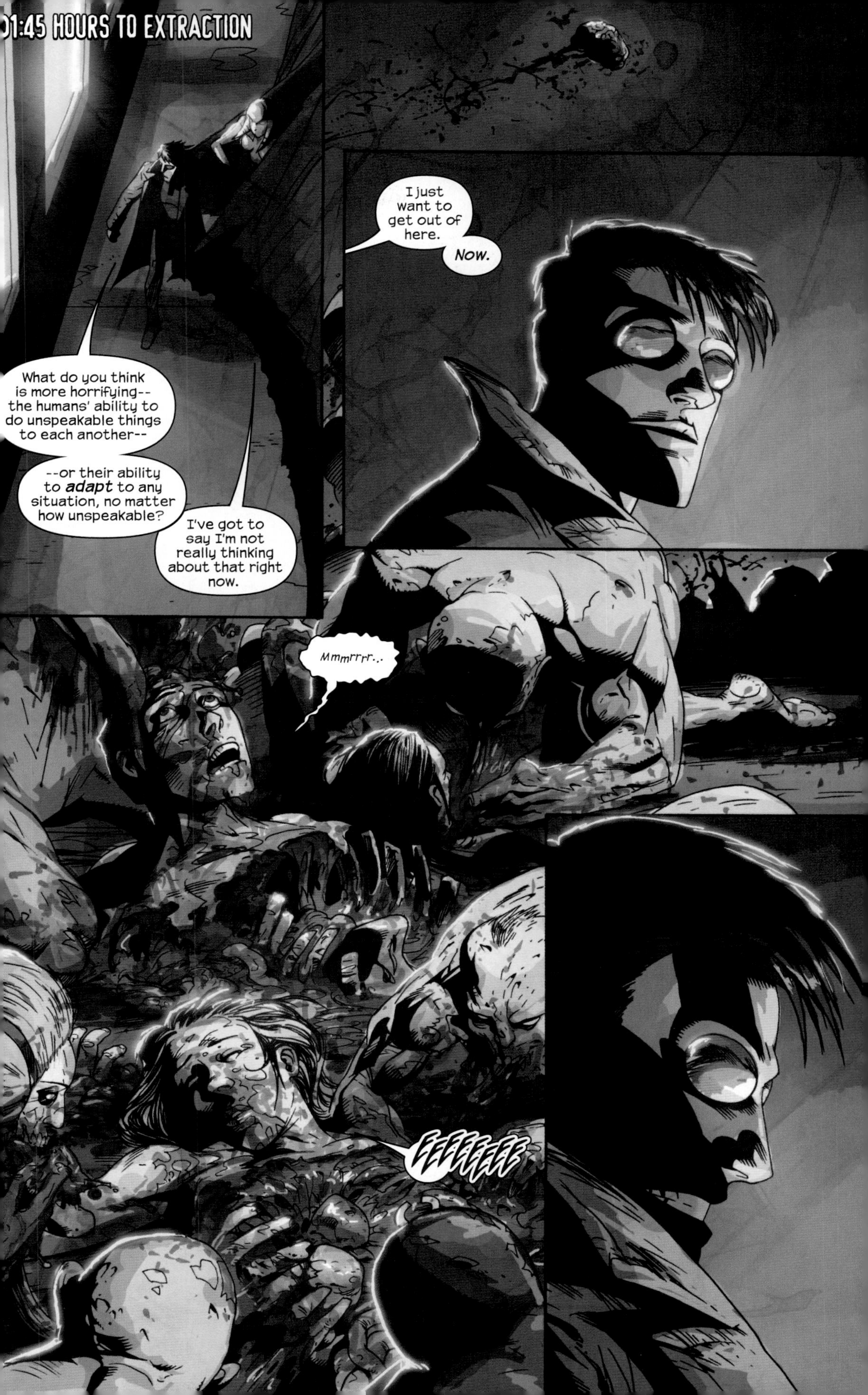
01:45 HOURS TO EXTRACTION
What do you think is more horrifying-- the humans' ability to do unspeakable things to each another--
--or their ability to *adapt* to any situation, no matter how unspeakable?
I've got to say I'm not really thinking about that right now.
I just want to get out of here.
Now.
Mmmrrrr...
EEEEEEEE

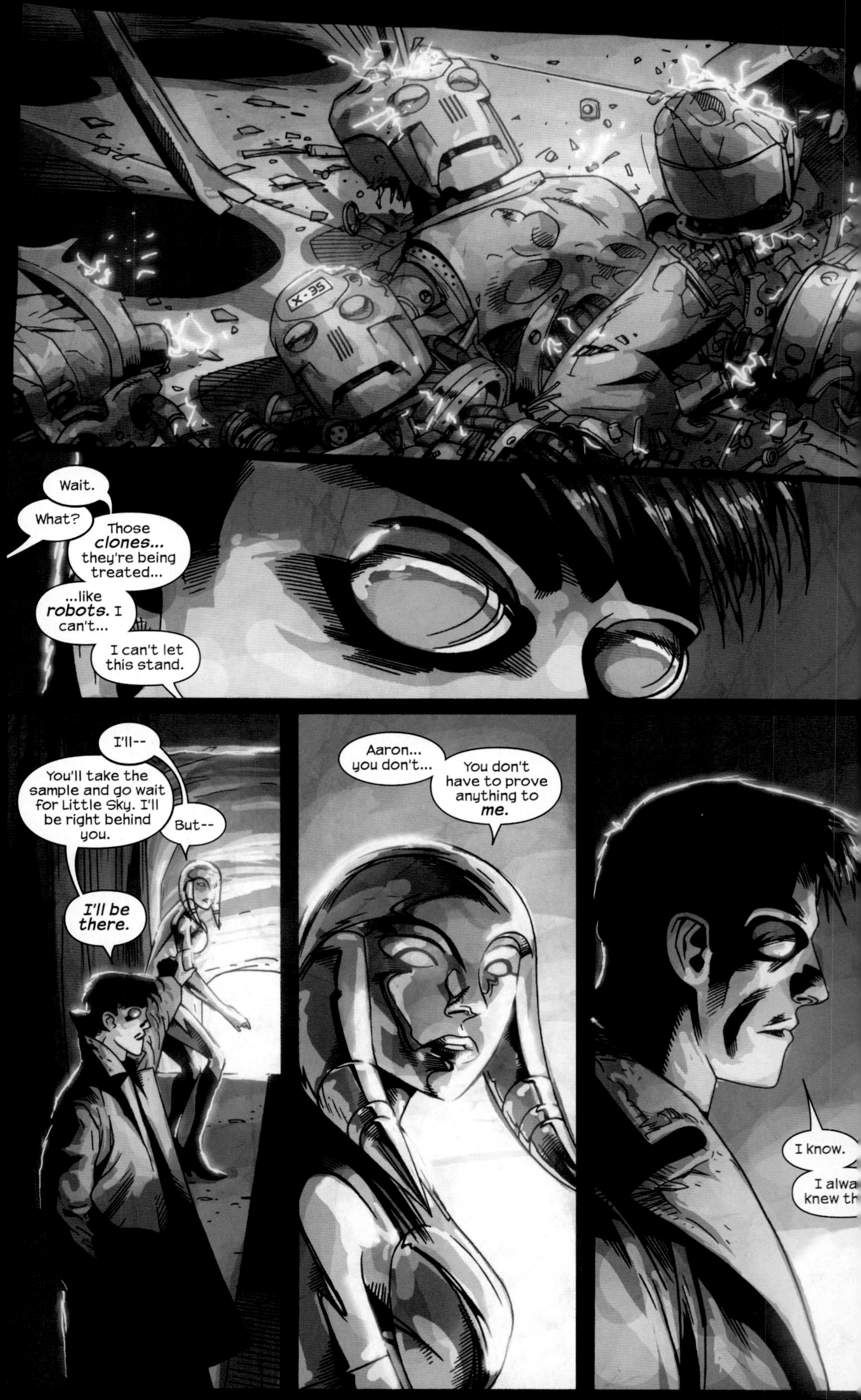

X-35
Wait.
What?
Those *clones...* they're being treated...
...like *robots.* I can't...
I can't let this stand.
I'll--
You'll take the sample and go wait for Little Sky. I'll be right behind you.
But--
I'll be there.
Aaron... you don't...
You don't have to prove anything to *me.*
I know.

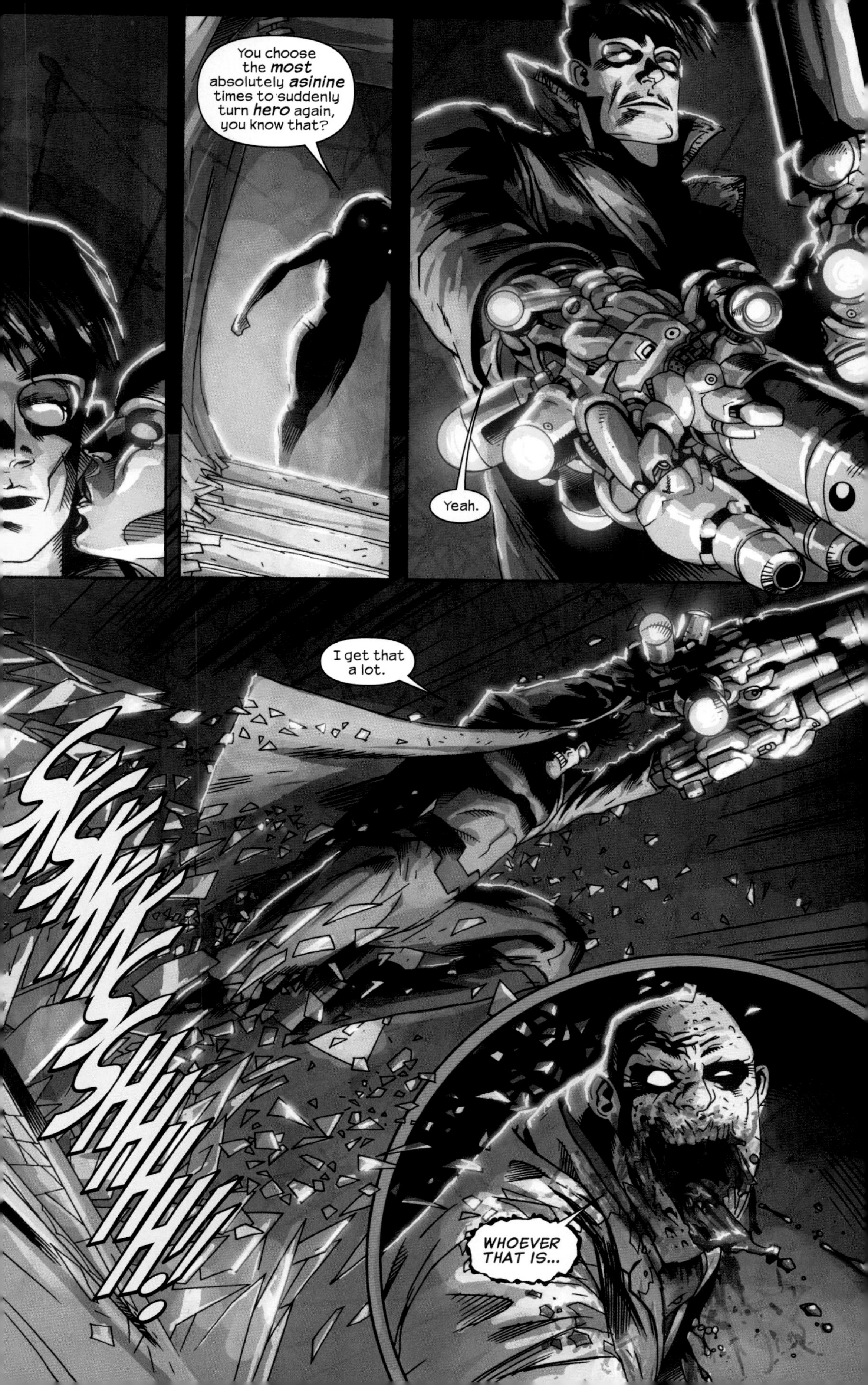

You choose the *most* absolutely *asinine* times to suddenly turn *hero* again, you know that?
Yeah.
I get that a lot.
SKSHHKSSHHH!!
WHOEVER THAT IS...

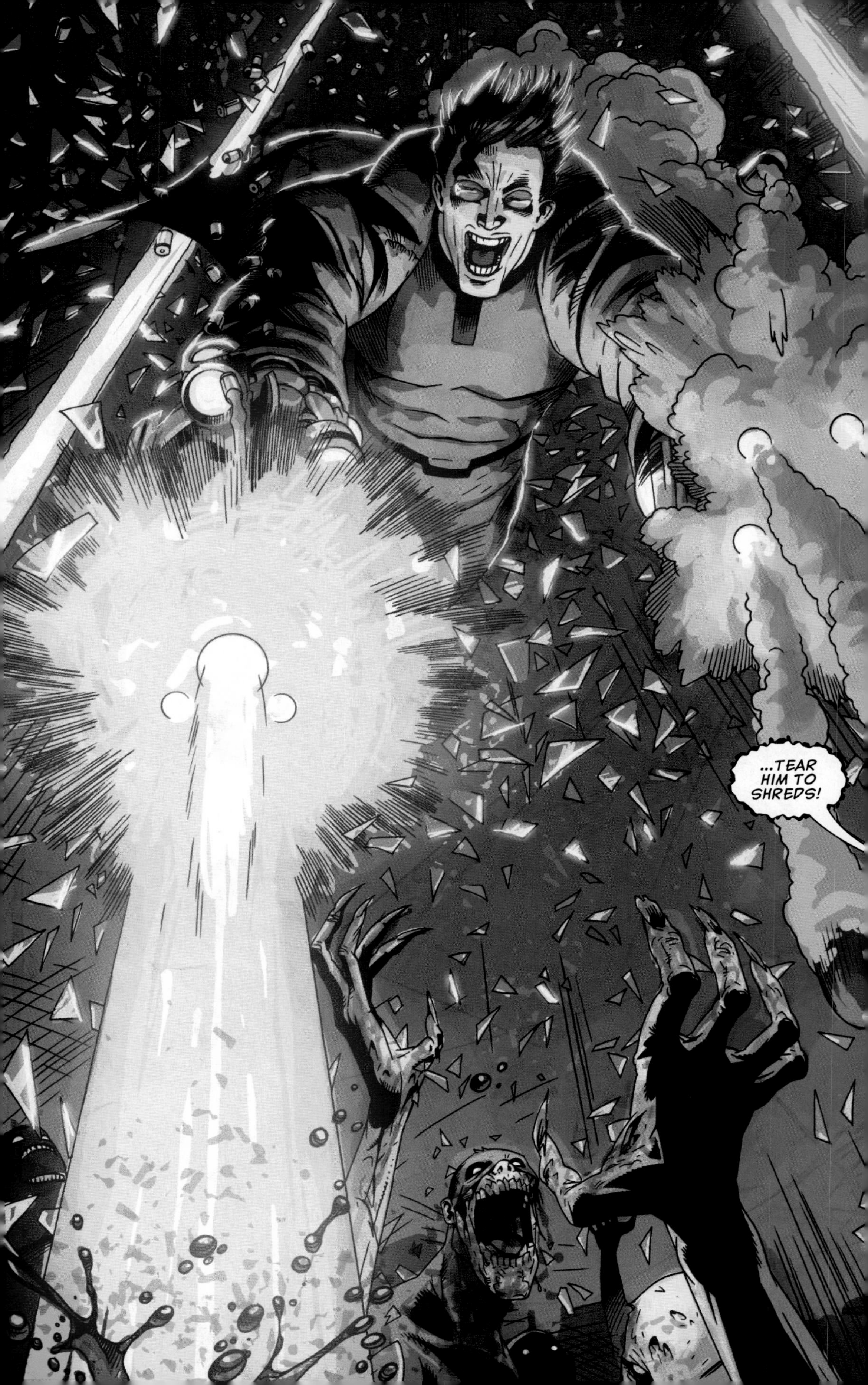
...TEAR HIM TO SHREDS!

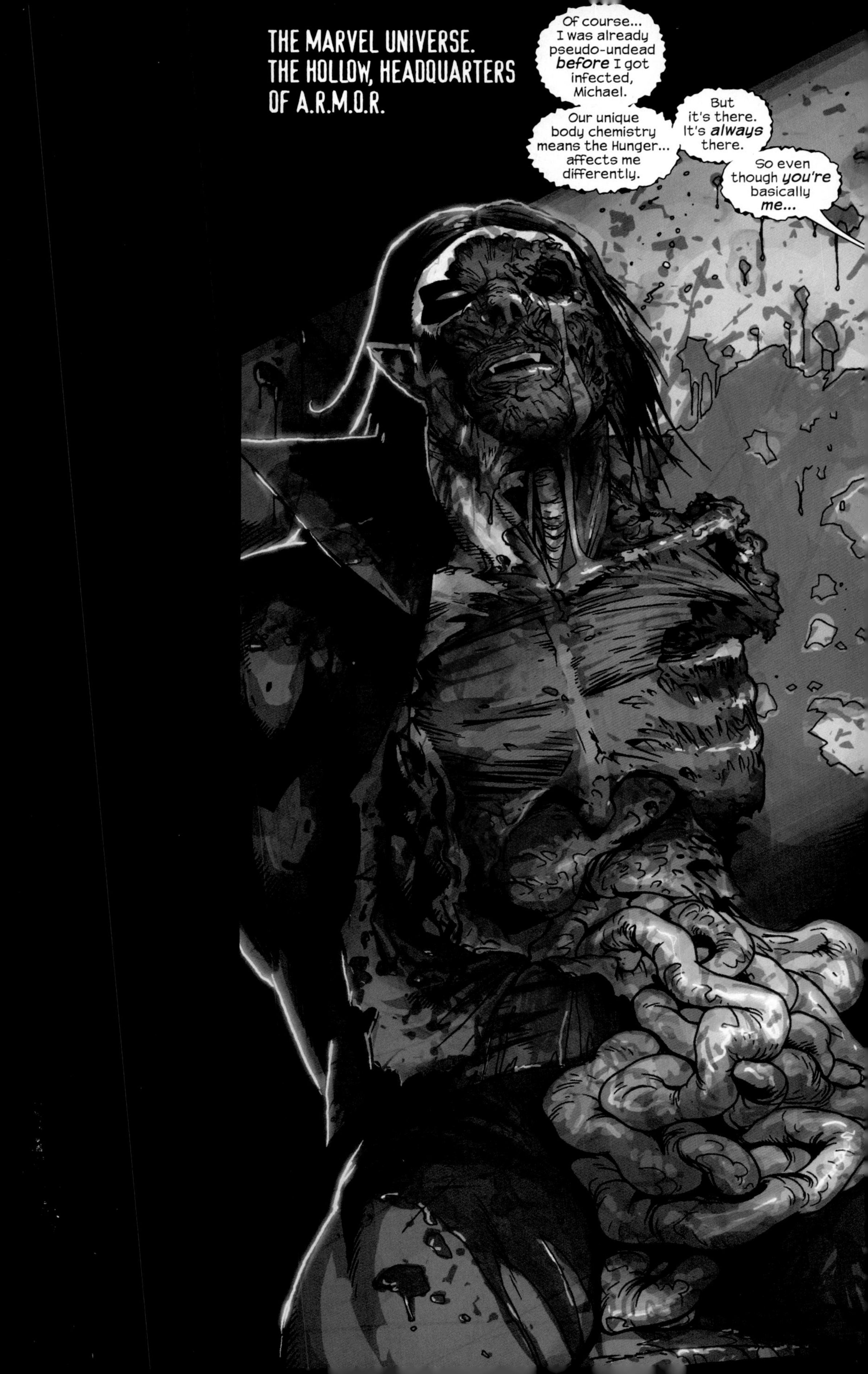
THE MARVEL UNIVERSE.
THE HOLLOW, HEADQUARTERS OF A.R.M.O.R.
Of course... I was already pseudo-undead *before* I got infected, Michael.
Our unique body chemistry means the Hunger... affects me differently.
But it's there. It's *always* there.
So even though *you're* basically *me...*

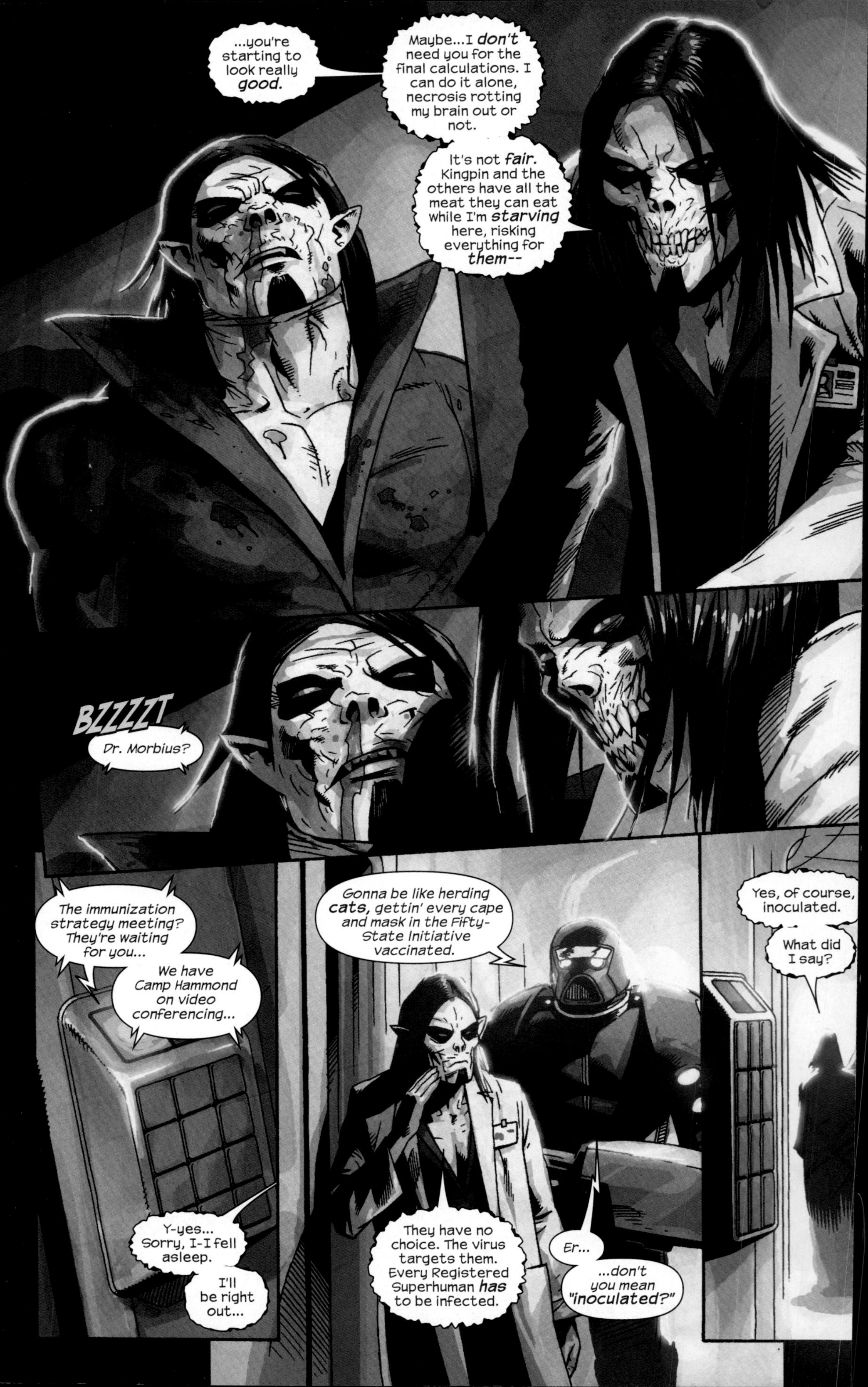
...you're starting to look really good.
Maybe...I don't need you for the final calculations. I can do it alone, necrosis rotting my brain out or not.
It's not fair. Kingpin and the others have all the meat they can eat while I'm starving here, risking everything for them--
BZZZZT
Dr. Morbius?
The immunization strategy meeting? They're waiting for you...
We have Camp Hammond on video conferencing...
Y-yes... Sorry, I-I fell asleep.
I'll be right out...
Gonna be like herding cats, gettin' every cape and mask in the Fifty-State Initiative vaccinated.
They have no choice. The virus targets them. Every Registered Superhuman has to be infected.
Er...
...don't you mean "inoculated?"
Yes, of course, inoculated.
What did I say?

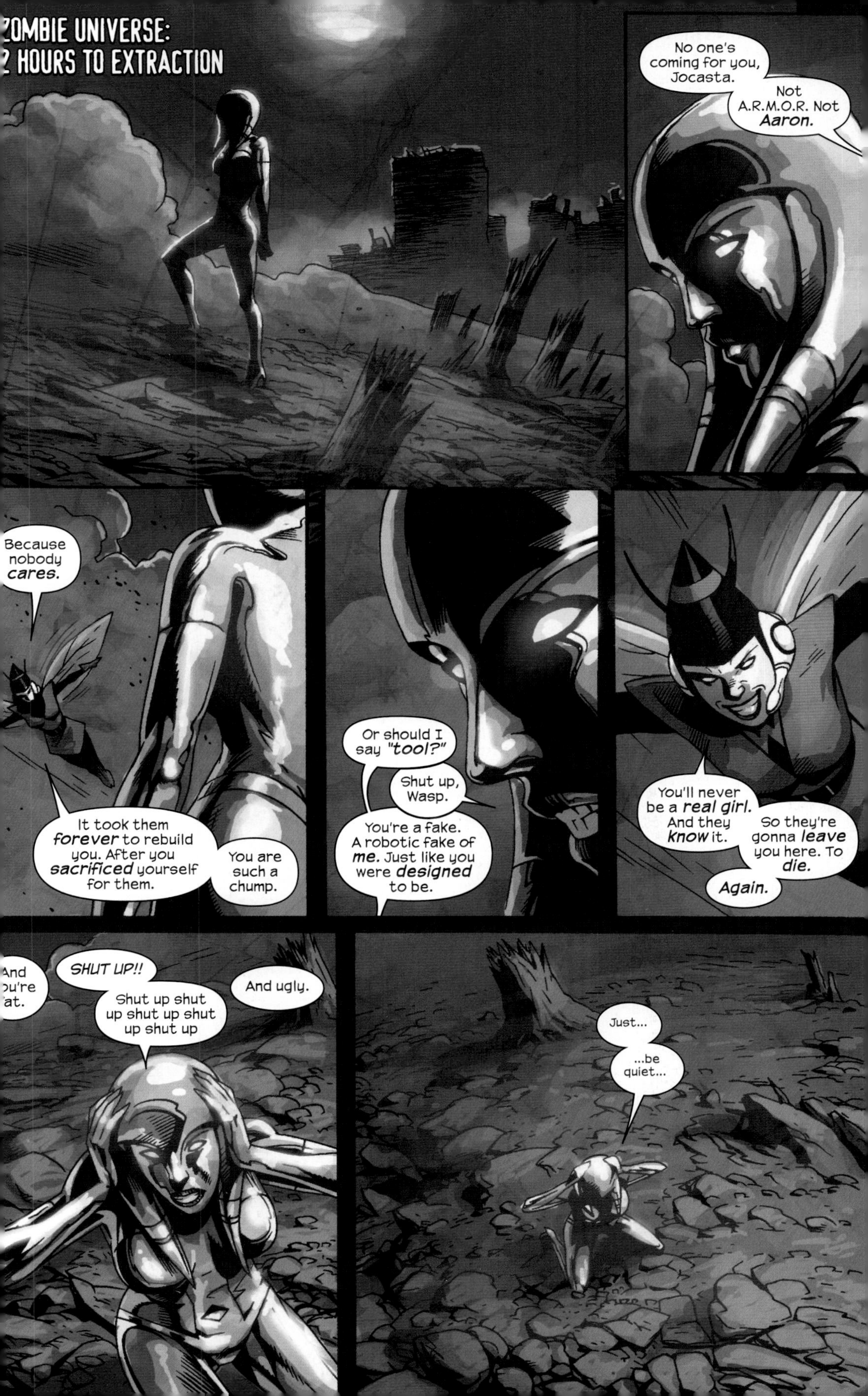
ZOMBIE UNIVERSE:
2 HOURS TO EXTRACTION
No one's coming for you, Jocasta.
Not A.R.M.O.R. Not Aaron.
Because nobody cares.
It took them forever to rebuild you. After you sacrificed yourself for them.
You are such a chump.
Or should I say "tool?"
Shut up, Wasp.
You're a fake. A robotic fake of me. Just like you were designed to be.
You'll never be a real girl. And they know it.
So they're gonna leave you here. To die.
Again.
And you're fat.
SHUT UP!!
Shut up shut up shut up shut up shut up
And ugly.
Just...
...be quiet...

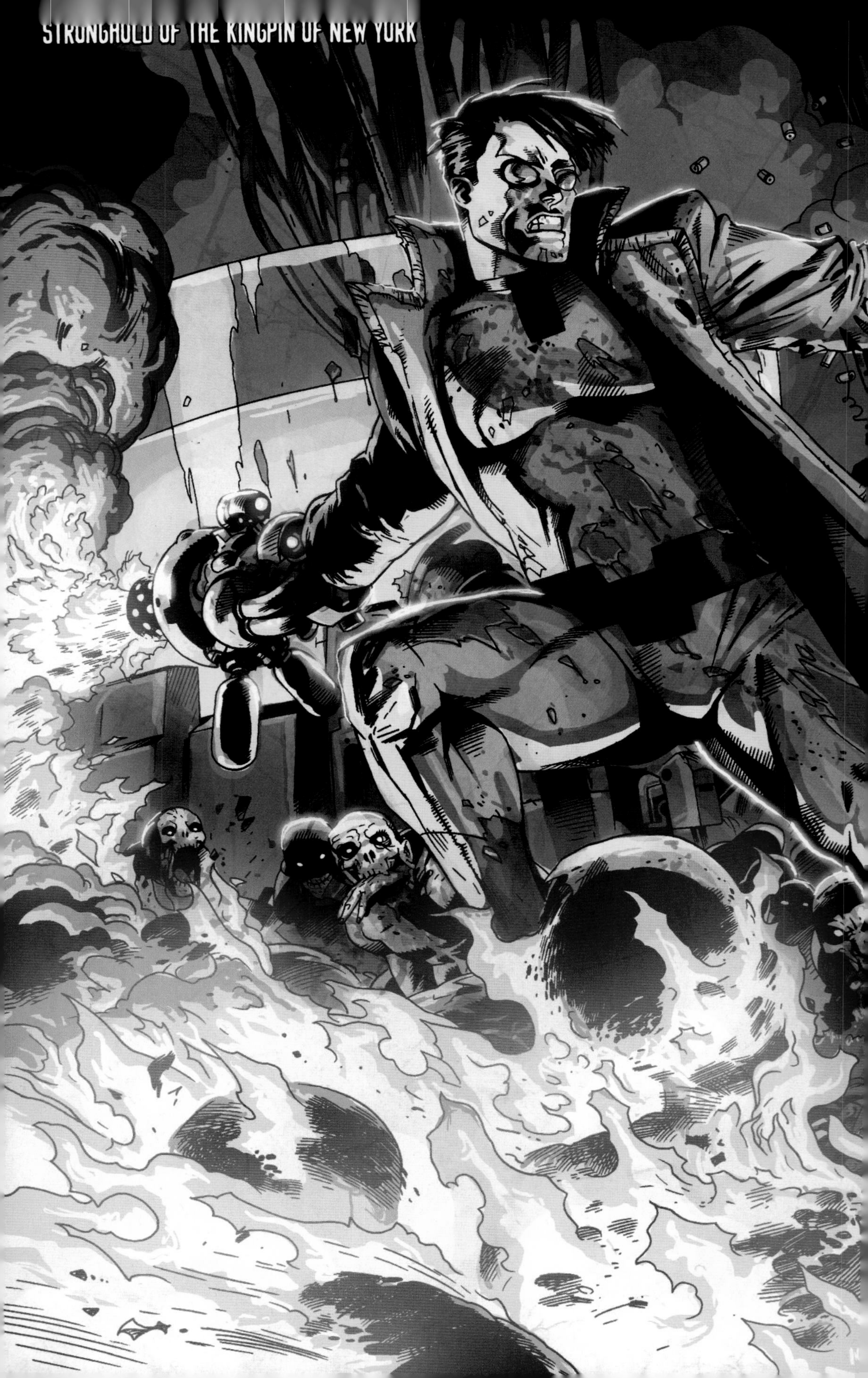
STRONGHOLD OF THE KINGPIN OF NEW YORK

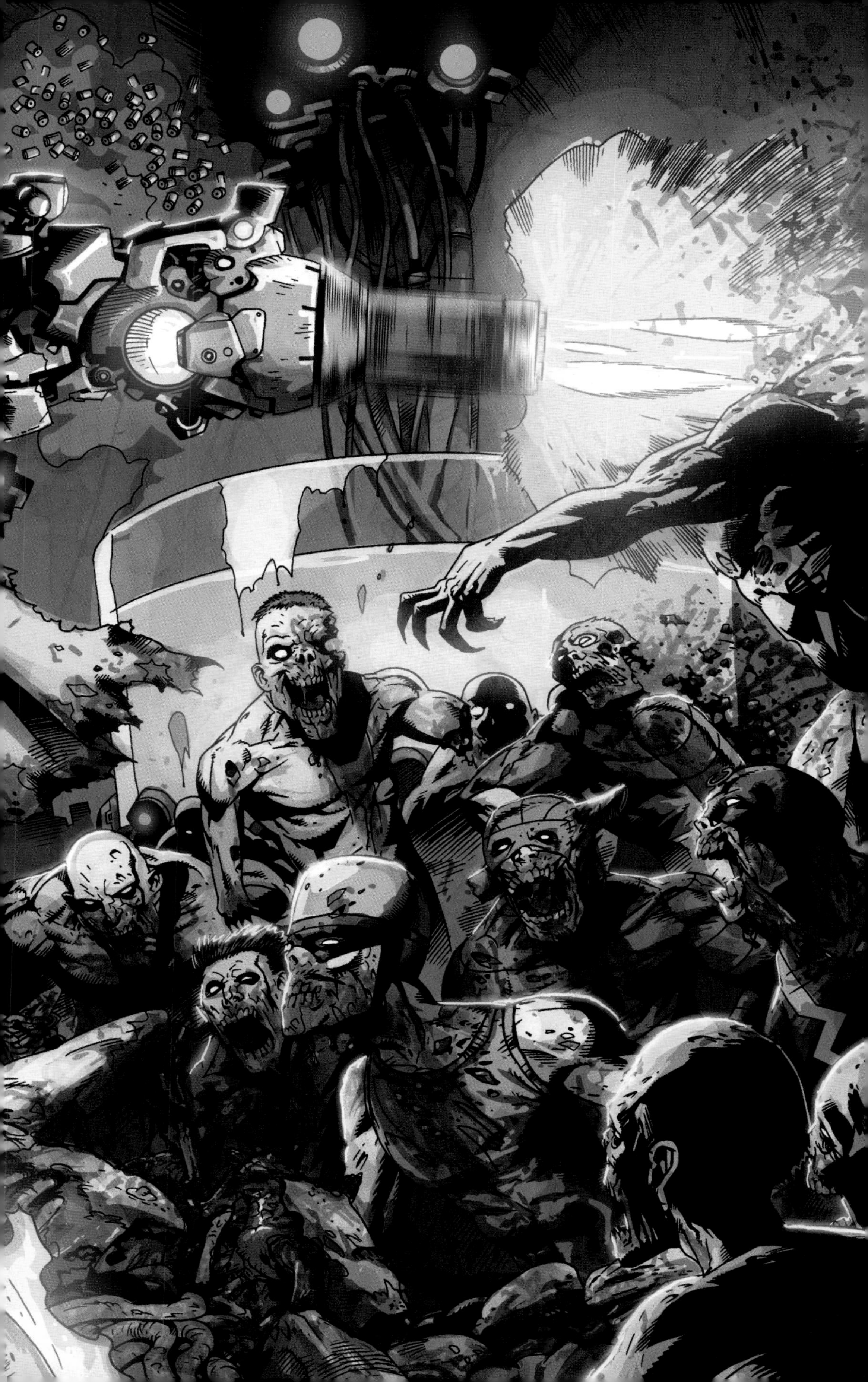

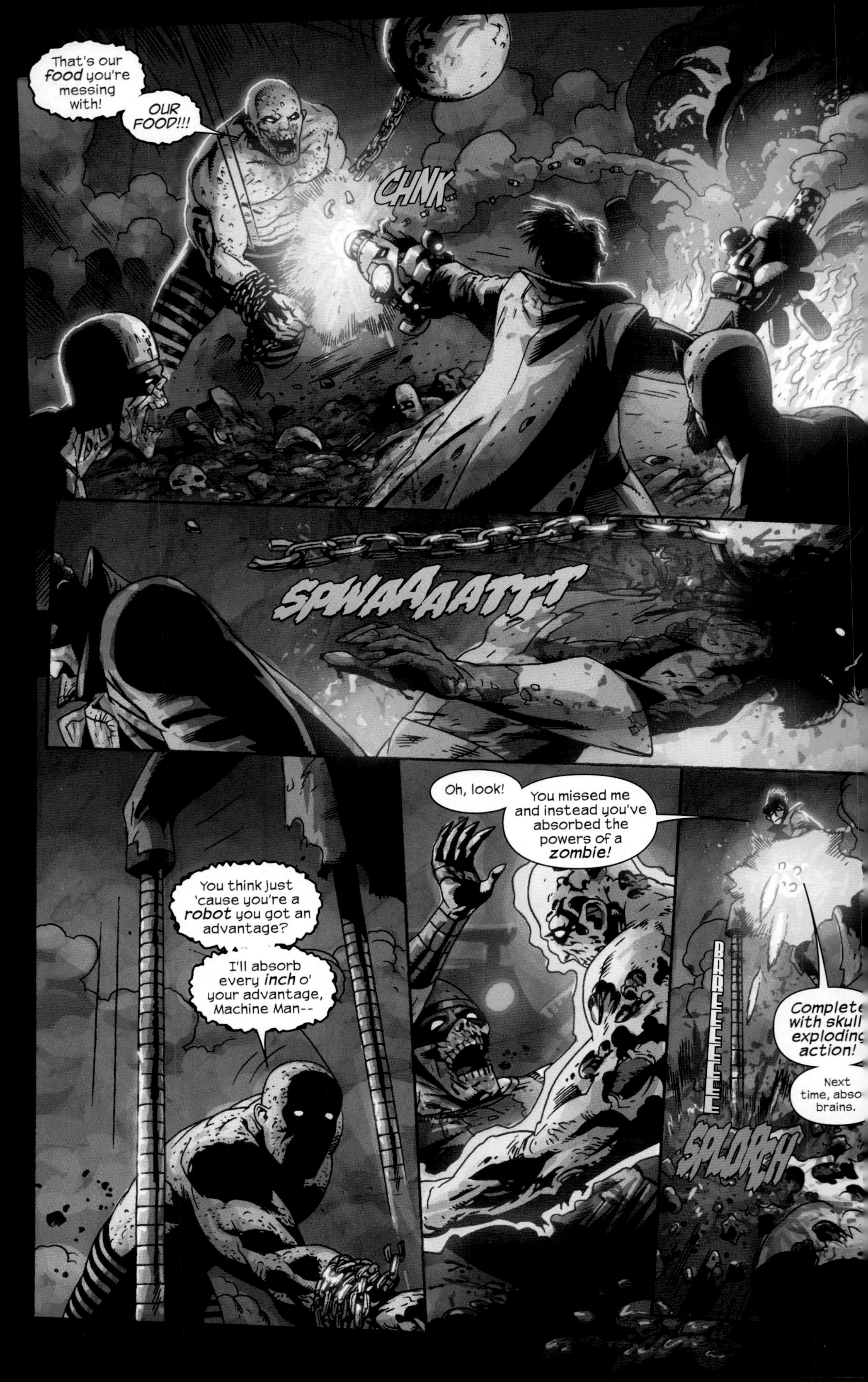
That's our food you're messing with!
OUR FOOD!!!
CHNK
SPWAAAATTT!
You think just 'cause you're a robot you got an advantage?
I'll absorb every inch o' your advantage, Machine Man--
Oh, look!
You missed me and instead you've absorbed the powers of a zombie!
Complete with skull exploding action!
Next time, abso brains.
BRREEEEEEE
SPLORCH

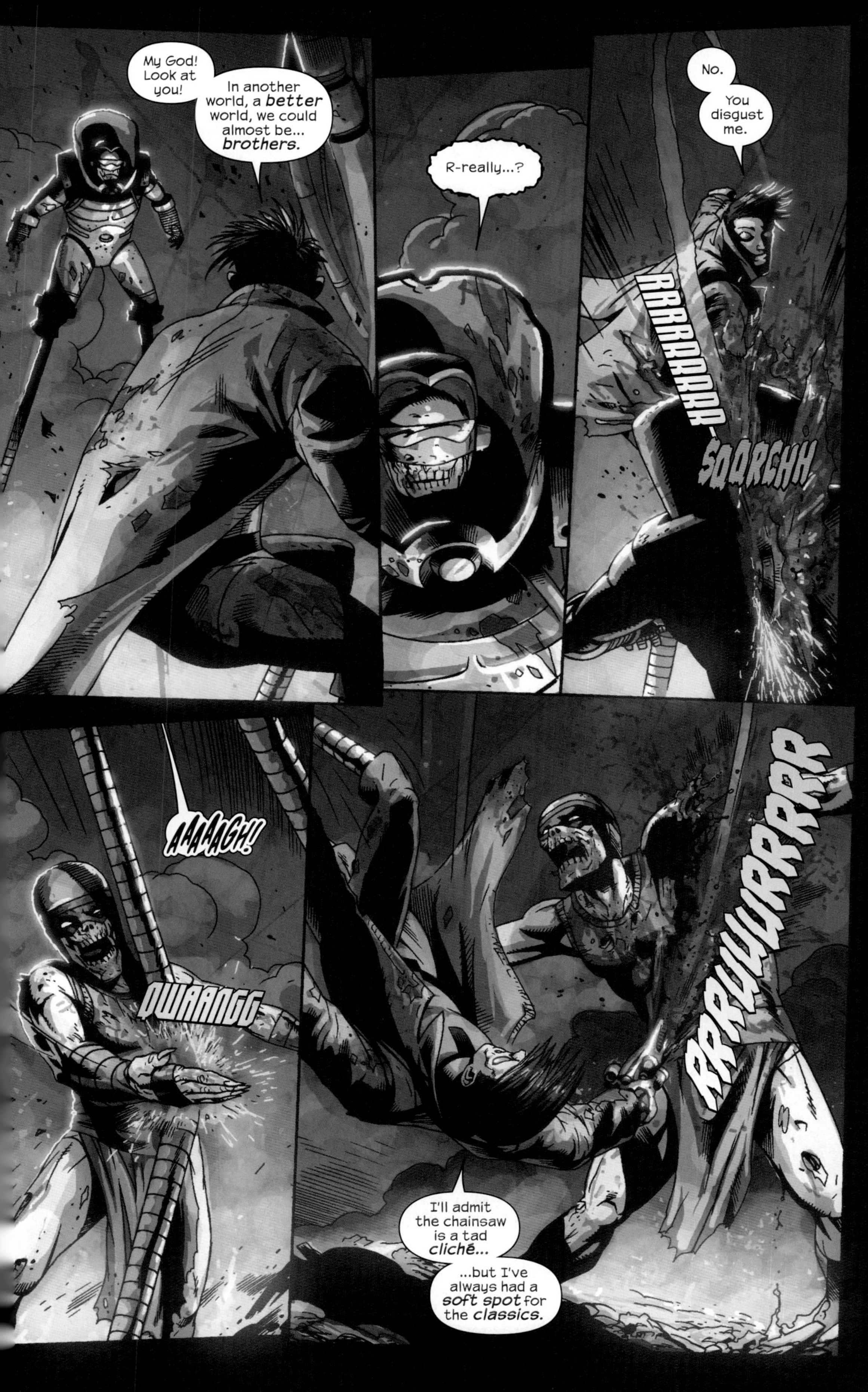
My God! Look at you!
In another world, a *better* world, we could almost be... *brothers.*
R-really...?
No.
You disgust me.
RRRRRRRRR
SQRCHH
AAAAAGH!
DWAANGG
BRRUURRRRR
I'll admit the chainsaw is a tad *cliché*...
...but I've always had a *soft spot* for the *classics.*

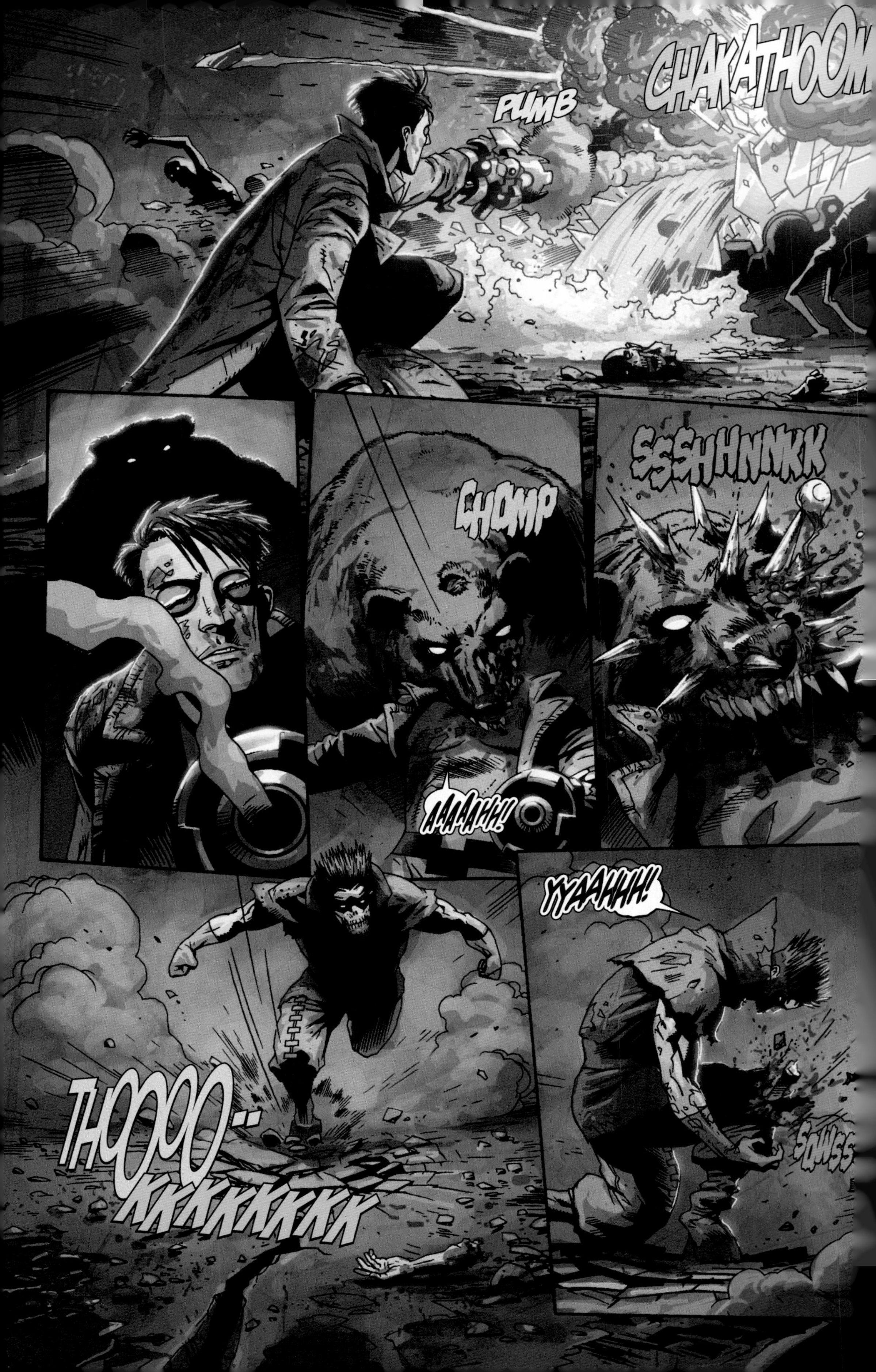
PUMB
CHAKATHOOM
CHOMP
AAAAHH!
SSSHHNNKK
THOOOO--
KKKKKKKKK
YYAAHHH!

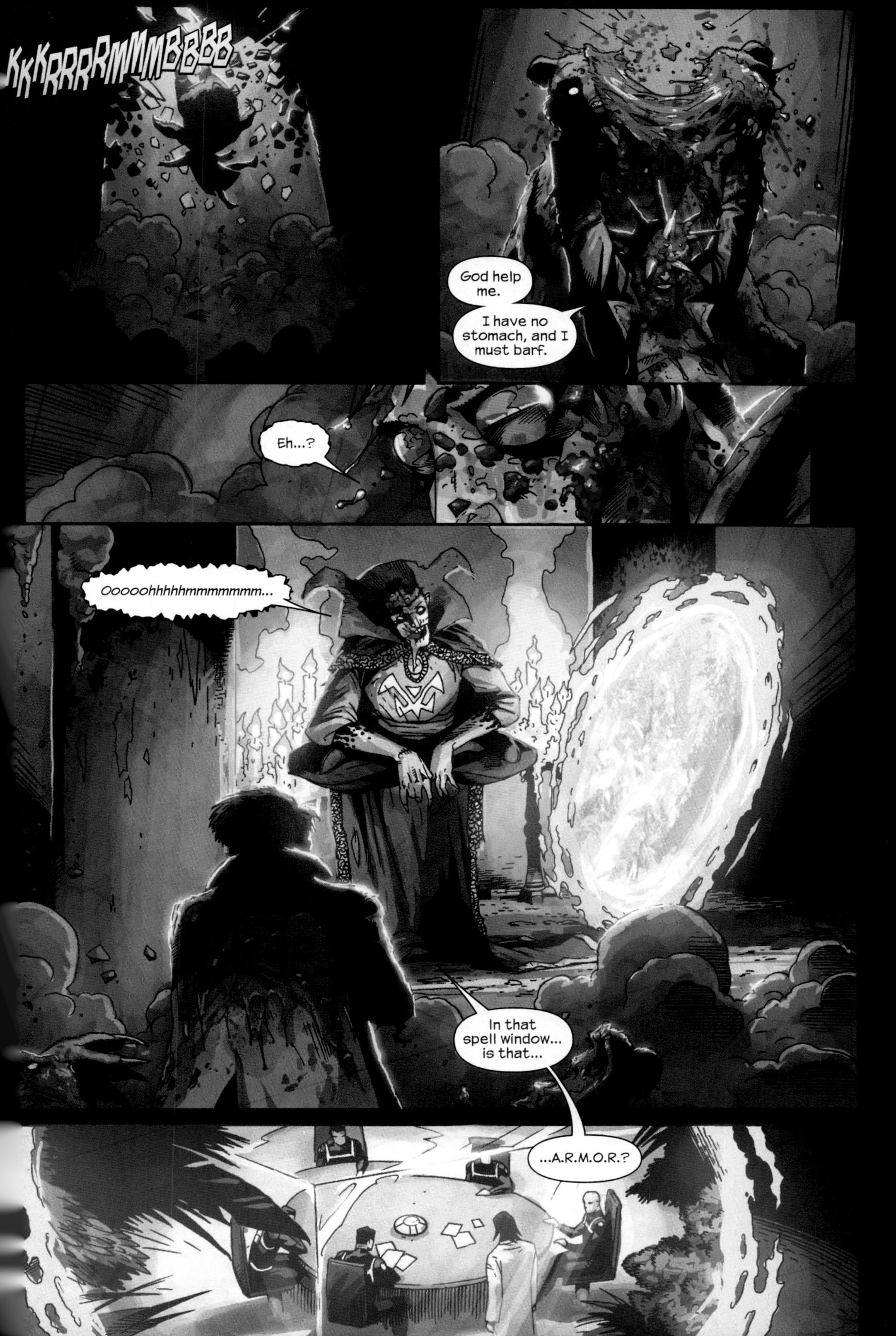
KKKRRRRMMMBBBB
God help me.
I have no stomach, and I must barf.
Eh...?
Ooooohhhhhmmmmmmm...
In that spell window... is that...
...A.R.M.O.R.?

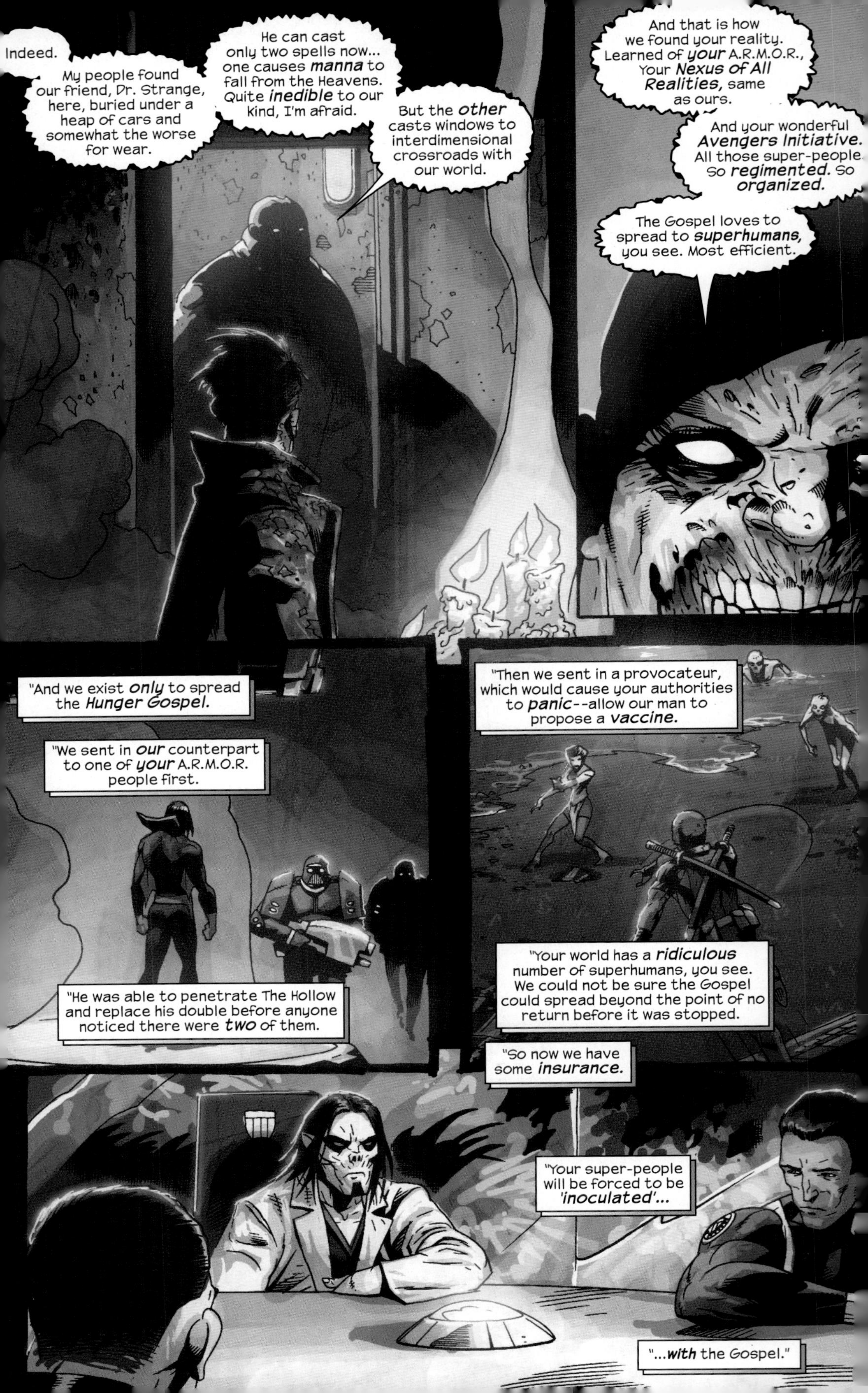
Indeed.
My people found our friend, Dr. Strange, here, buried under a heap of cars and somewhat the worse for wear.
He can cast only two spells now... one causes manna to fall from the Heavens. Quite inedible to our kind, I'm afraid.
But the other casts windows to interdimensional crossroads with our world.
And that is how we found your reality. Learned of your A.R.M.O.R., Your Nexus of All Realities, same as ours.
And your wonderful Avengers Initiative. All those super-people. So regimented. So organized.
The Gospel loves to spread to superhumans, you see. Most efficient.
"And we exist only to spread the Hunger Gospel.
"We sent in our counterpart to one of your A.R.M.O.R. people first.
"He was able to penetrate The Hollow and replace his double before anyone noticed there were two of them.
"Then we sent in a provocateur, which would cause your authorities to panic--allow our man to propose a vaccine.
"Your world has a ridiculous number of superhumans, you see. We could not be sure the Gospel could spread beyond the point of no return before it was stopped.
"So now we have some insurance.
"Your super-people will be forced to be 'inoculated'...
"...with the Gospel."

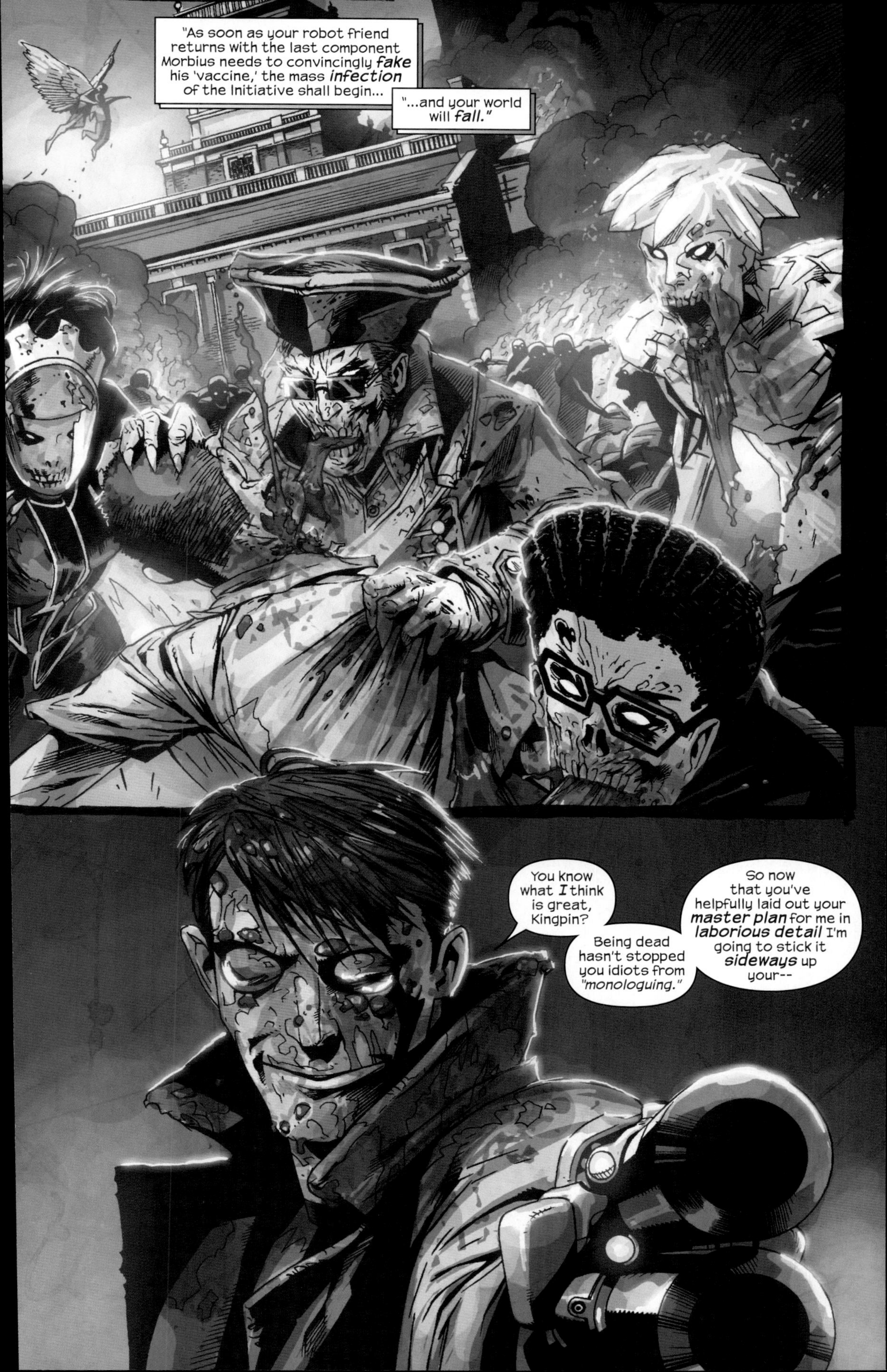
"As soon as your robot friend returns with the last component Morbius needs to convincingly *fake* his 'vaccine,' the mass *infection* of the Initiative shall begin...
"...and your world will *fall.*"
You know what *I* think is great, Kingpin?
Being dead hasn't stopped you idiots from "monologuing."
So now that you've helpfully laid out your *master plan* for me in *laborious detail* I'm going to stick it *sideways* up your--

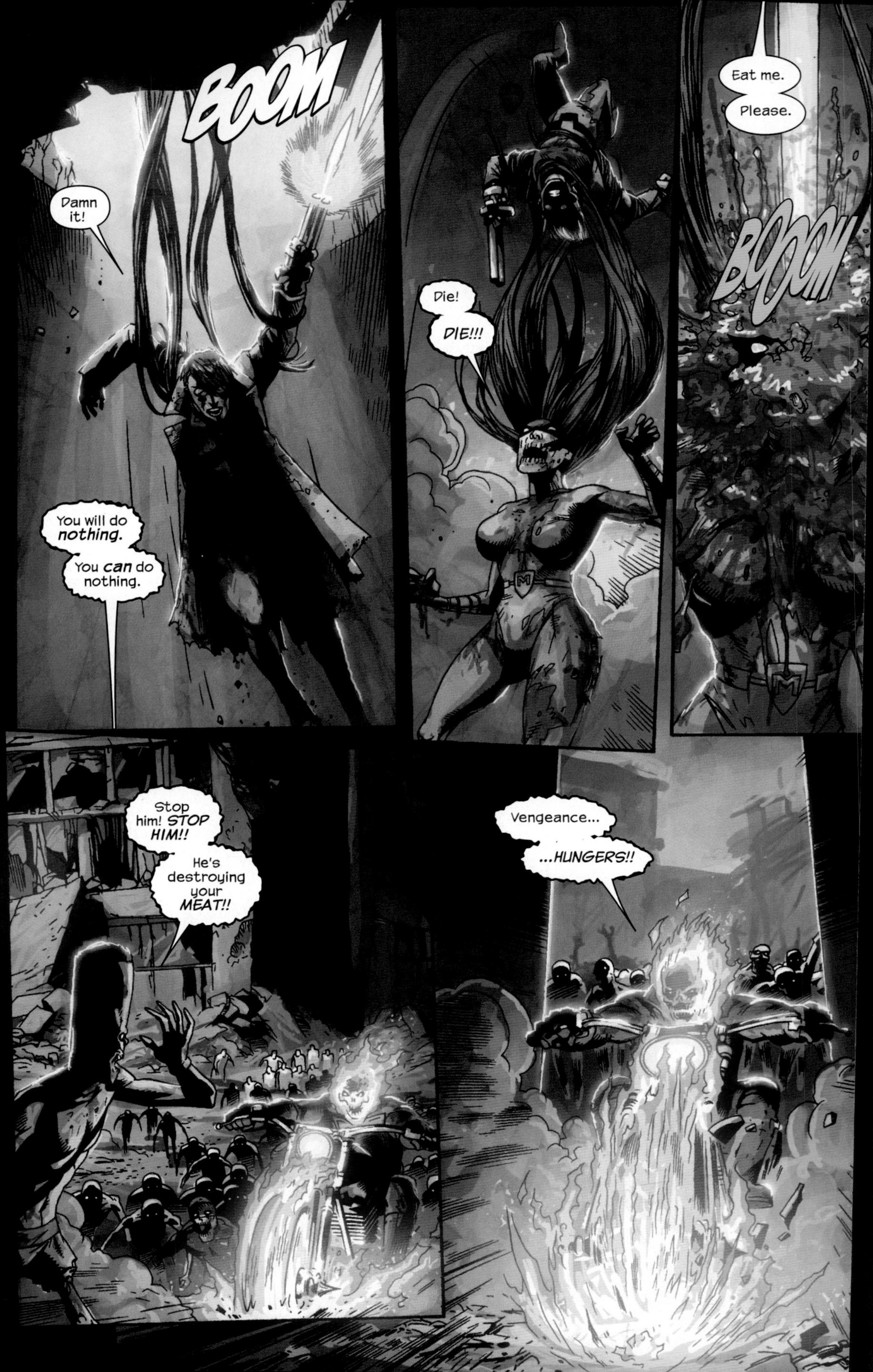
BOOM
Damn it!
You will do nothing.
You can do nothing.
Die!
DIE!!!
Eat me.
Please.
BOOOM
Stop him! STOP HIM!!
He's destroying your MEAT!!
Vengeance...
...HUNGERS!!

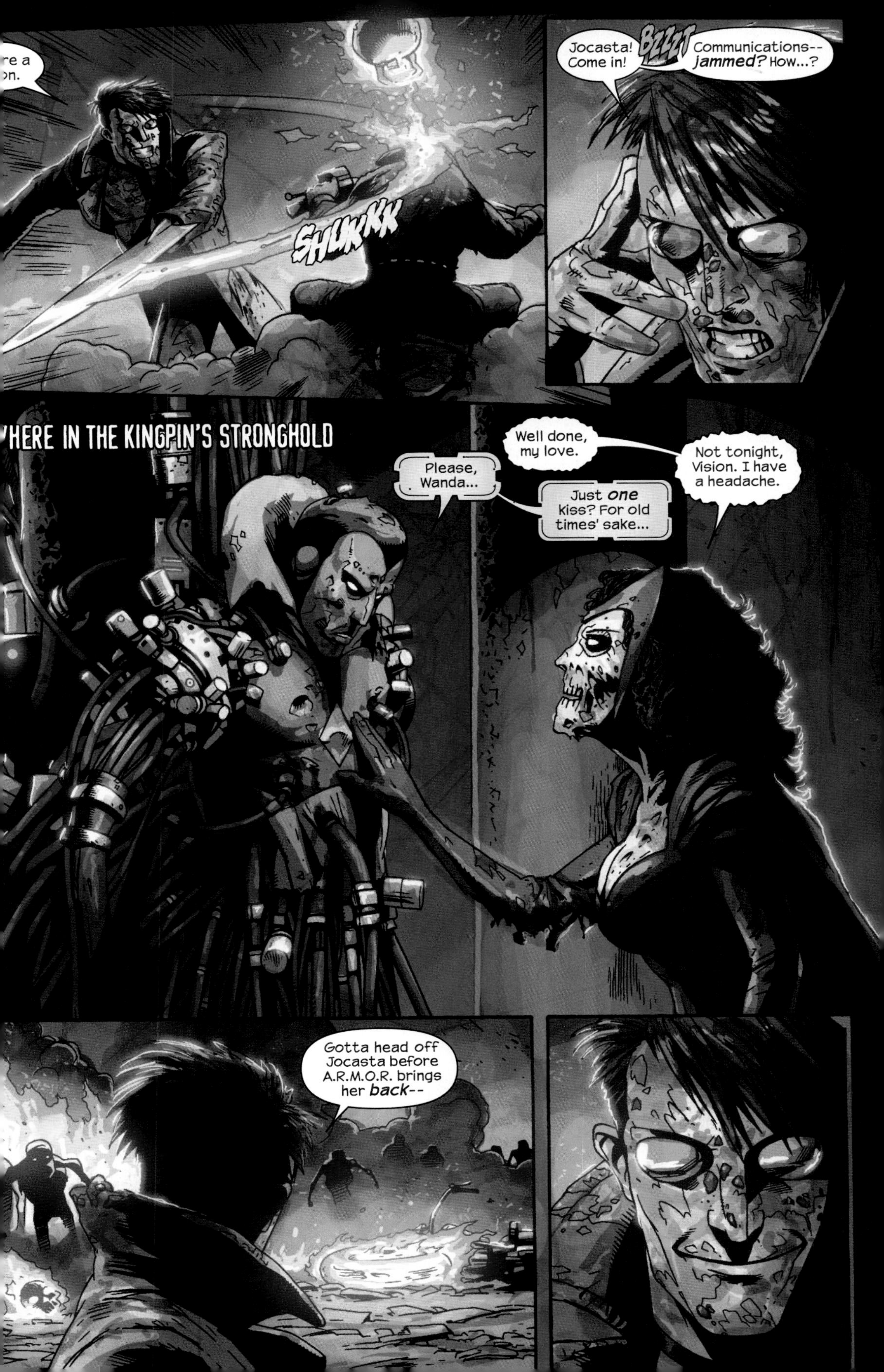

re a
on.
SHUKKK
Jocasta! Come in!
BZZZT
Communications-- *jammed?* How...?
'HERE IN THE KINGPIN'S STRONGHOLD
Please, Wanda...
Well done, my love.
Just *one* kiss? For old times' sake...
Not tonight, Vision. I have a headache.
Gotta head off Jocasta before A.R.M.O.R. brings her *back*--

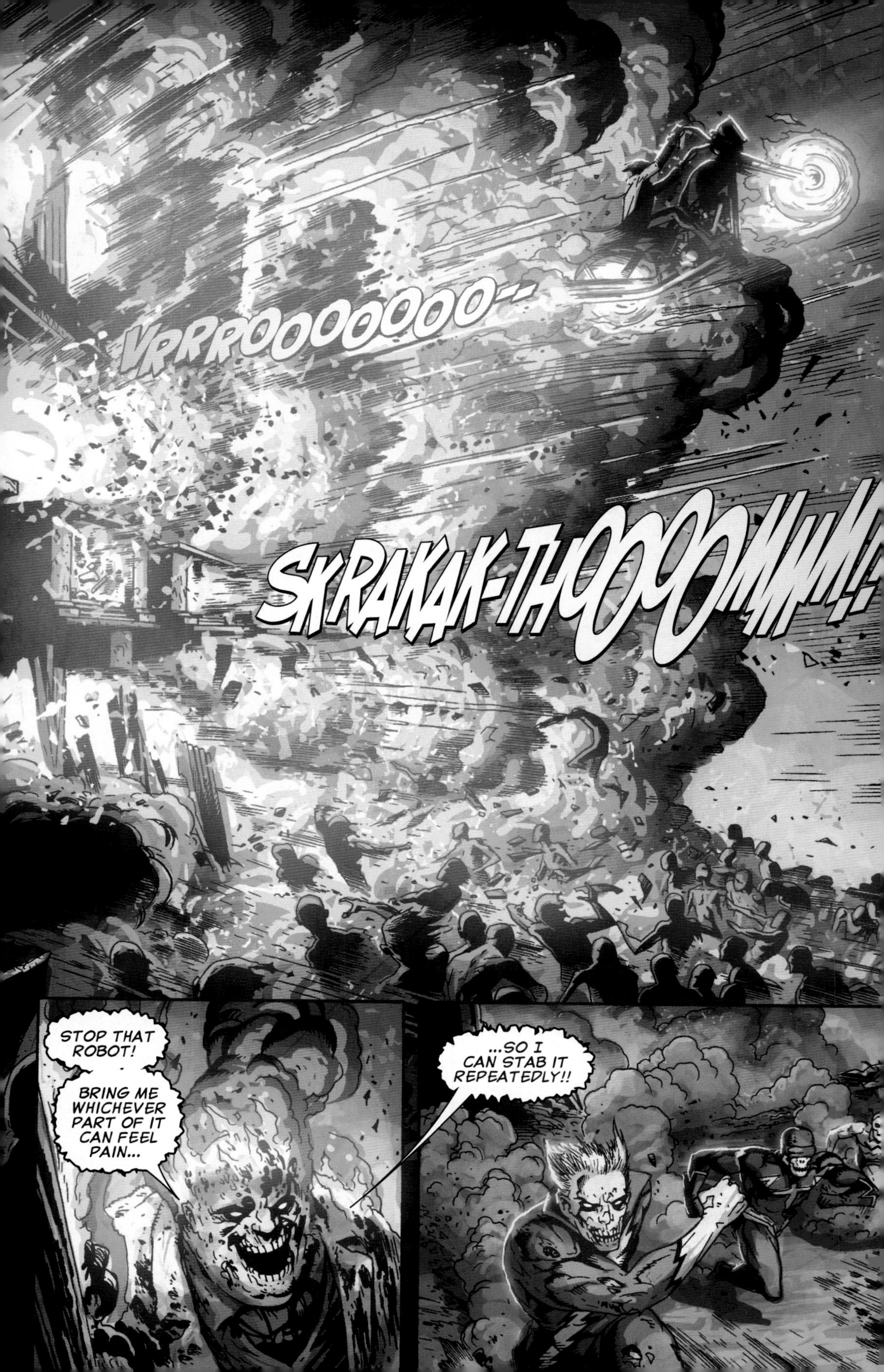
VRRROOOOOOOO--
SKRAKAK-THOOOOMMM!!
STOP THAT ROBOT!
BRING ME WHICHEVER PART OF IT CAN FEEL PAIN...
...SO I CAN STAB IT REPEATEDLY!!

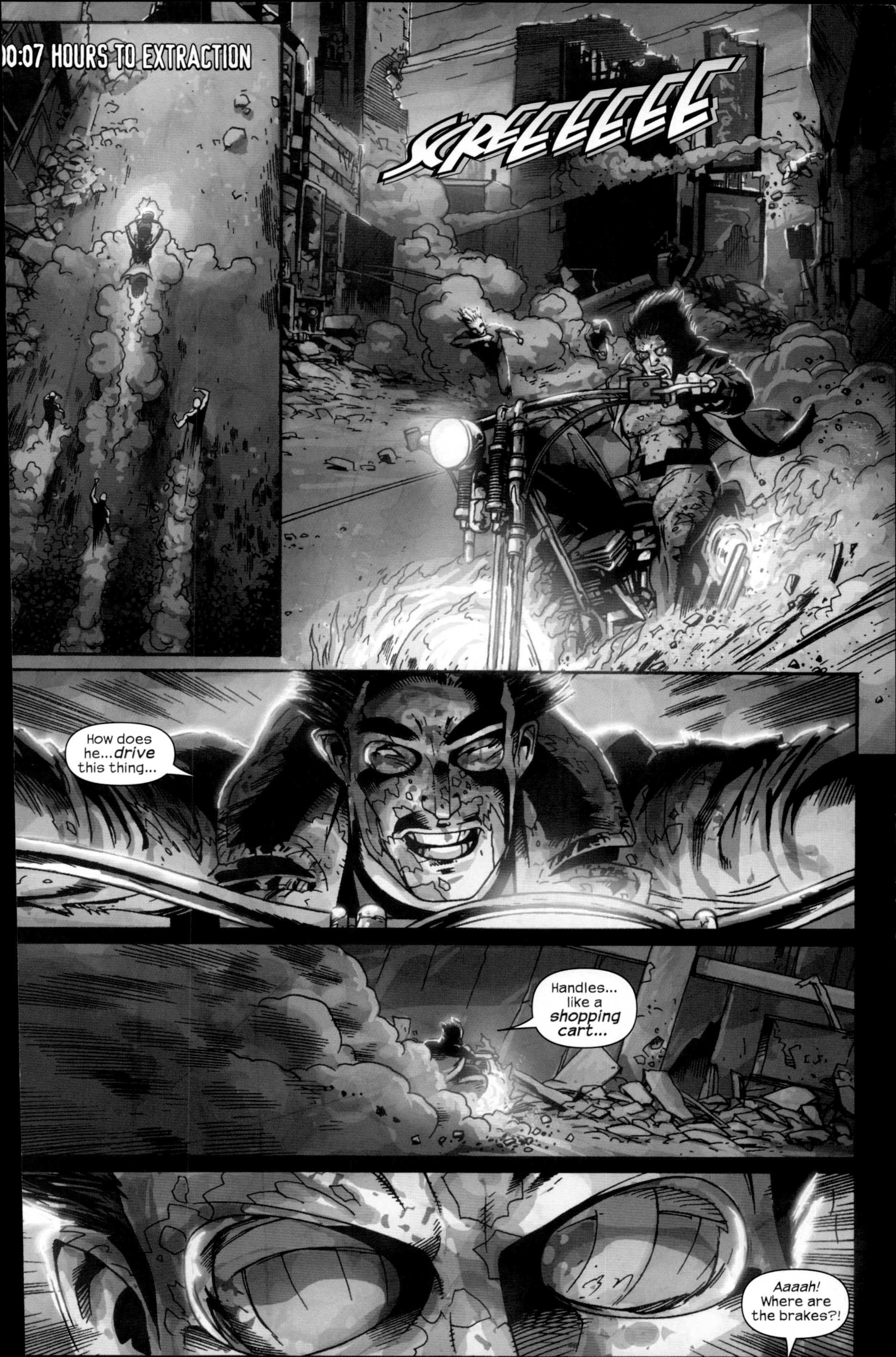

00:07 HOURS TO EXTRACTION
SCREEEEEEE
How does he...*drive* this thing...
Handles... like a *shopping cart*...
Aaaah! Where are the brakes?!

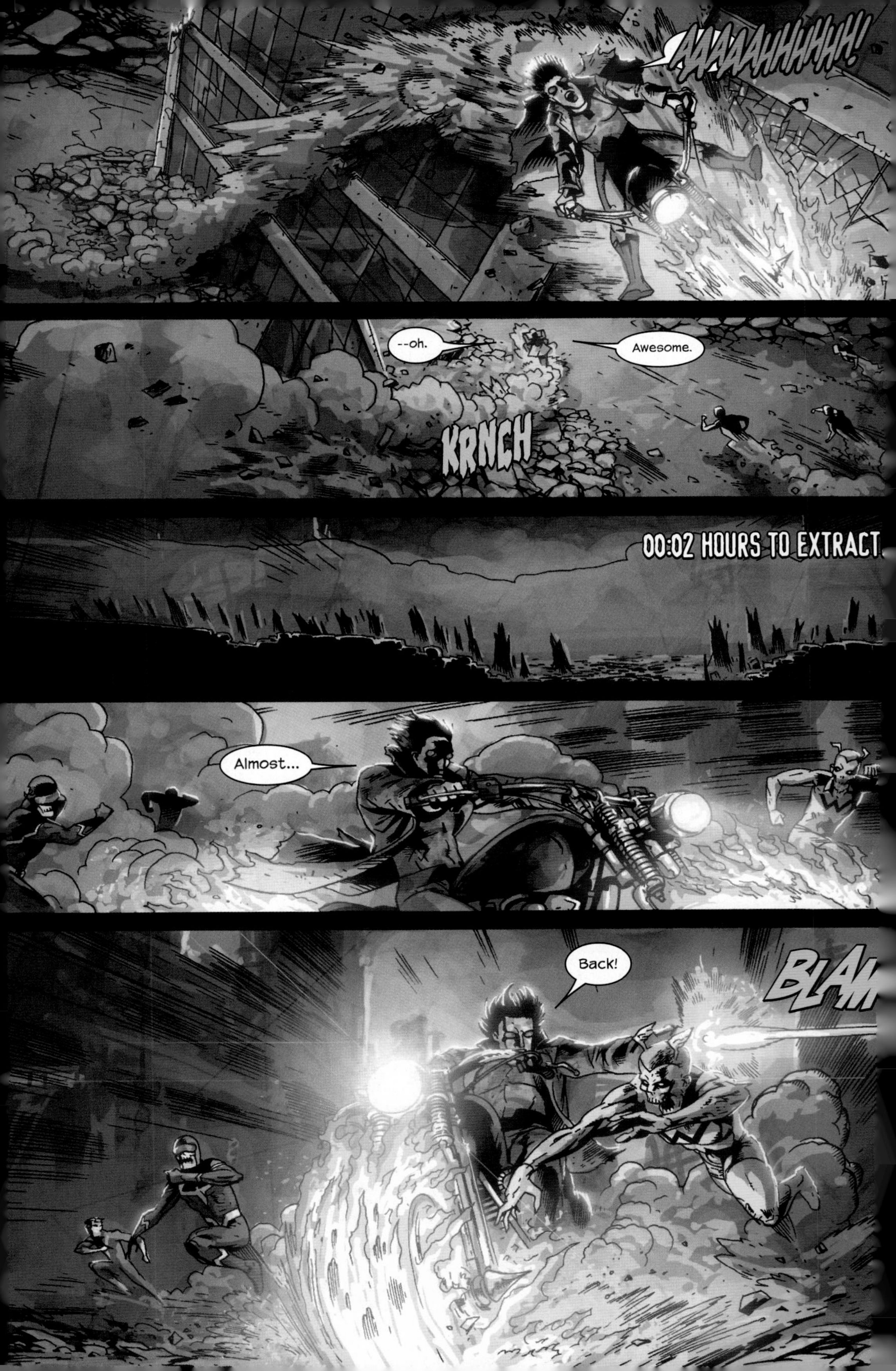
AAAAAHHHHH!
--oh.
Awesome.
KRNCH
00:02 HOURS TO EXTRACT
Almost...
Back!
BLAM

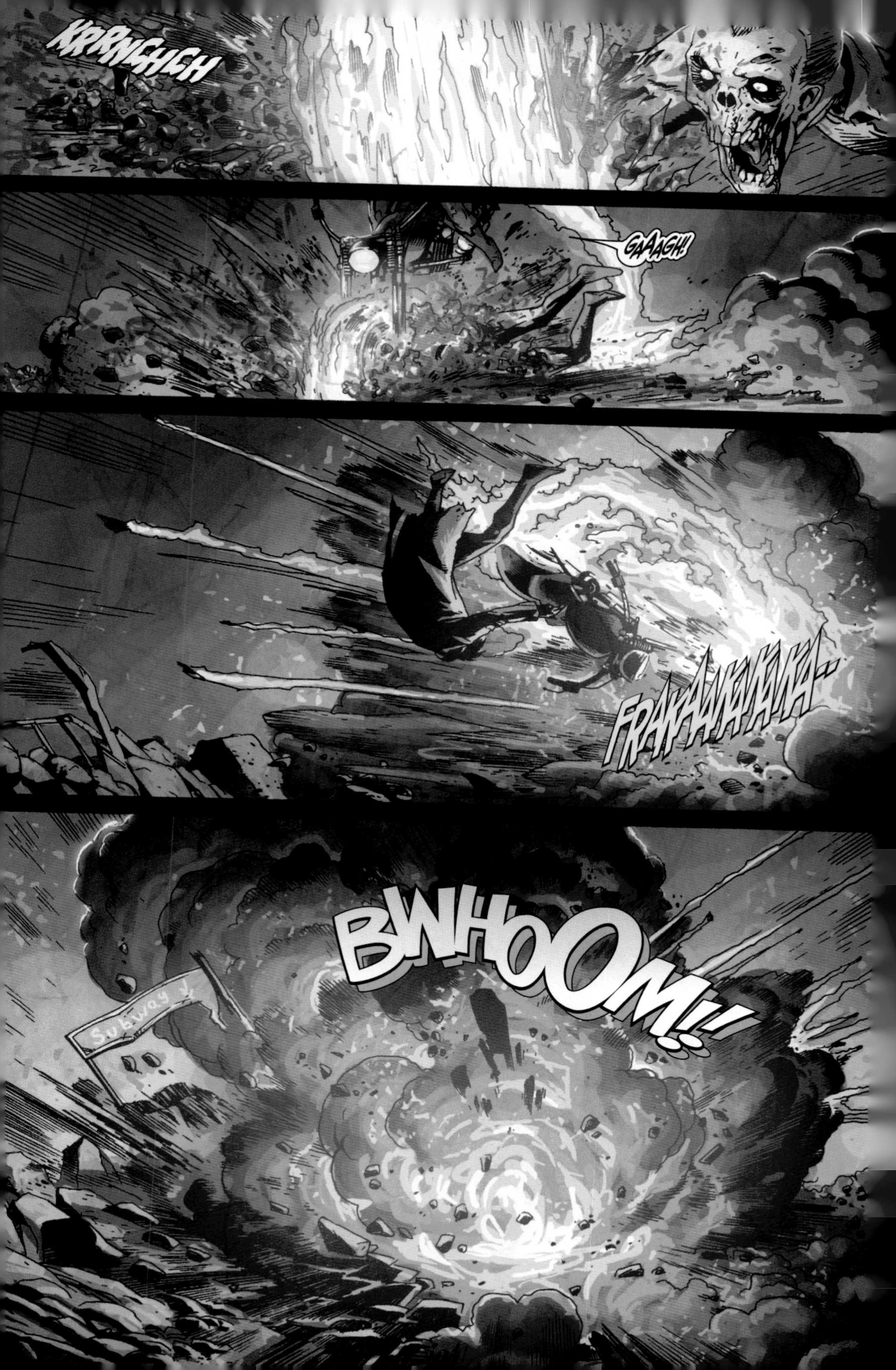
KRRNCHCH
GAAAGH!
FRAKAAKAKAKA--
Subway
BWHOOOM!!

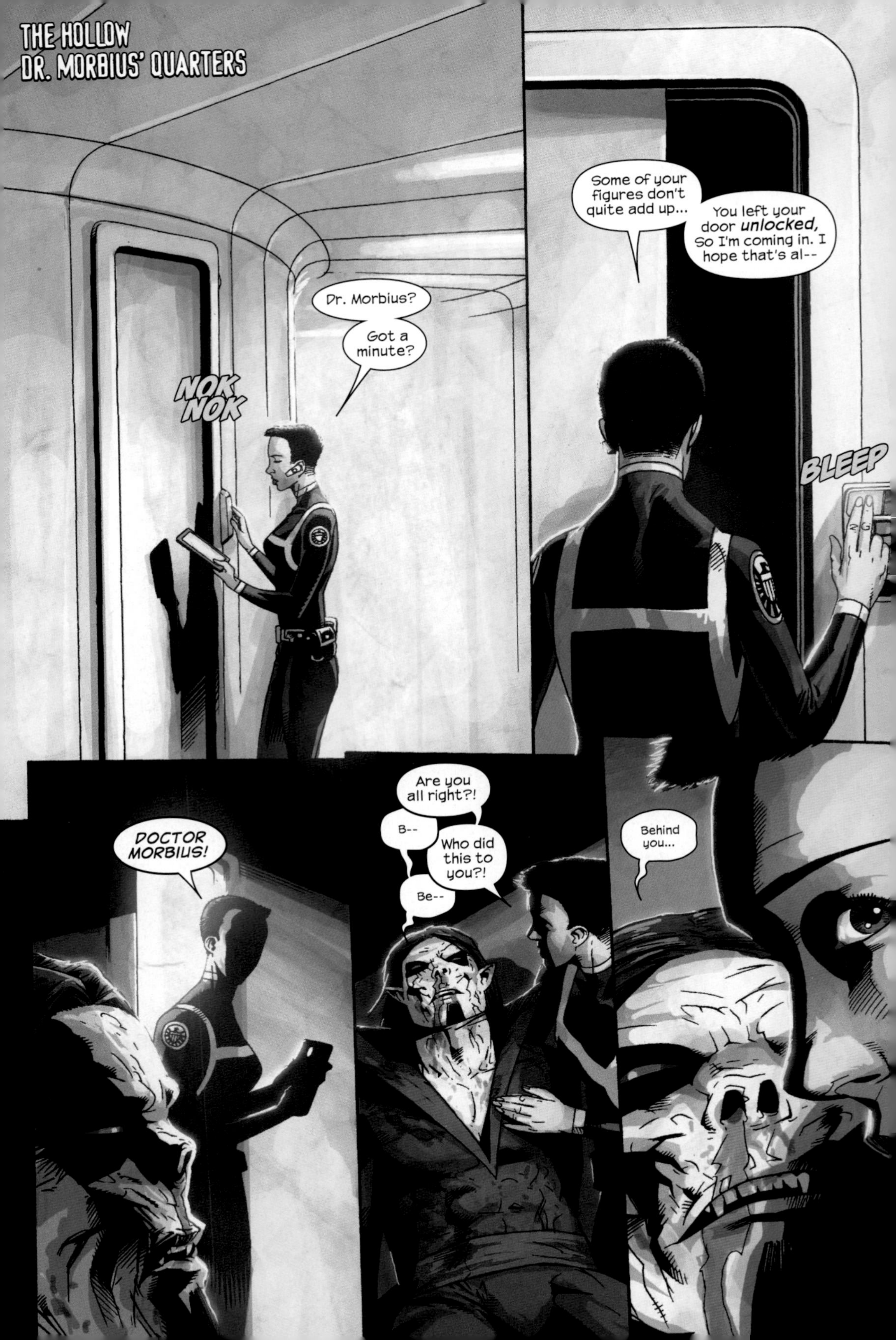
THE HOLLOW
DR. MORBIUS' QUARTERS
NOK NOK
Dr. Morbius?
Got a minute?
Some of your figures don't quite add up...
You left your door unlocked, So I'm coming in. I hope that's al--
BLEEP
DOCTOR MORBIUS!
Are you all right?!
B--
Who did this to you?!
Be--
Behind you...

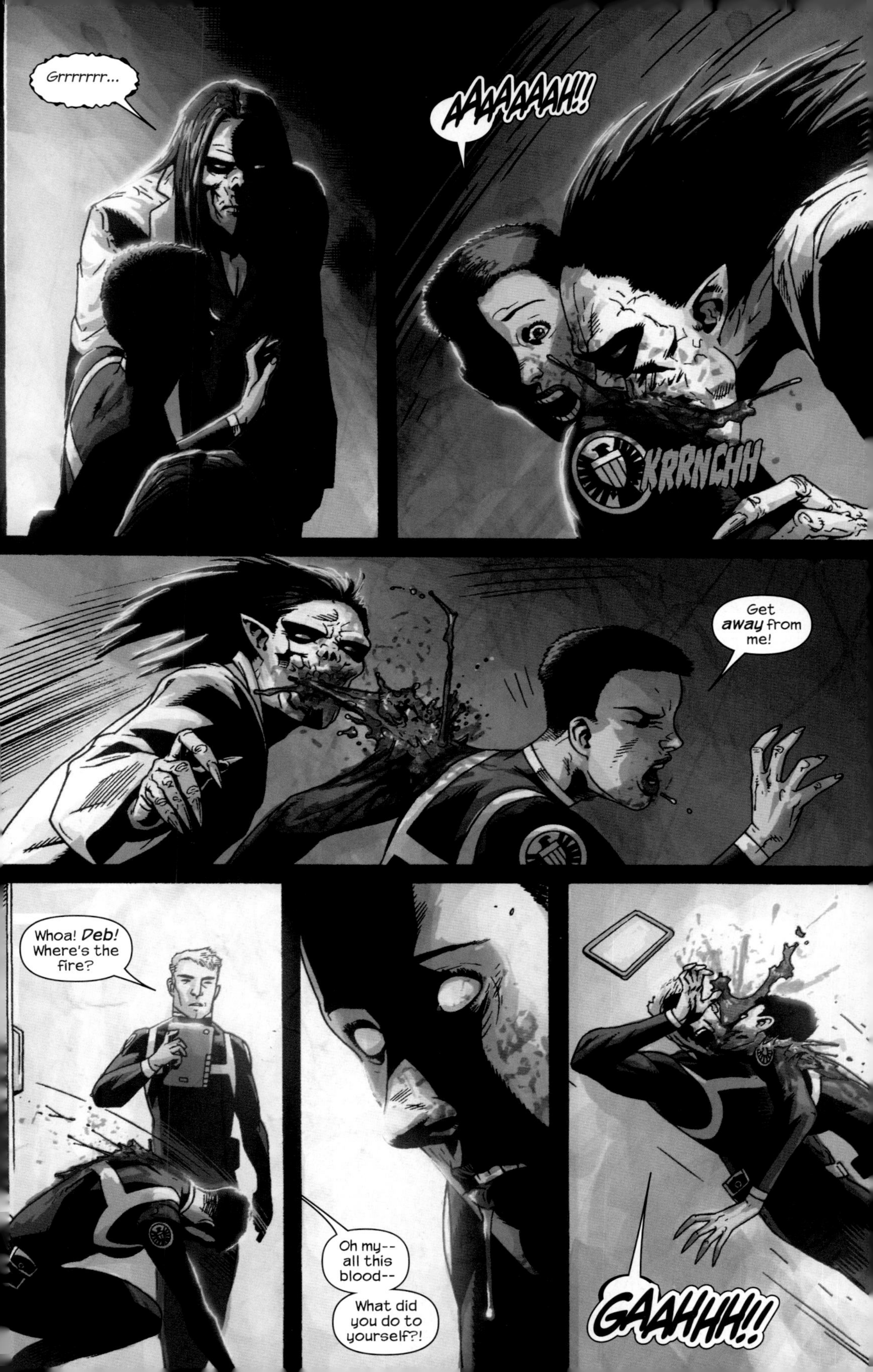
Grrrrrrr...
AAAAAAAH!!
KRRNCHH
Get away from me!
Whoa! Deb! Where's the fire?
Oh my-- all this blood--
What did you do to yourself?!
GAAHHH!!

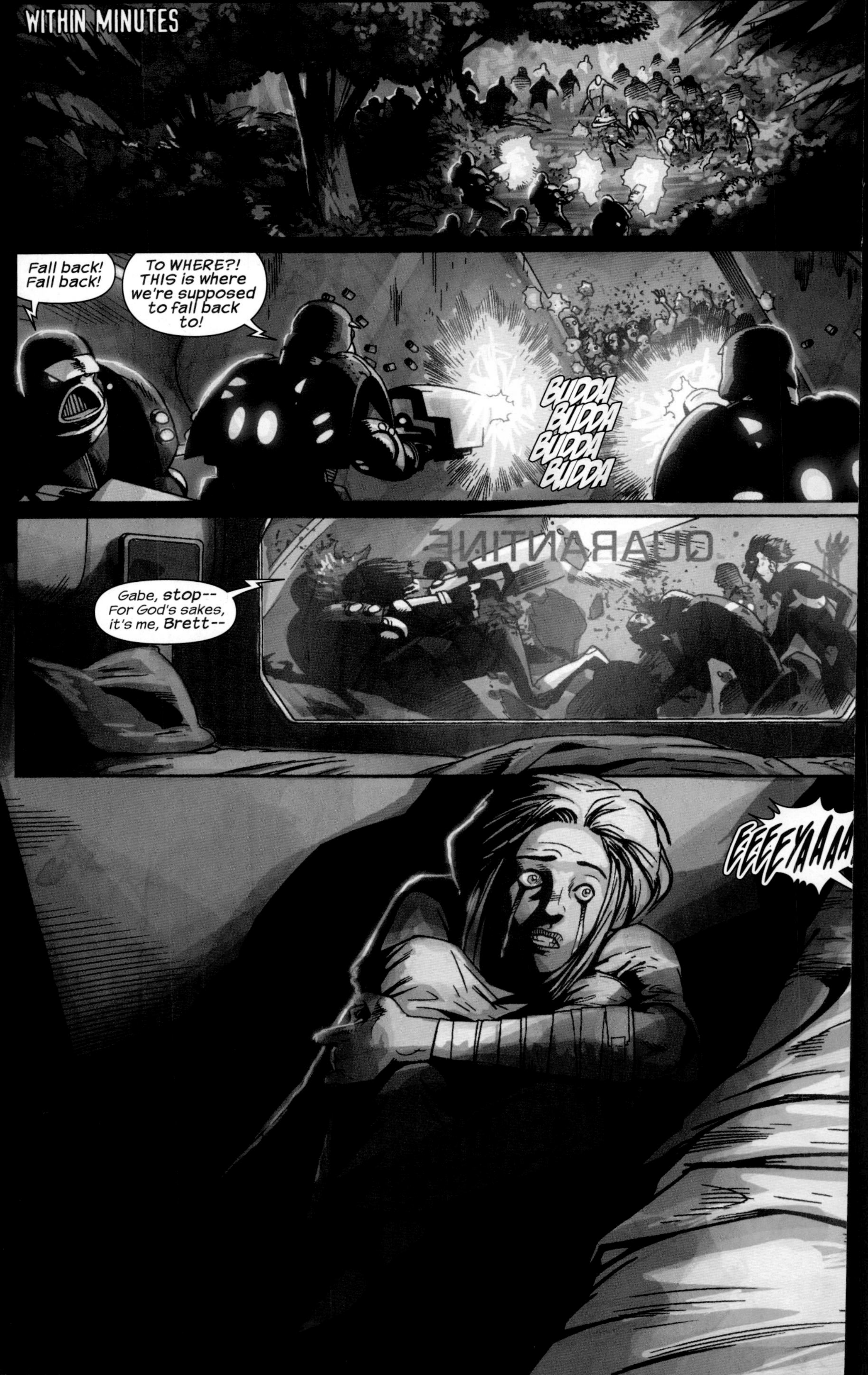
WITHIN MINUTES
Fall back! Fall back!
TO WHERE?! THIS is where we're supposed to fall back to!
BUDDA BUDDA BUDDA BUDDA
QUARANTINE
Gabe, stop-- For God's sakes, it's me, Brett--

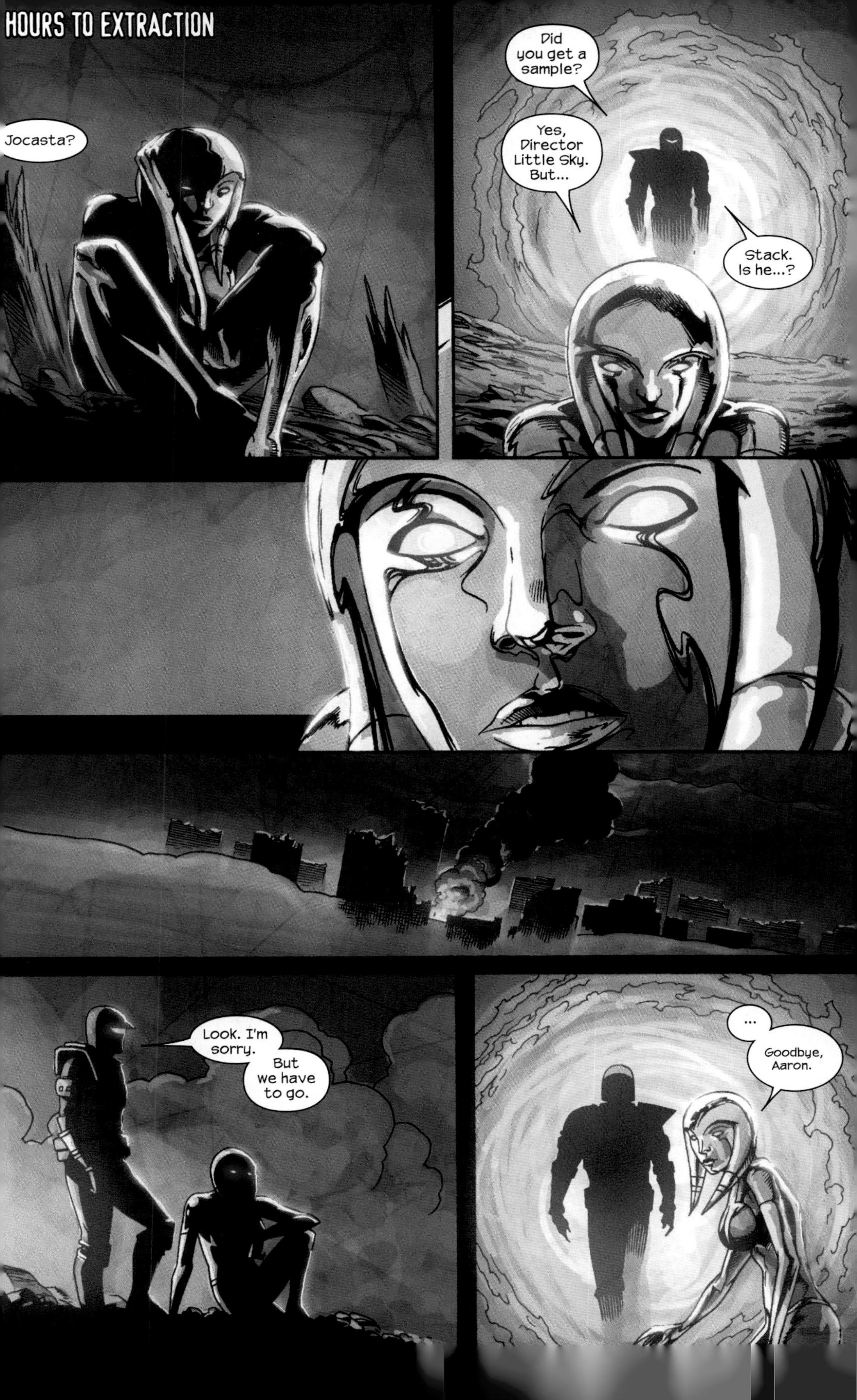
HOURS TO EXTRACTION
Jocasta?
Did you get a sample?
Yes, Director Little Sky. But...
Stack. Is he...?
Look. I'm sorry.
But we have to go.
...
Goodbye, Aaron.

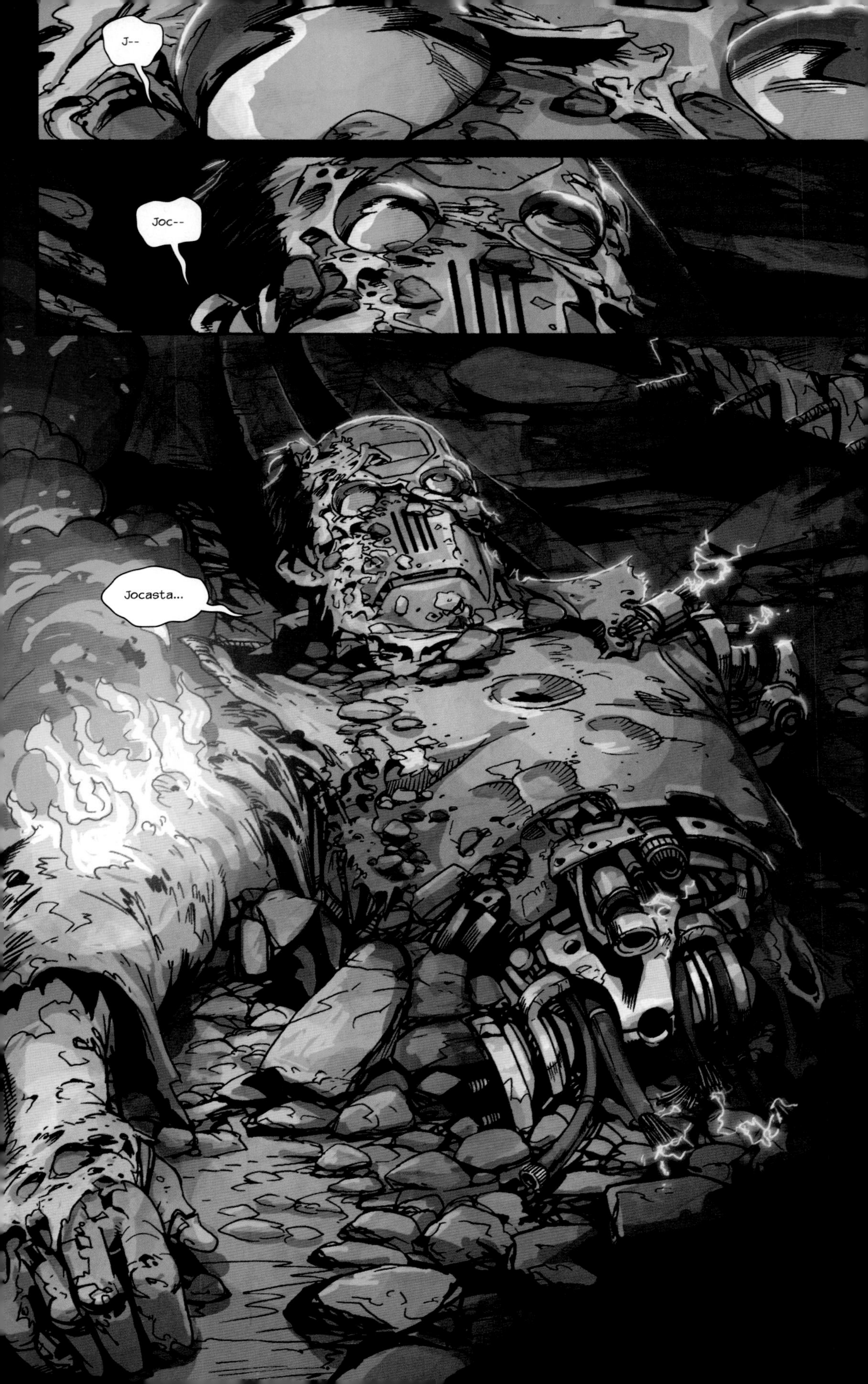
J--
Joc--
Jocasta...

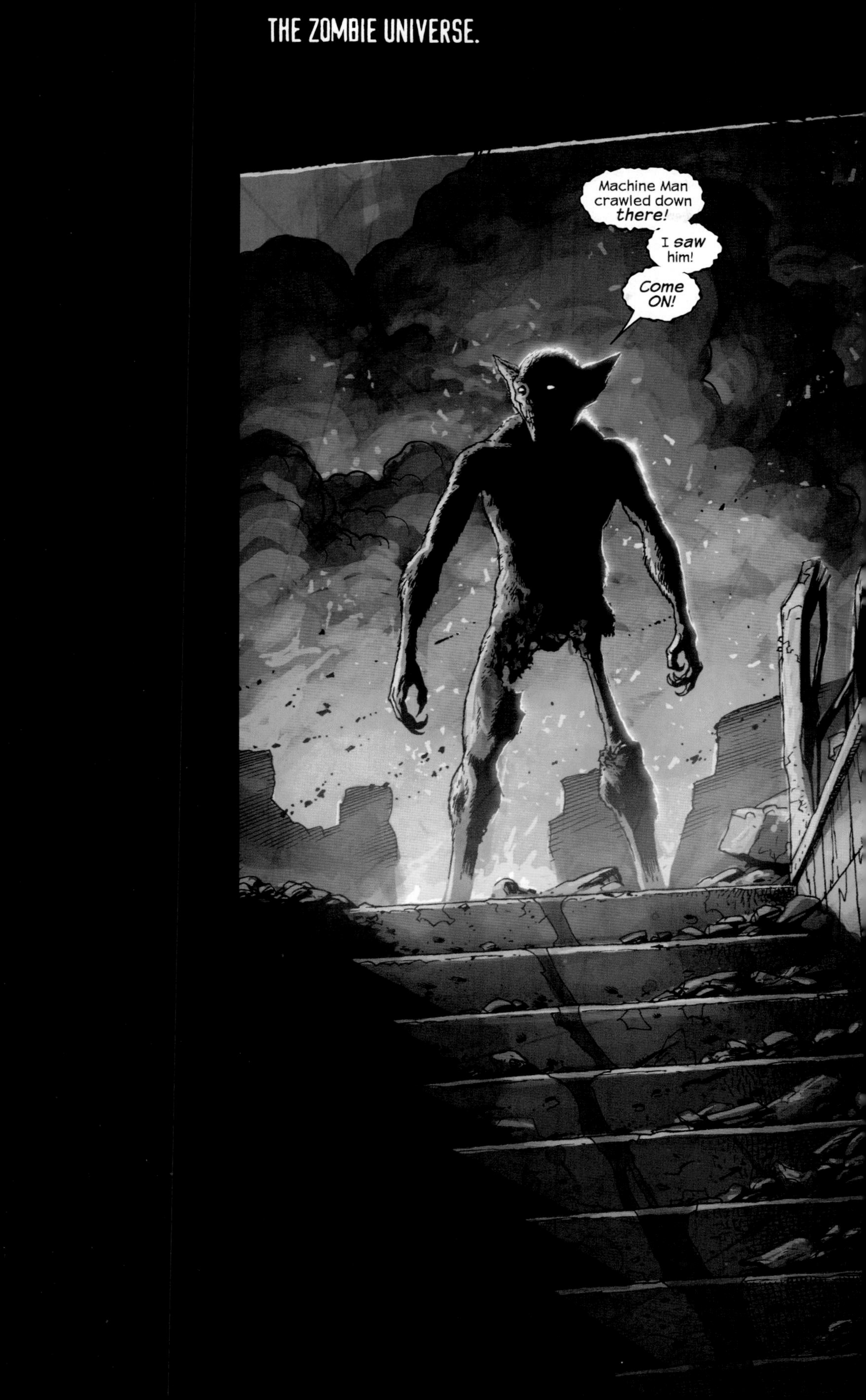
THE ZOMBIE UNIVERSE.
Machine Man crawled down there!
I saw him!
Come ON!

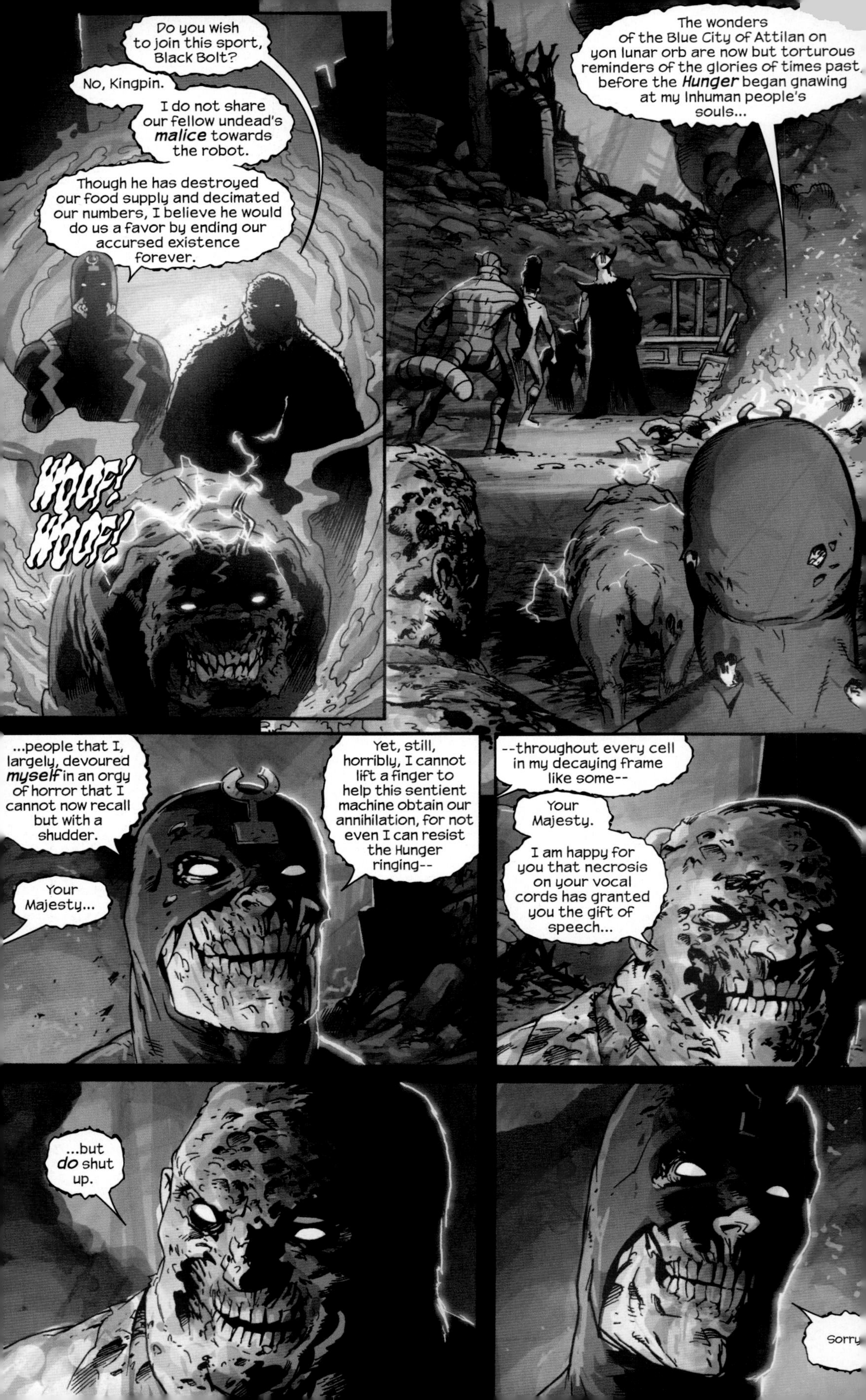
Do you wish to join this sport, Black Bolt?
No, Kingpin.
I do not share our fellow undead's *malice* towards the robot.
Though he has destroyed our food supply and decimated our numbers, I believe he would do us a favor by ending our accursed existence forever.
WOOF! WOOF!
The wonders of the Blue City of Attilan on yon lunar orb are now but torturous reminders of the glories of times past, before the *Hunger* began gnawing at my Inhuman people's souls...
...people that I, largely, devoured *myself* in an orgy of horror that I cannot now recall but with a shudder.
Your Majesty...
Yet, still, horribly, I cannot lift a finger to help this sentient machine obtain our annihilation, for not even I can resist the Hunger ringing--
--throughout every cell in my decaying frame like some--
Your Majesty.
I am happy for you that necrosis on your vocal cords has granted you the gift of speech...
...but *do* shut up.
Sorry

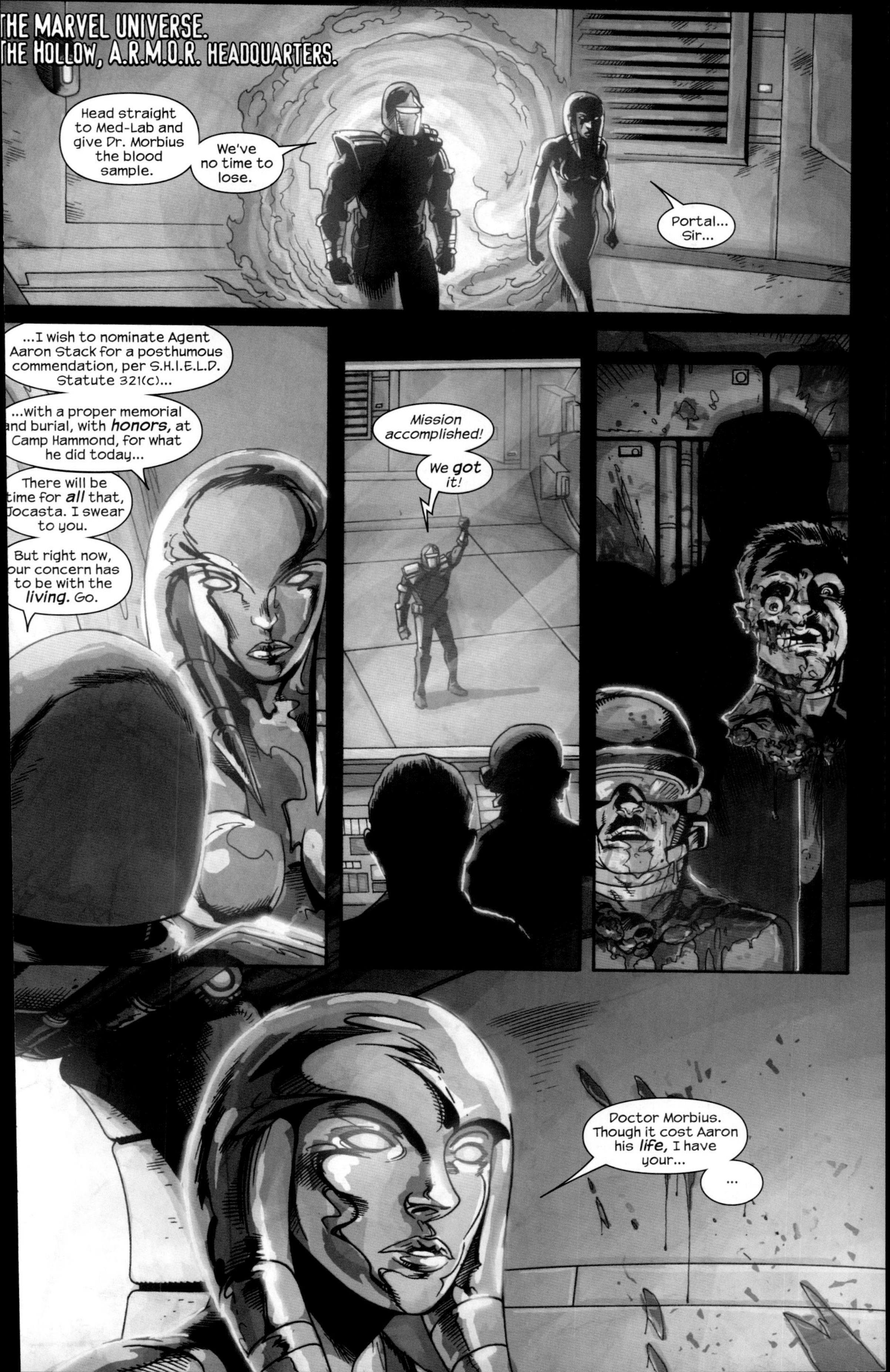
THE MARVEL UNIVERSE.
THE HOLLOW, A.R.M.O.R. HEADQUARTERS.
Head straight to Med-Lab and give Dr. Morbius the blood sample.
We've no time to lose.
Portal... Sir...
...I wish to nominate Agent Aaron Stack for a posthumous commendation, per S.H.I.E.L.D. Statute 321(c)...
...with a proper memorial and burial, with *honors,* at Camp Hammond, for what he did today...
There will be time for *all* that, Jocasta. I swear to you.
But right now, our concern has to be with the *living.* Go.
Mission accomplished!
We ***got*** *it!*
Doctor Morbius. Though it cost Aaron his *life,* I have your...
...

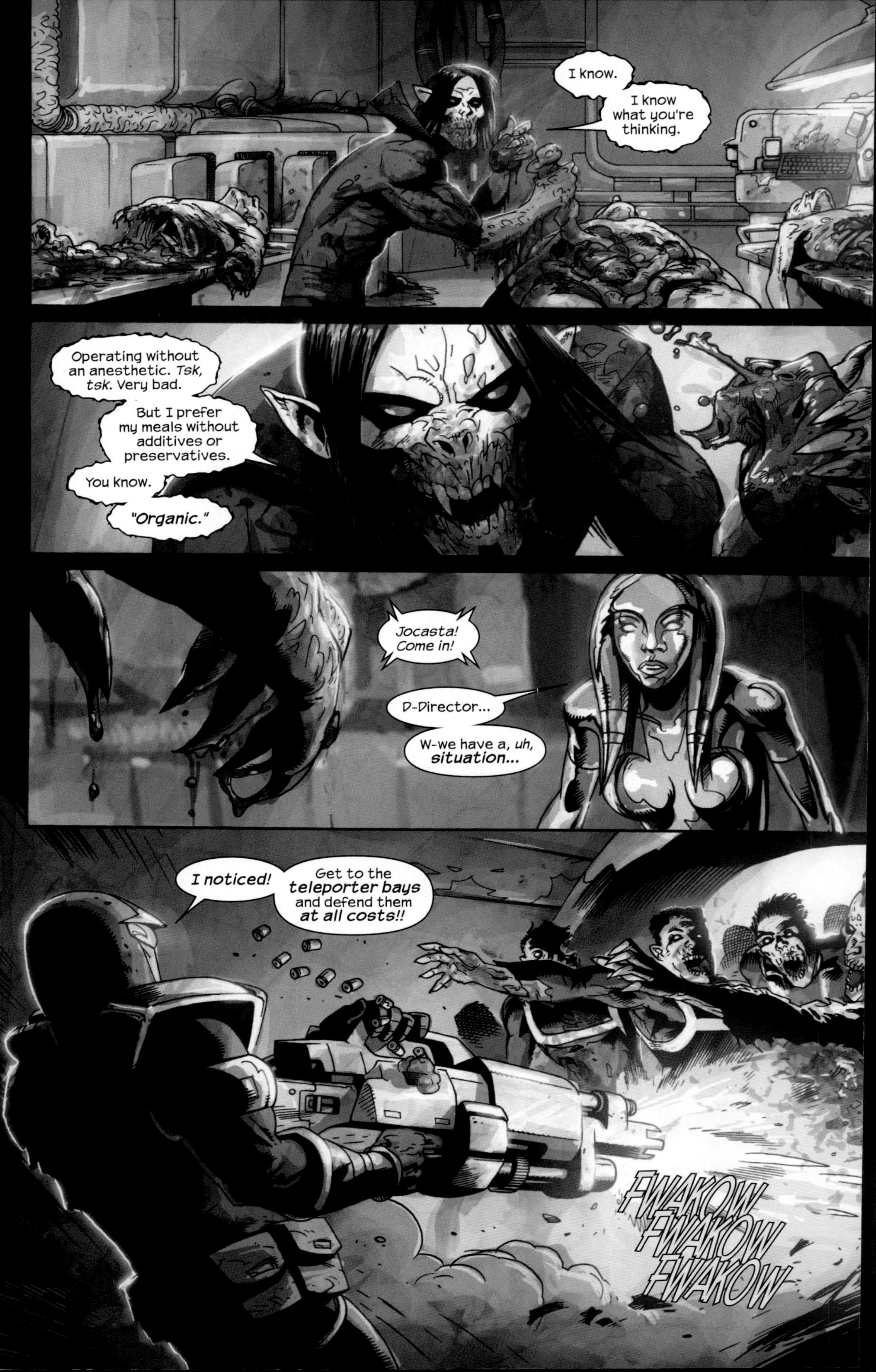
I know.
I know what you're thinking.
Operating without an anesthetic. Tsk, tsk. Very bad.
But I prefer my meals without additives or preservatives.
You know.
"Organic."
Jocasta! Come in!
D-Director...
W-we have a, uh, situation...
I noticed!
Get to the teleporter bays and defend them at all costs!!
FWAKOW
FWAKOW
FWAKOW

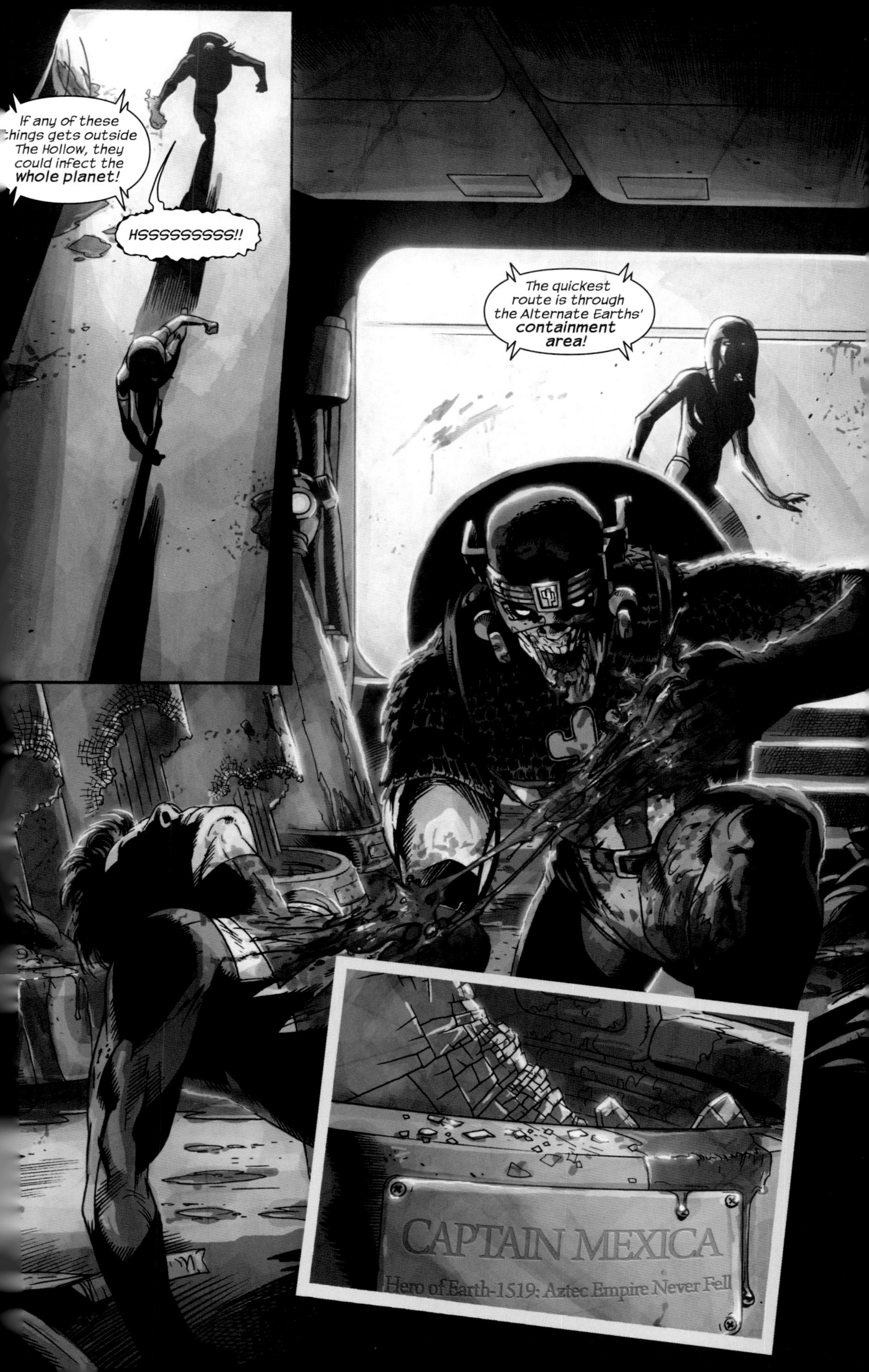
If any of these things gets outside The Hollow, they could infect the whole planet!
HSSSSSSSSS!!
The quickest route is through the Alternate Earths' containment area!
CAPTAIN MEXICA
Hero of Earth-1519: Aztec Empire Never Fell

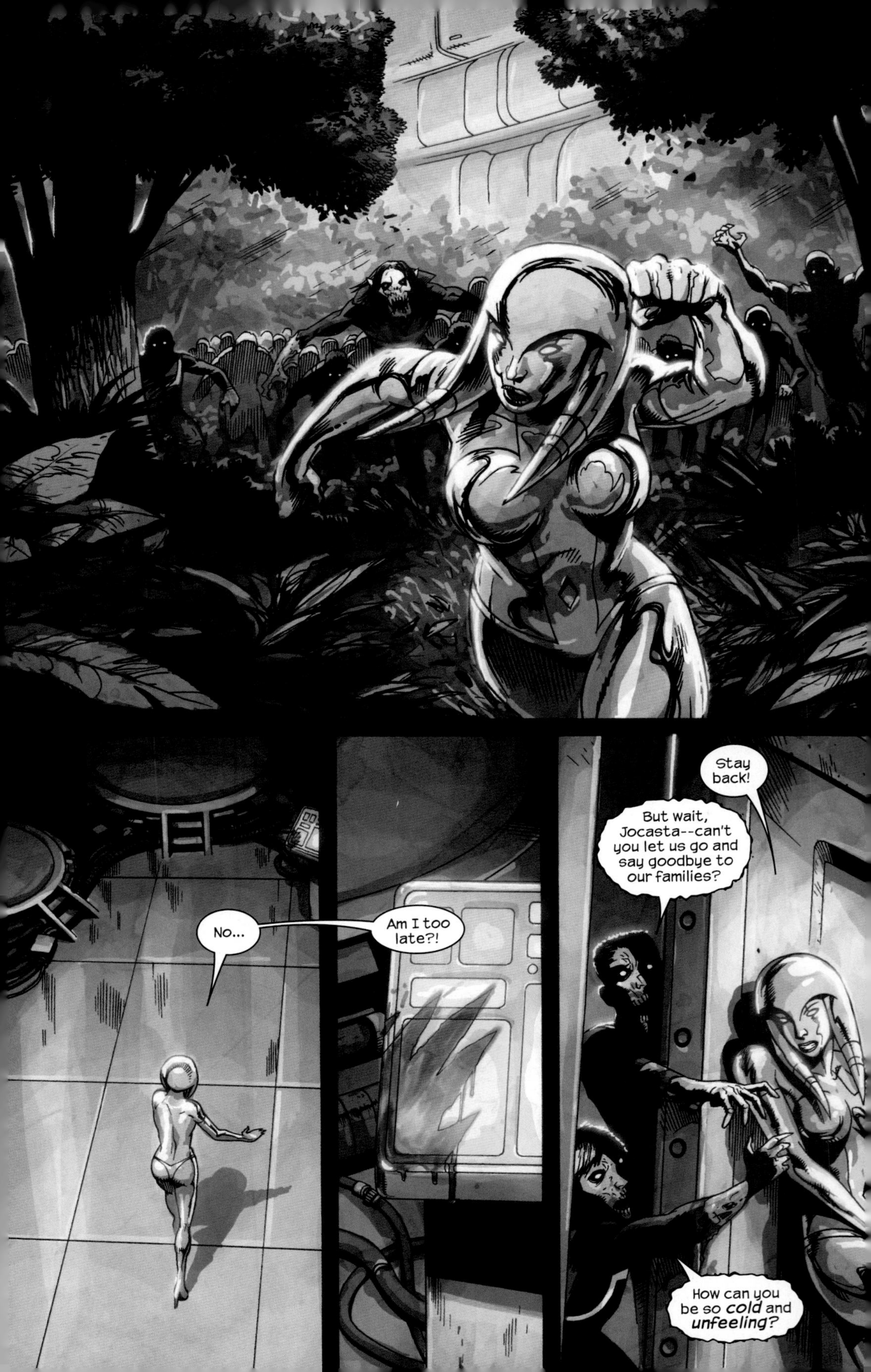
No...
Am I too late?!
Stay back!
But wait, Jocasta--can't you let us go and say goodbye to our families?
How can you be so *cold* and *unfeeling*?

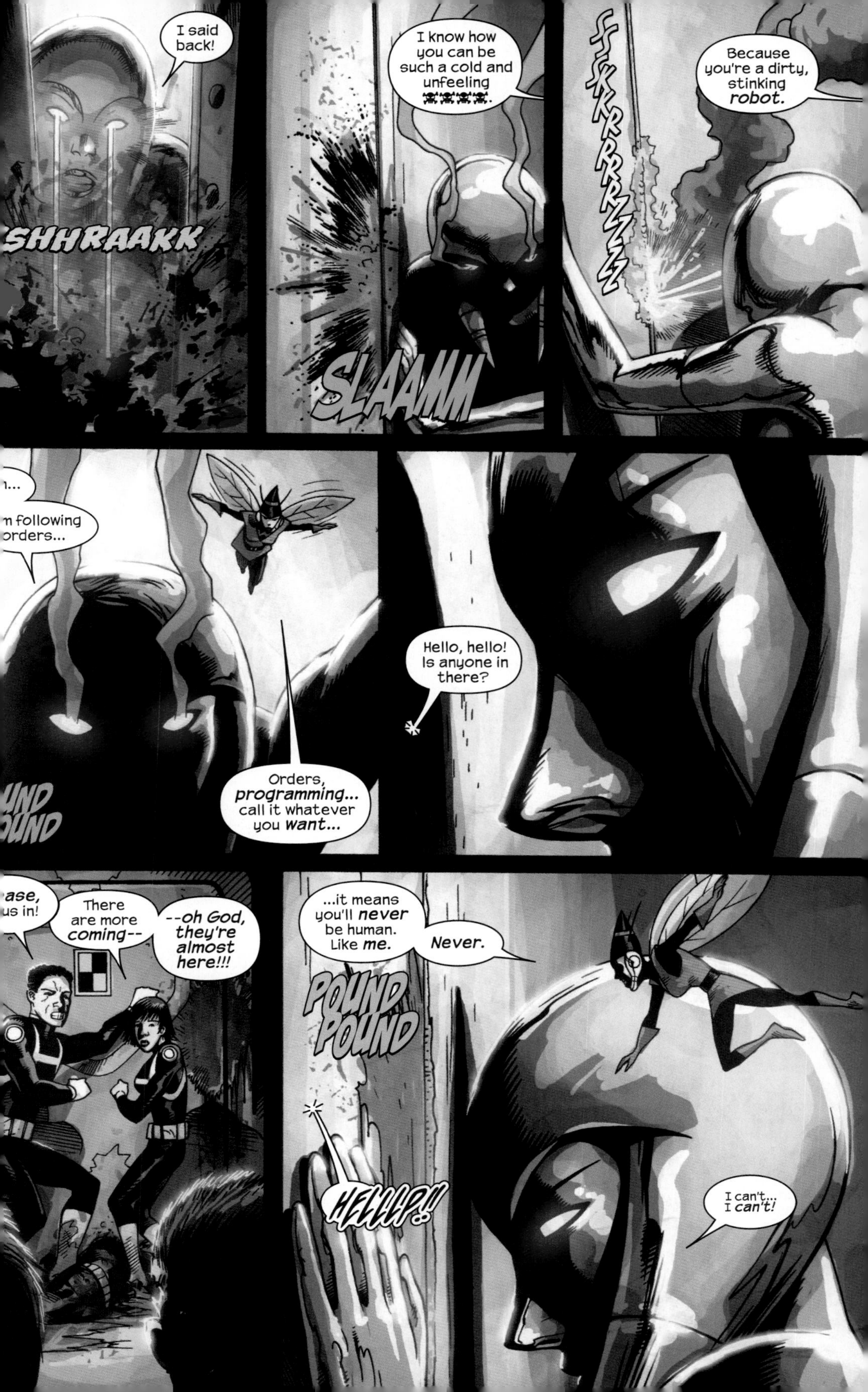
I said back!
SHHRAAKK
I know how you can be such a cold and unfeeling ☠☠☠☠.
SLAAMM
SSKRRRZZZ
Because you're a dirty, stinking robot.
n...
n following orders...
Orders, programming... call it whatever you want...
UND
OUND
Hello, hello! Is anyone in there?
ase, us in!
There are more coming--
--oh God, they're almost here!!!
...it means you'll never be human. Like me.
Never.
POUND POUND
HELLLP!!
I can't... I can't!

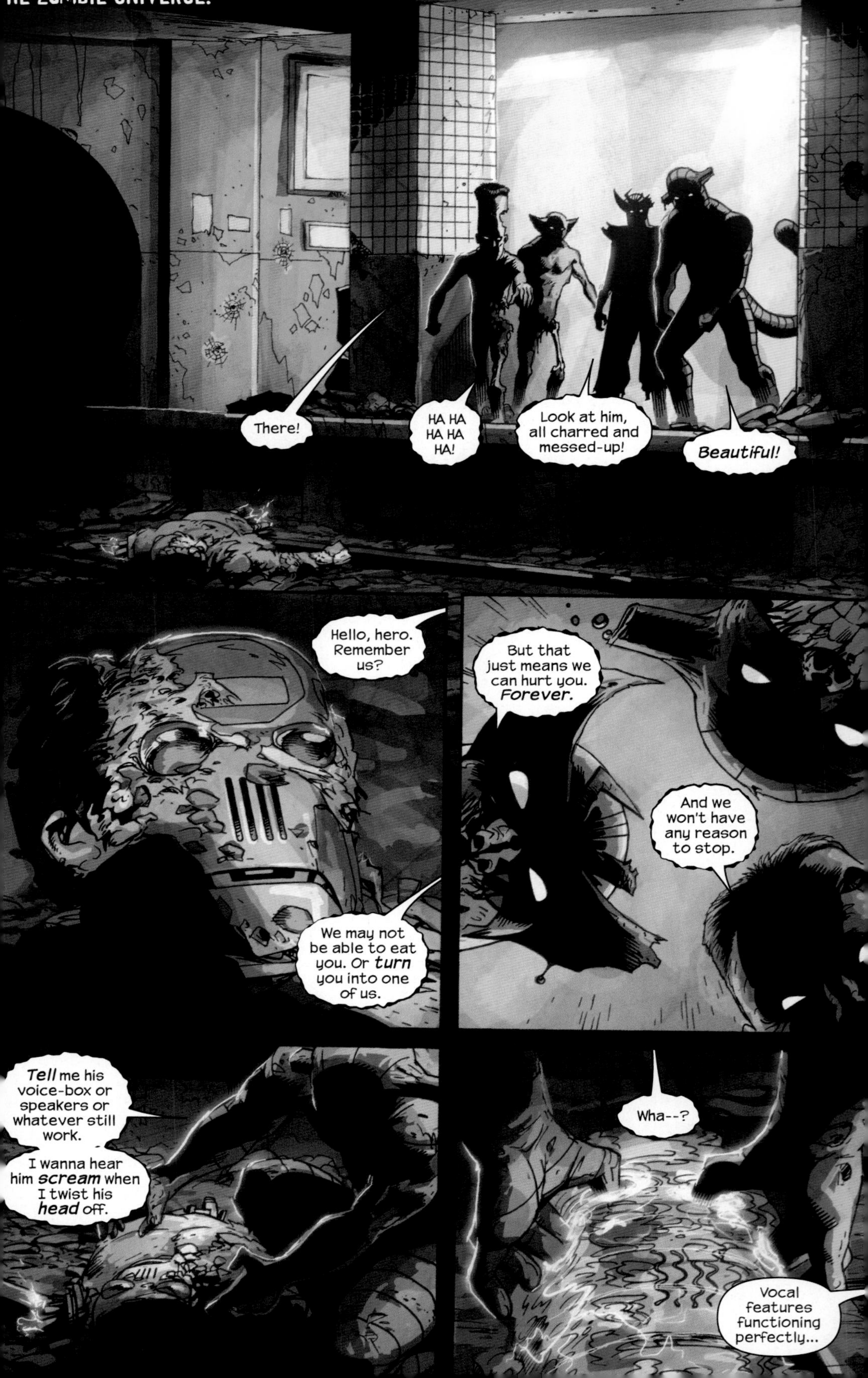
There!
HA HA HA HA HA!
Look at him, all charred and messed-up!
Beautiful!
Hello, hero. Remember us?
We may not be able to eat you. Or turn you into one of us.
But that just means we can hurt you. Forever.
And we won't have any reason to stop.
Tell me his voice-box or speakers or whatever still work.
I wanna hear him scream when I twist his head off.
Wha--?
Vocal features functioning perfectly...

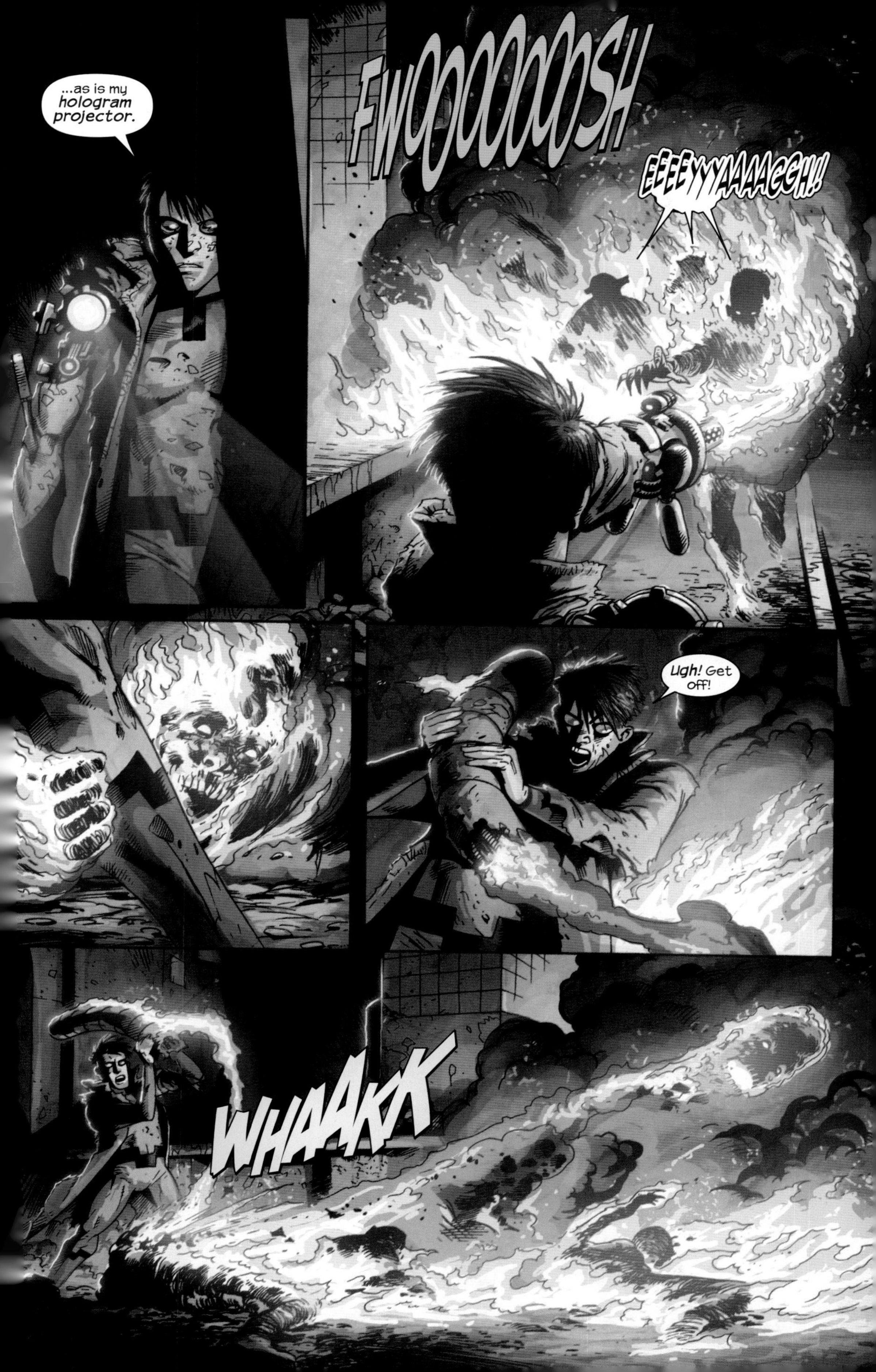
...as is my *hologram projector.*
FWOOOOOOOSH
EEEEYYAAAAGGH!!
Ugh! Get off!
WHAAKK

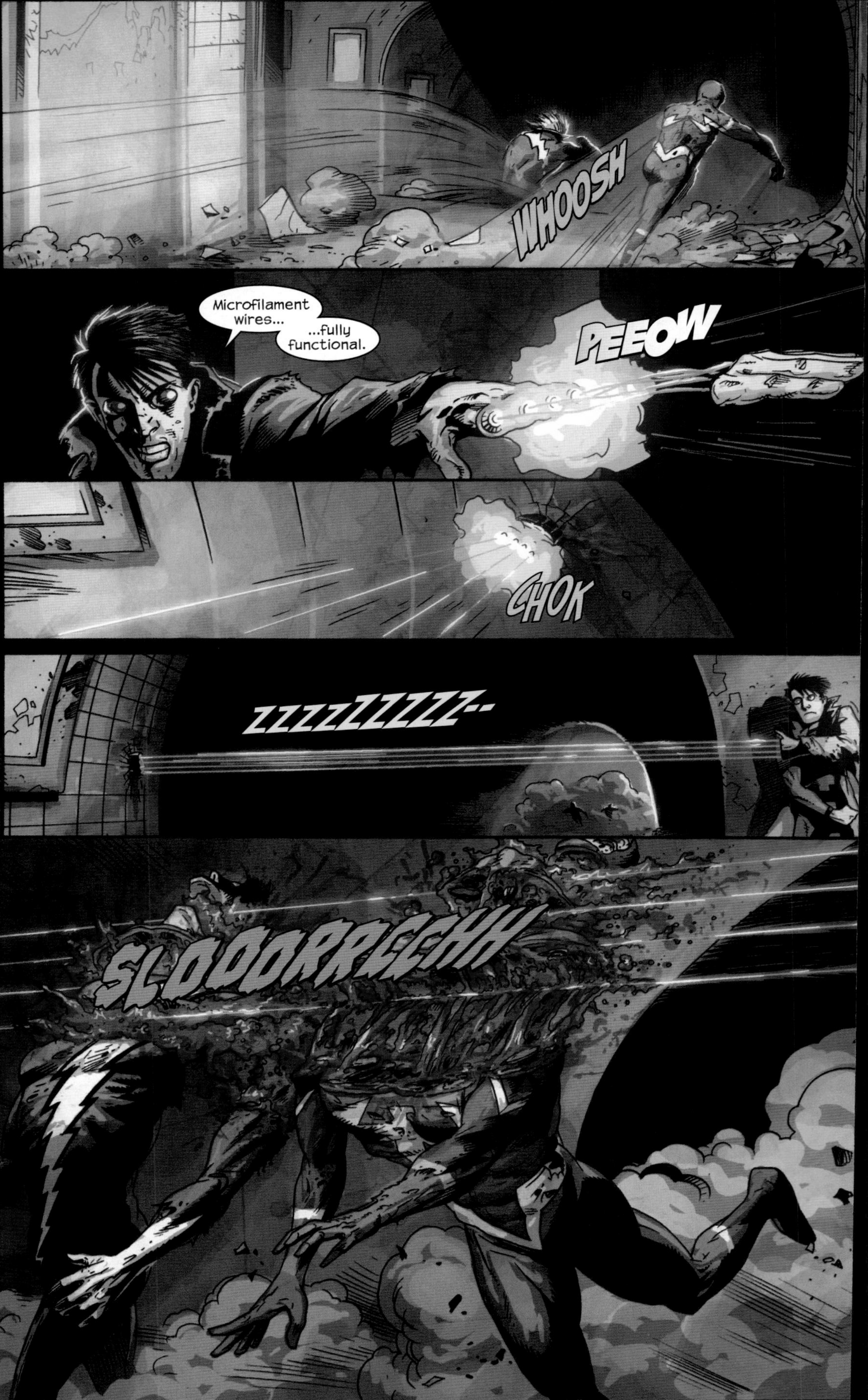
WHOOSH
Microfilament wires...
...fully functional.
PEEOW
CHOK
ZZZZZZZZZZ--
SLOORRCHH

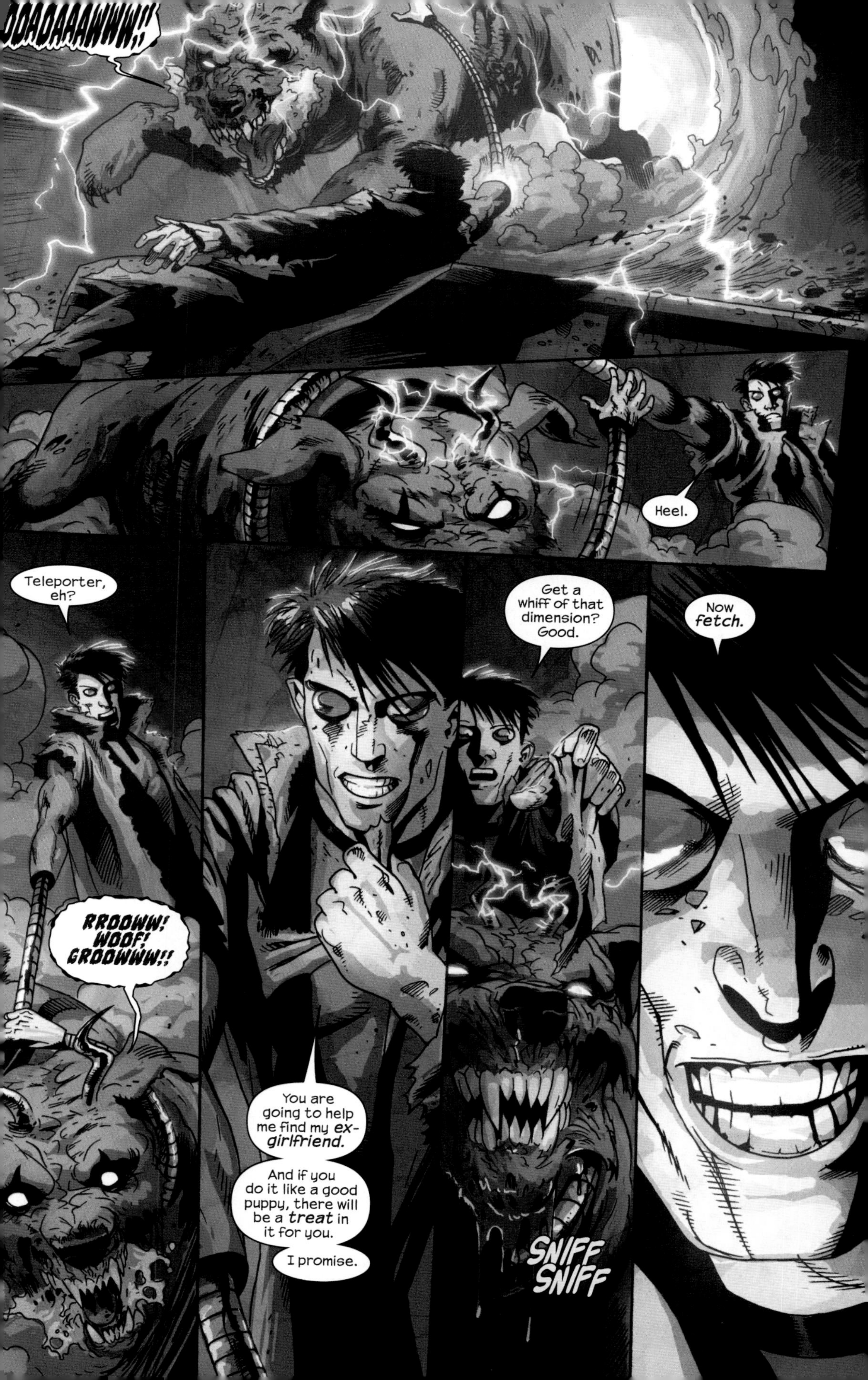

ODADAAAWWW!!
Heel.
Teleporter, eh?
RROOWW! WOOF! GROOWWW!!
You are going to help me find my ex-girlfriend.
And if you do it like a good puppy, there will be a treat in it for you.
I promise.
Get a whiff of that dimension? Good.
SNIFF SNIFF
Now fetch.

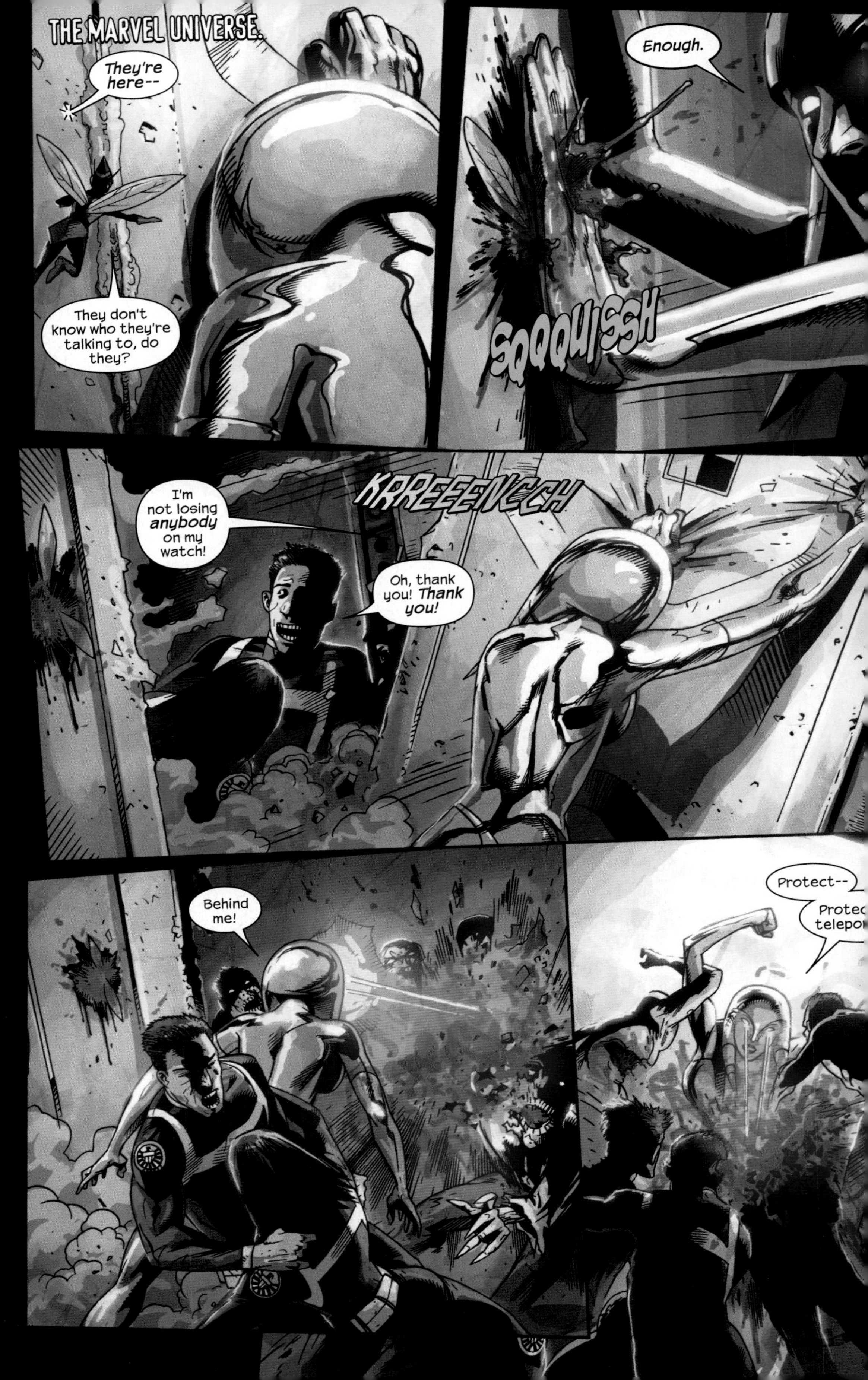
THE MARVEL UNIVERSE.
They're here--
They don't know who they're talking to, do they?
Enough.
SQQQUISSH
KRREEEENCCH
I'm not losing *anybody* on my watch!
Oh, thank you! *Thank you!*
Behind me!
Protect--

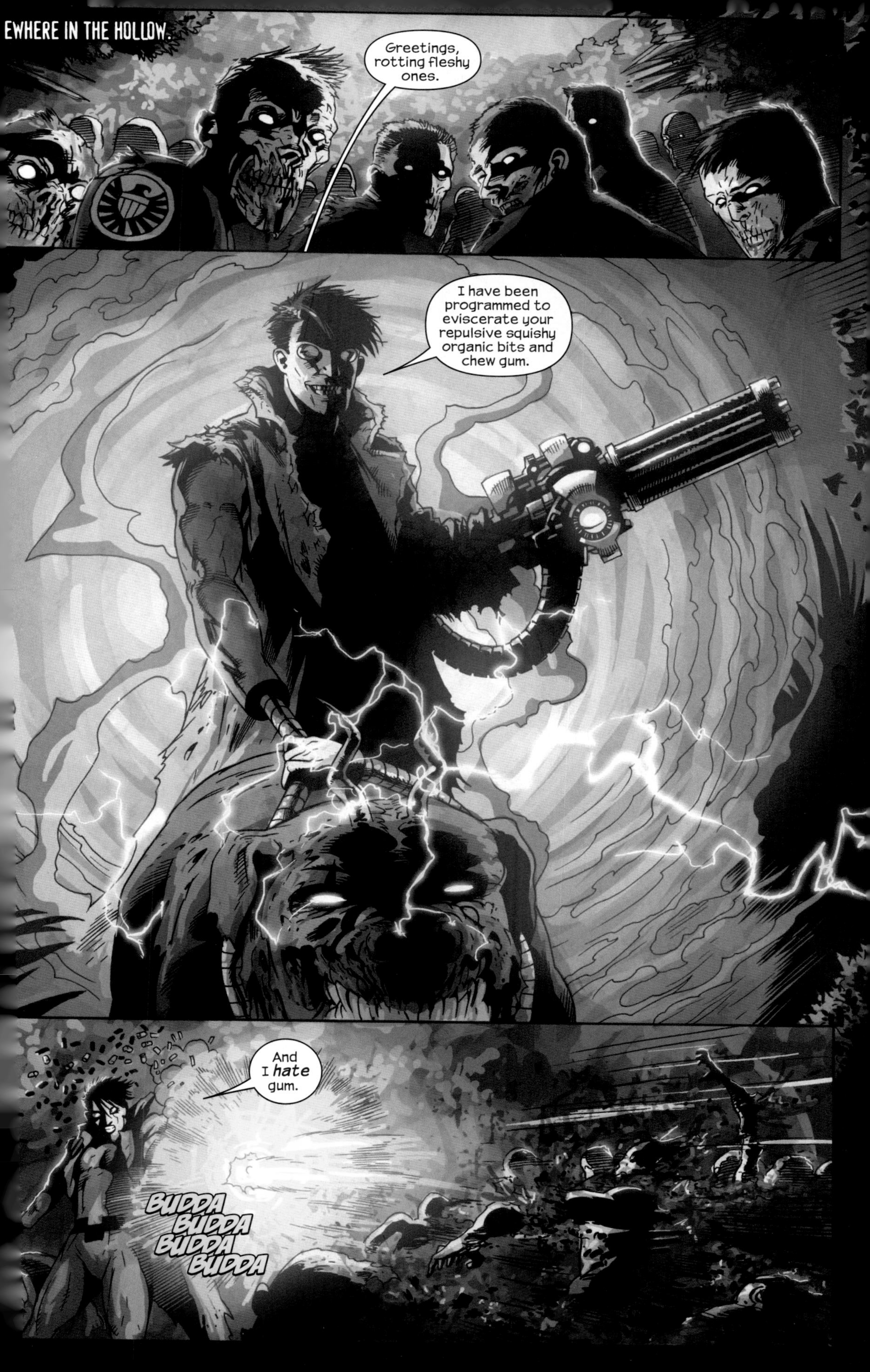
EWHERE IN THE HOLLOW.
Greetings, rotting fleshy ones.
I have been programmed to eviscerate your repulsive squishy organic bits and chew gum.
And I *hate* gum.
BUDDA BUDDA BUDDA BUDDA

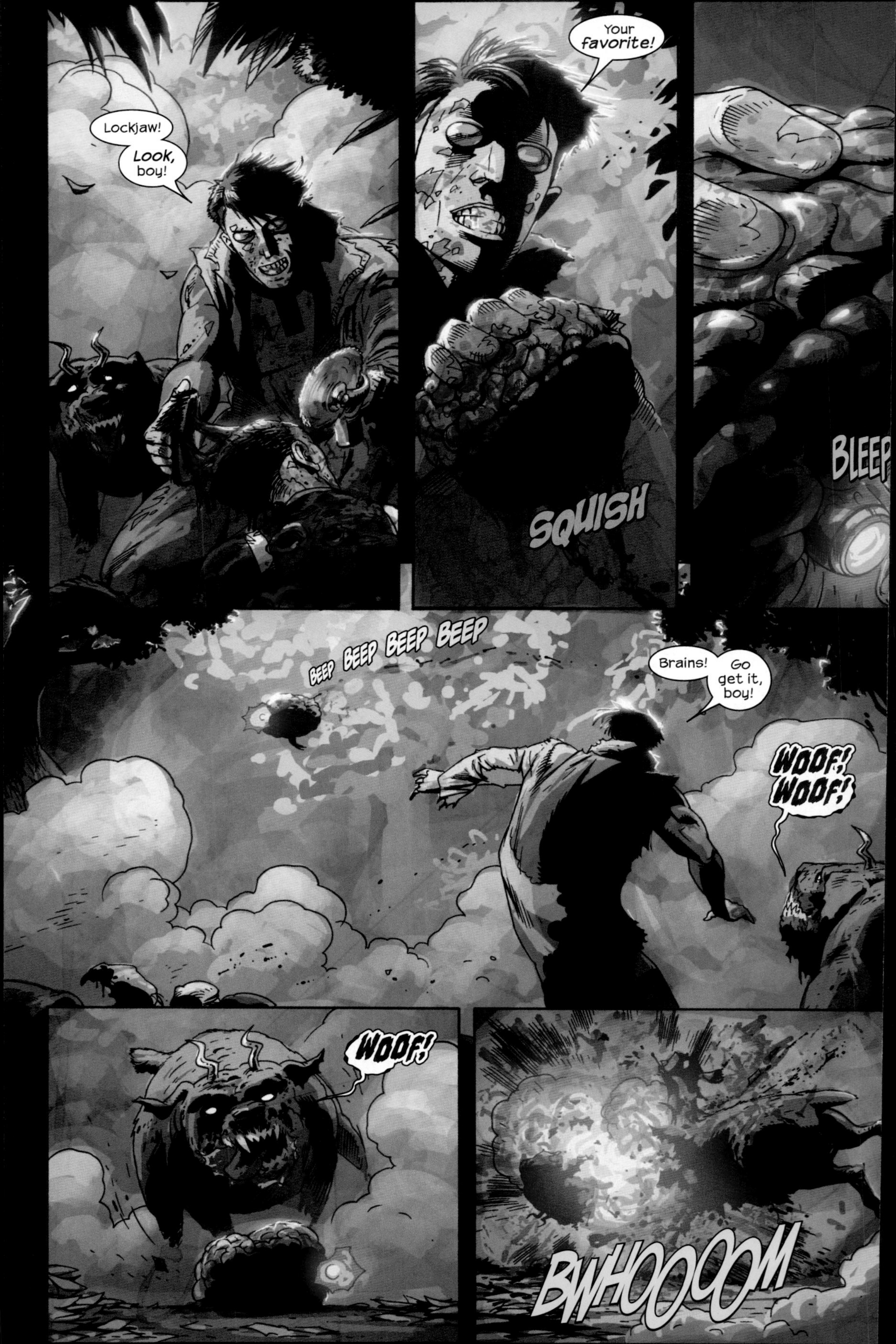
Lockjaw!
Look, boy!
Your favorite!
SQUISH
BLEEP
BEEP BEEP BEEP BEEP
Brains!
Go get it, boy!
WOOF! WOOF!
WOOF!
BWHOOOOM

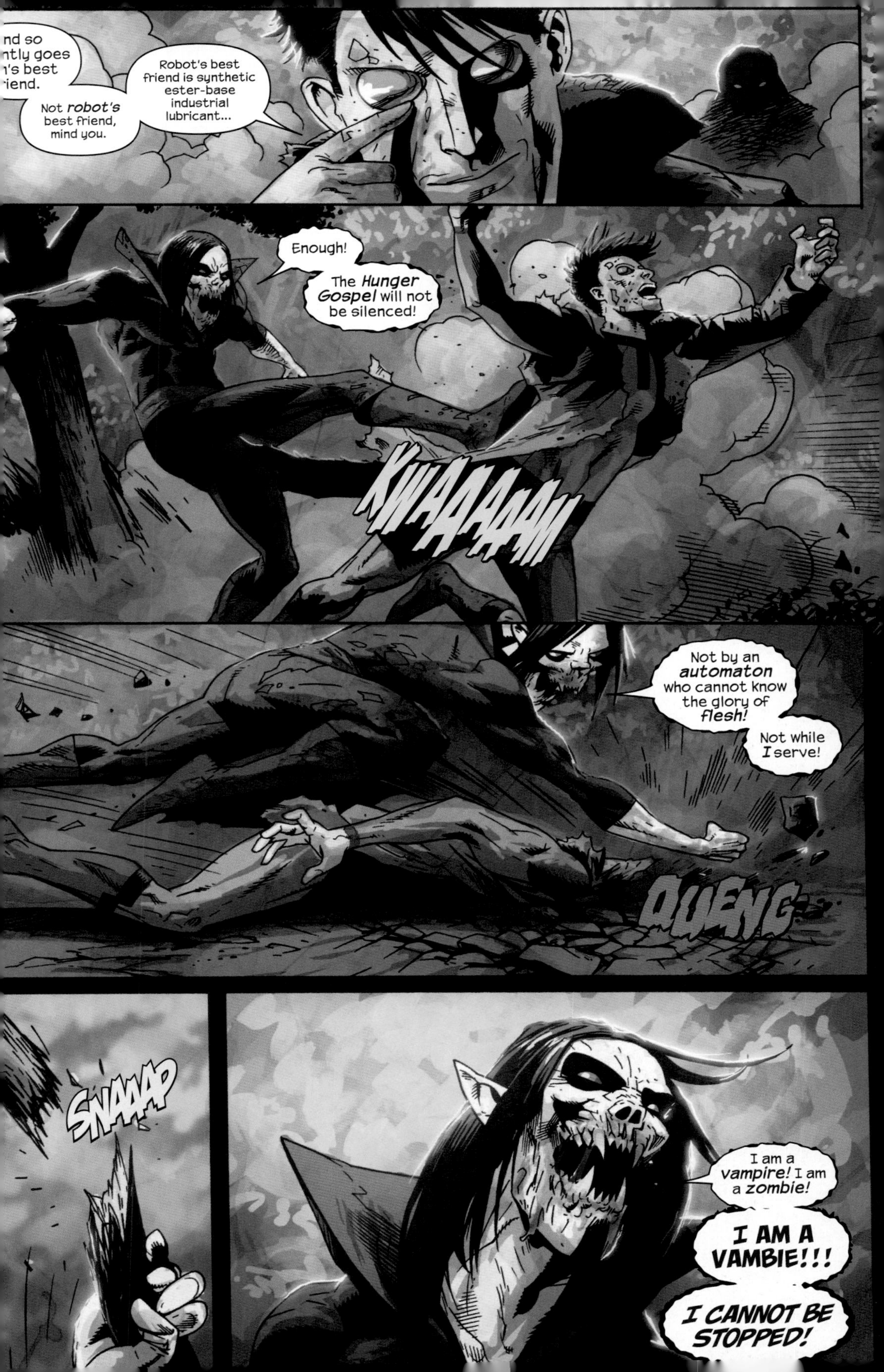

nd so
ntly goes
'n's best
riend.
Robot's best friend is synthetic ester-base industrial lubricant...
Not *robot's* best friend, mind you.
Enough!
The *Hunger Gospel* will not be silenced!
KWAAAAAM
Not by an *automaton* who cannot know the glory of *flesh!*
Not while *I* serve!
QUENG
SNAAAP
I am a *vampire!* I am a *zombie!*
I AM A VAMBIE!!!
I CANNOT BE STOPPED!

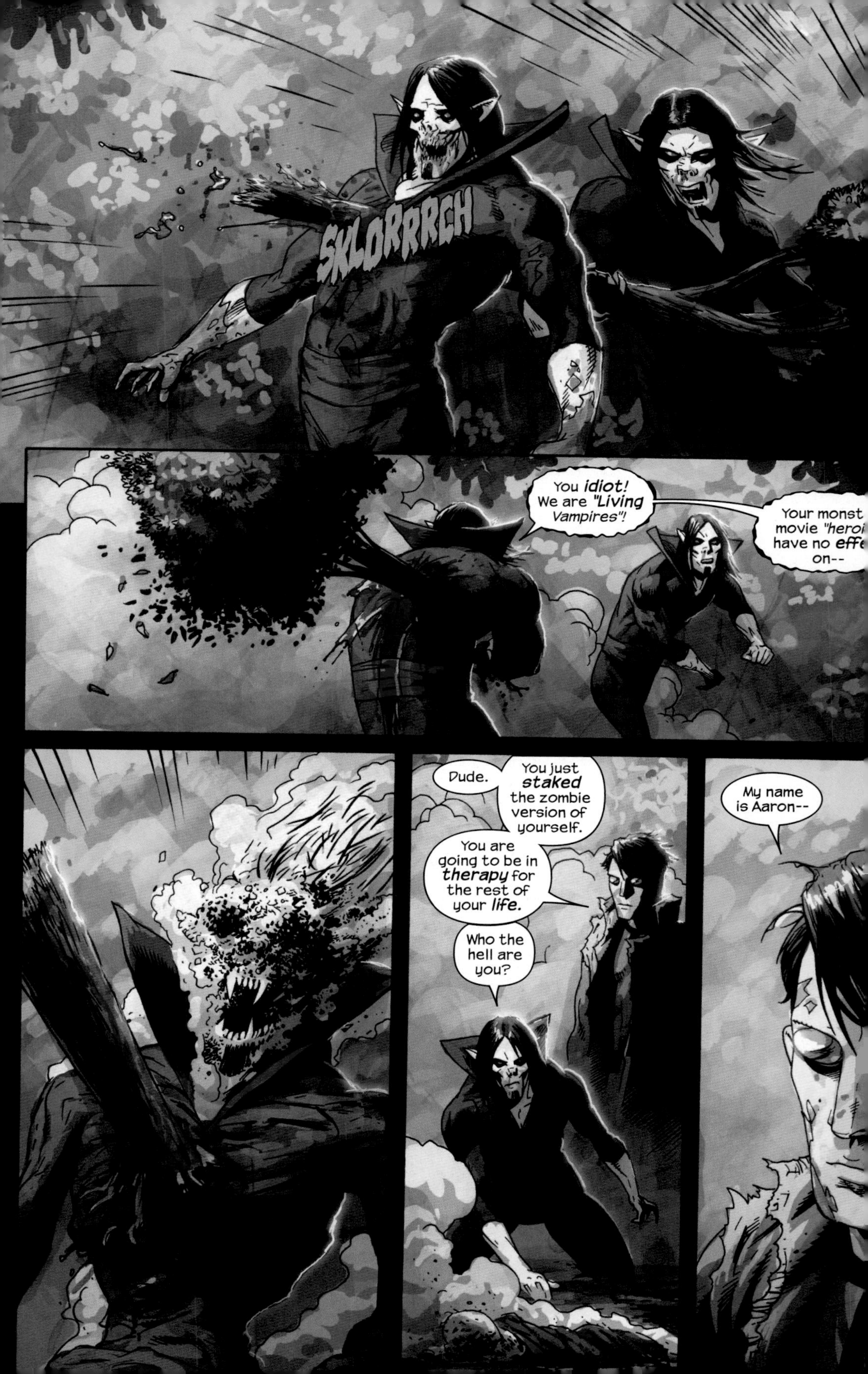
SKLORRRCH
You idiot! We are "Living Vampires"!
Your monst movie "heroi have no effe on--
Dude.
You just staked the zombie version of yourself.
You are going to be in therapy for the rest of your life.
Who the hell are you?
My name is Aaron--

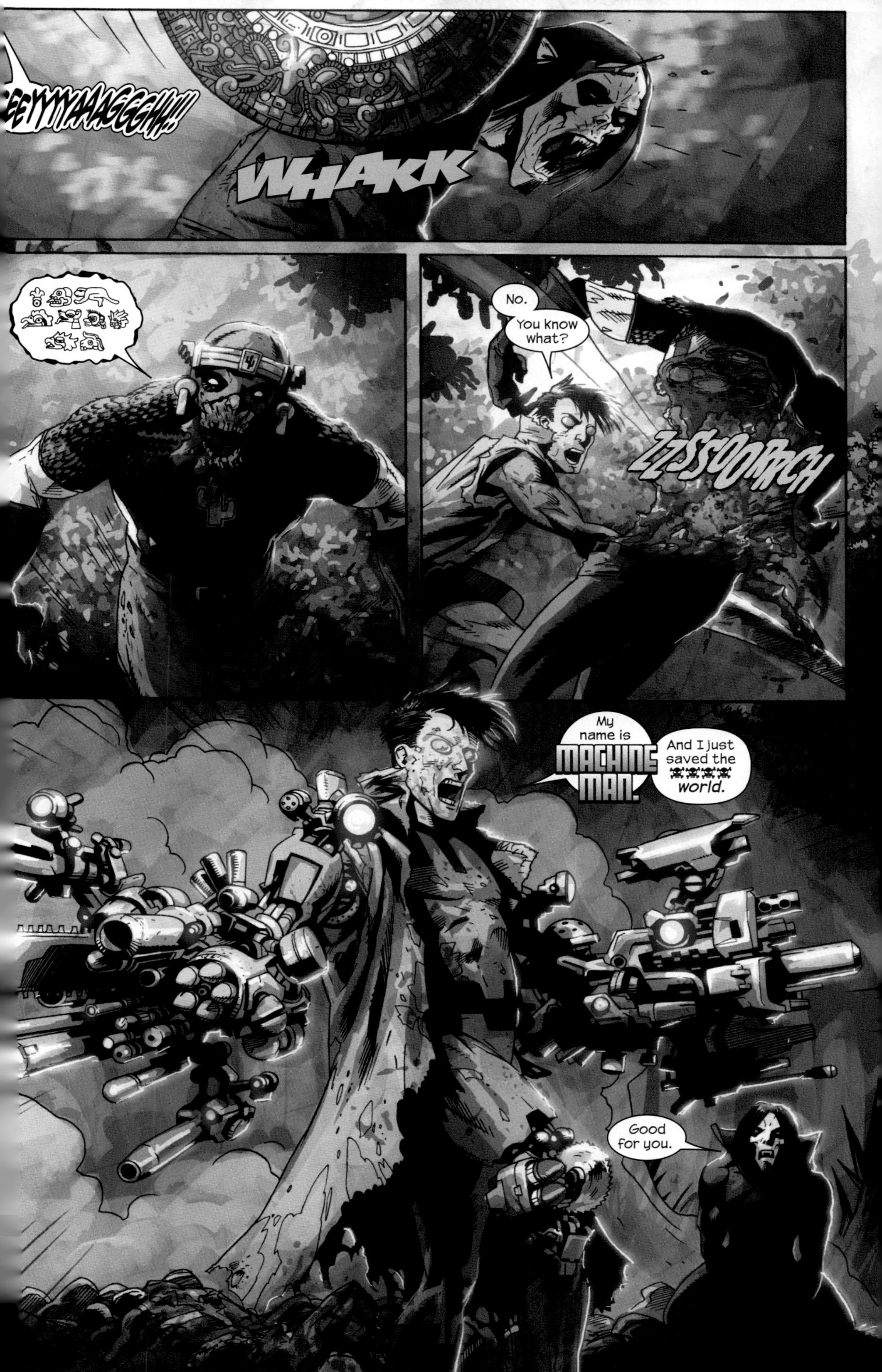
EEYYYYAAAGGGHH!!
WHAKK
No.
You know what?
ZZZSSOORRCH
My name is MACHINE MAN!
And I just saved the ☠☠☠☠ world.
Good for you.

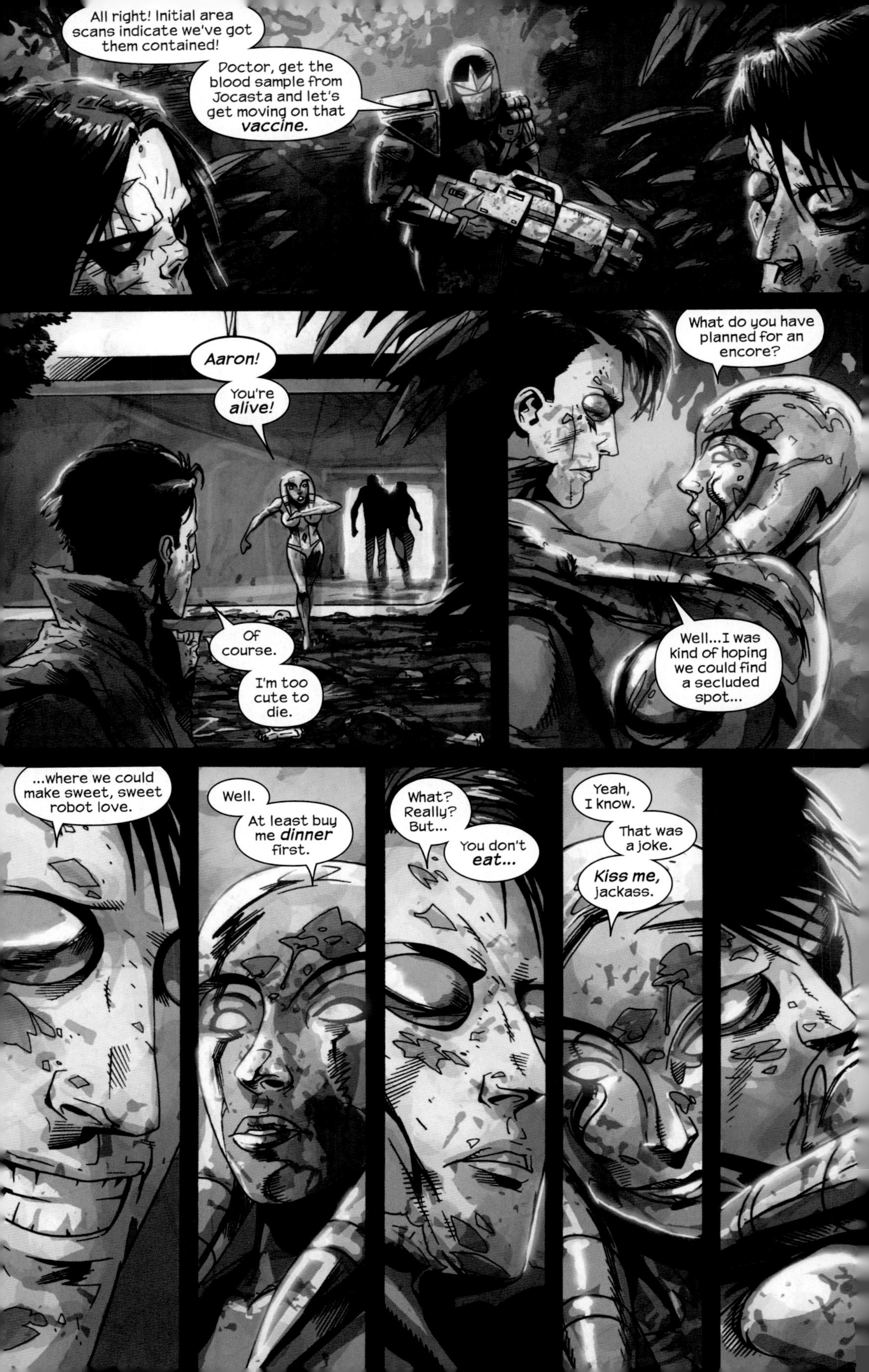
All right! Initial area scans indicate we've got them contained!
Doctor, get the blood sample from Jocasta and let's get moving on that *vaccine.*
Aaron!
You're *alive!*
Of course.
I'm too cute to die.
What do you have planned for an encore?
Well...I was kind of hoping we could find a secluded spot...
...where we could make sweet, sweet robot love.
Well.
At least buy me *dinner* first.
What? Really? But...
You don't *eat...*
Yeah, I know.
That was a joke.
Kiss me, jackass.

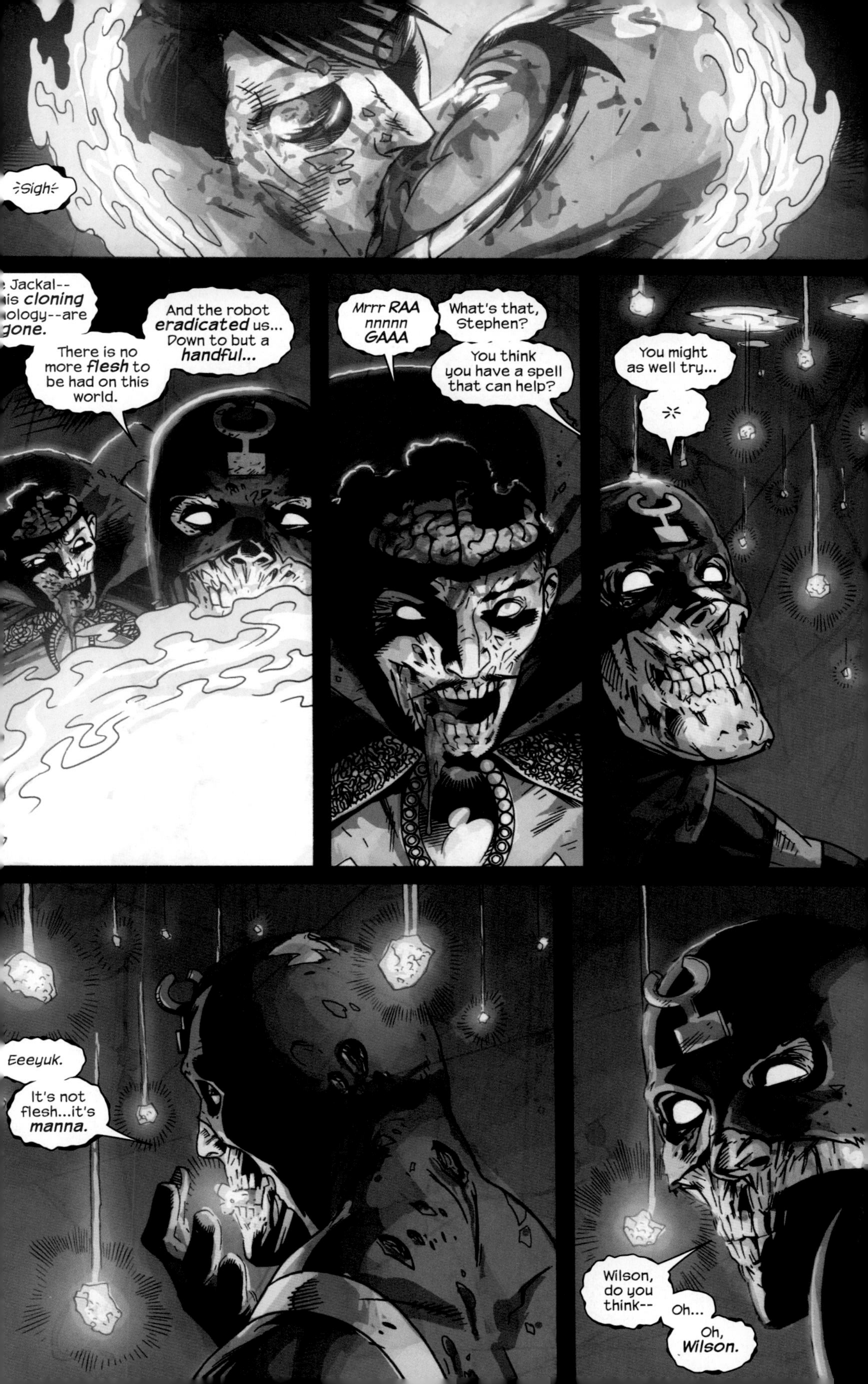

Sigh
Jackal--
is cloning
ology--are
gone.
There is no more flesh to be had on this world.
And the robot eradicated us... Down to but a handful...
Mrrr RAA nnnnn GAAA
What's that, Stephen?
You think you have a spell that can help?
You might as well try...
Eeeyuk.
It's not flesh...it's manna.
Wilson, do you think--
Oh...
Oh, Wilson.

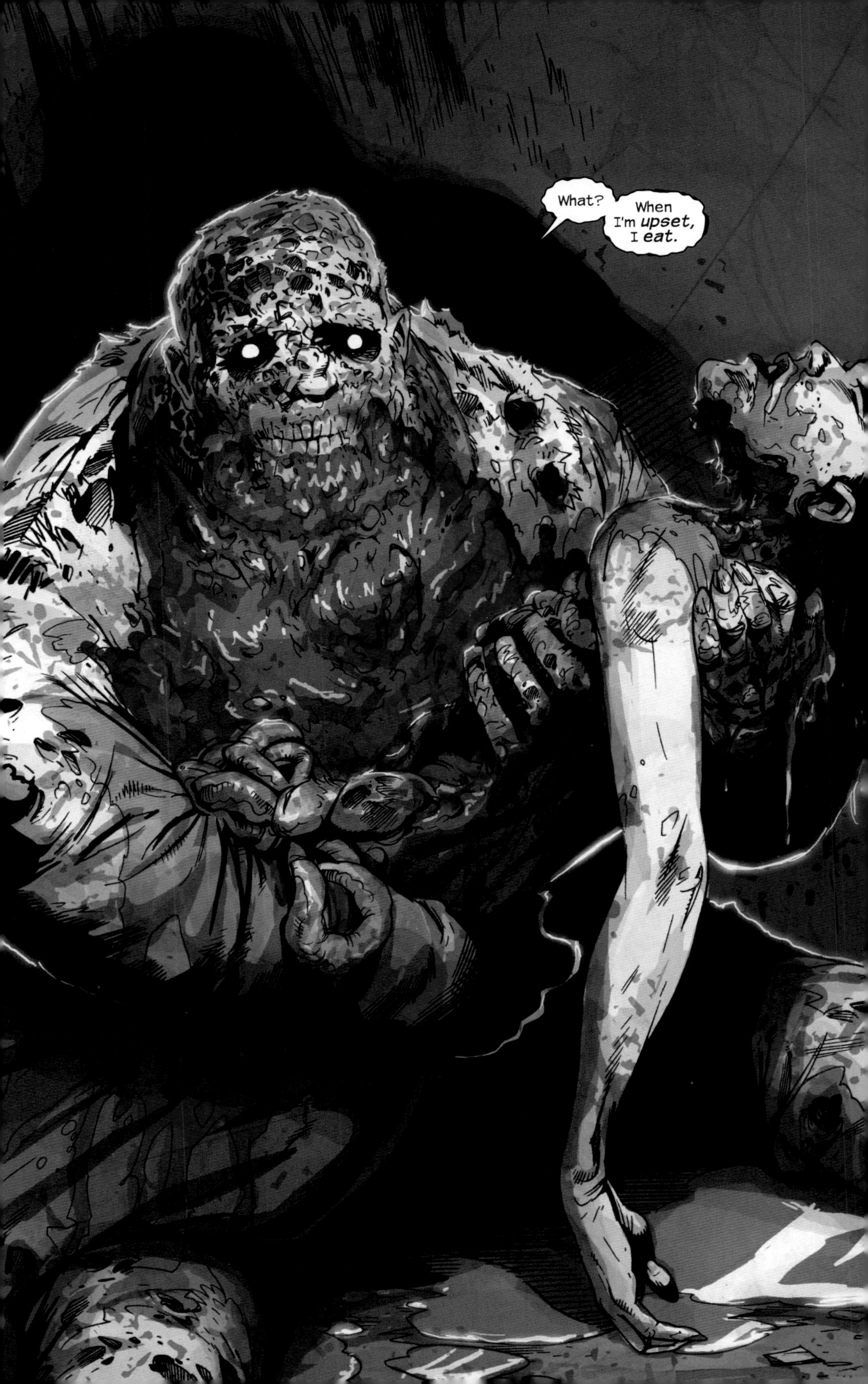
What?
When I'm *upset,* I *eat.*

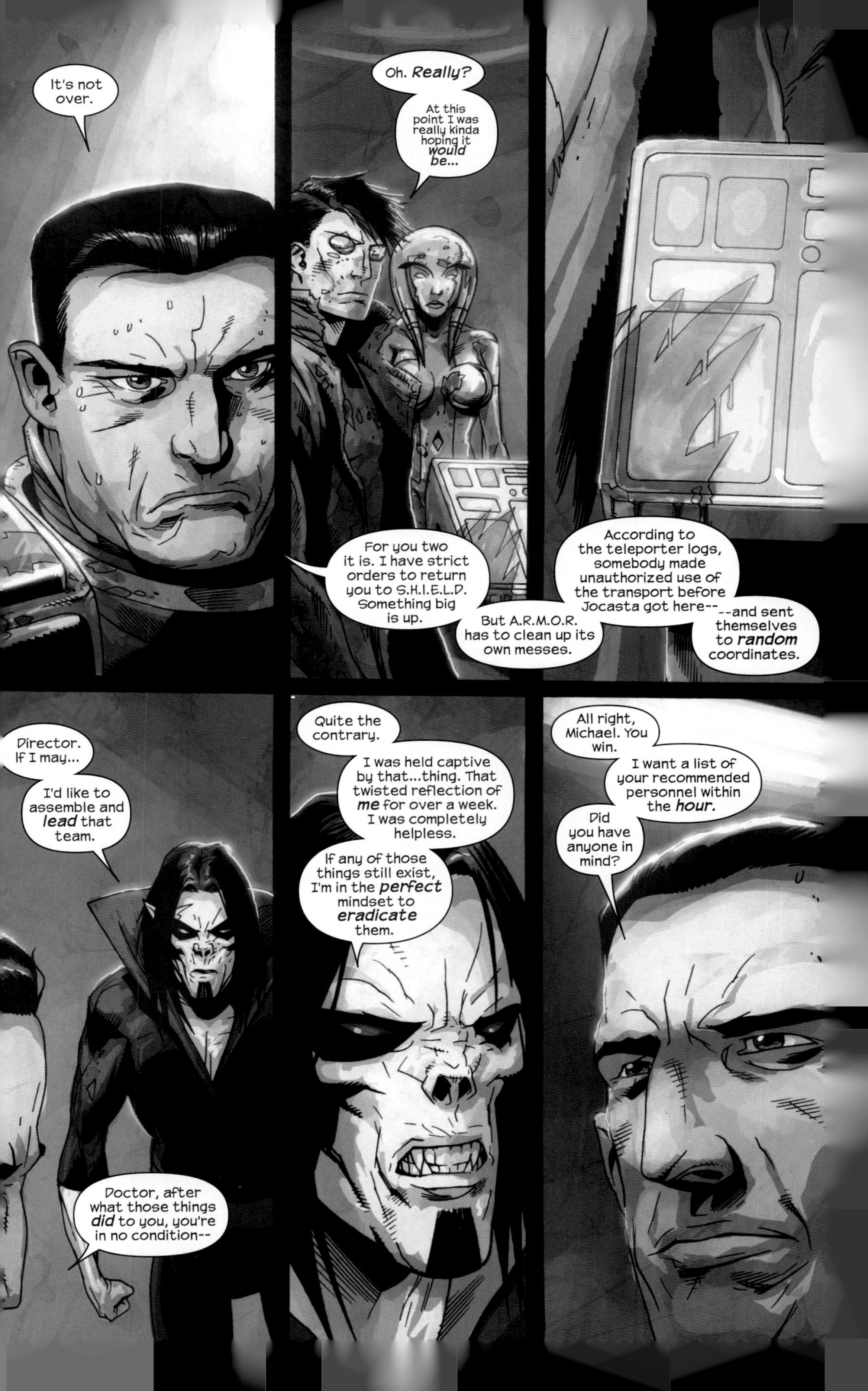
It's not over.
Oh. Really?
At this point I was really kinda hoping it would be...
For you two it is. I have strict orders to return you to S.H.I.E.L.D. Something big is up.
But A.R.M.O.R. has to clean up its own messes.
According to the teleporter logs, somebody made unauthorized use of the transport before Jocasta got here--
--and sent themselves to random coordinates.
Director. If I may...
I'd like to assemble and lead that team.
Doctor, after what those things did to you, you're in no condition--
Quite the contrary.
I was held captive by that...thing. That twisted reflection of me for over a week. I was completely helpless.
If any of those things still exist, I'm in the perfect mindset to eradicate them.
All right, Michael. You win.
I want a list of your recommended personnel within the hour.
Did you have anyone in mind?

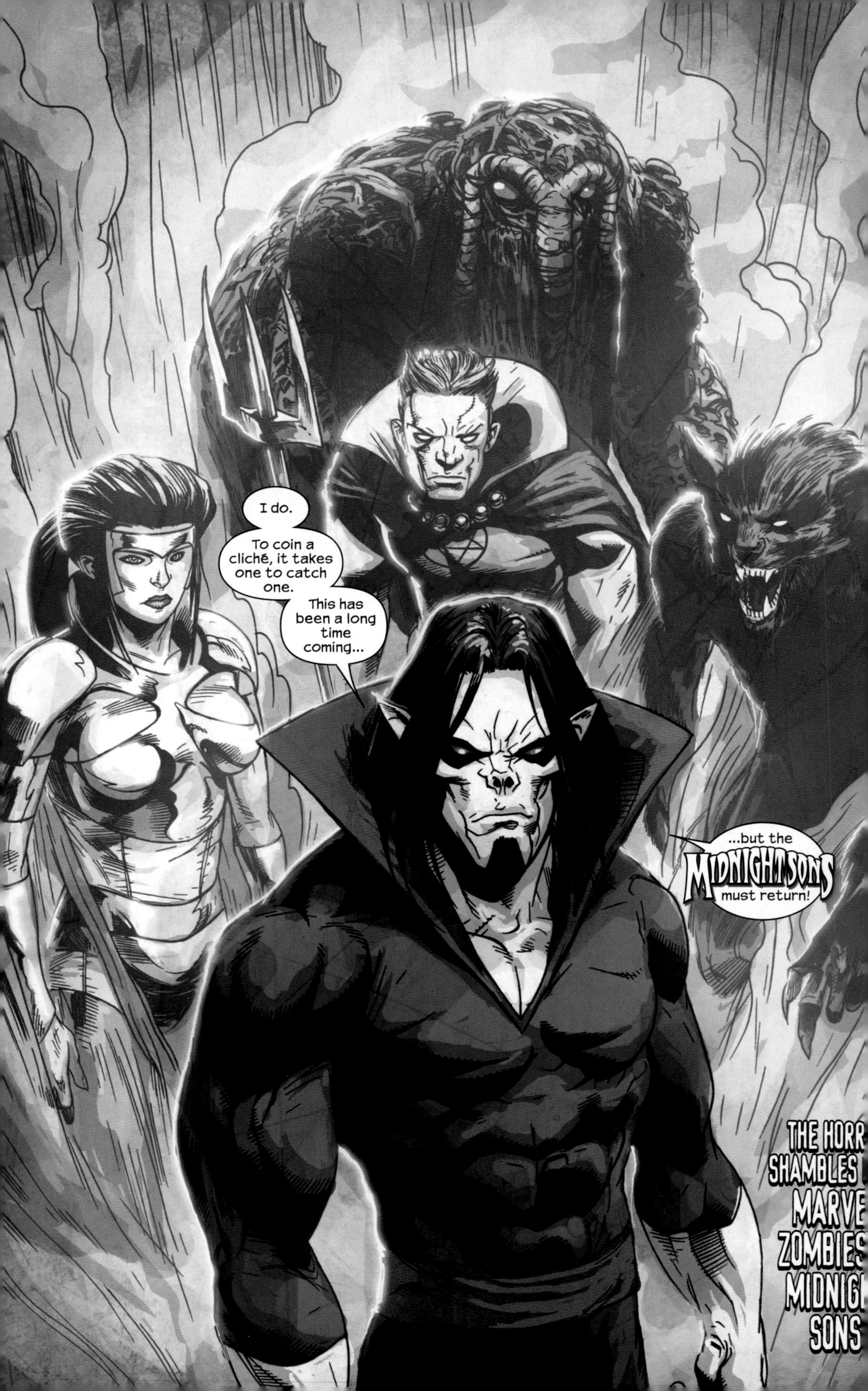
I do.
To coin a cliché, it takes one to catch one.
This has been a long time coming...
...but the MIDNIGHT SONS must return!
THE HORR
SHAMBLES
MARVE
ZOMBIES
MIDNIG
SONS

#1 VARIANT COVER BY ARTHUR SUYDAM

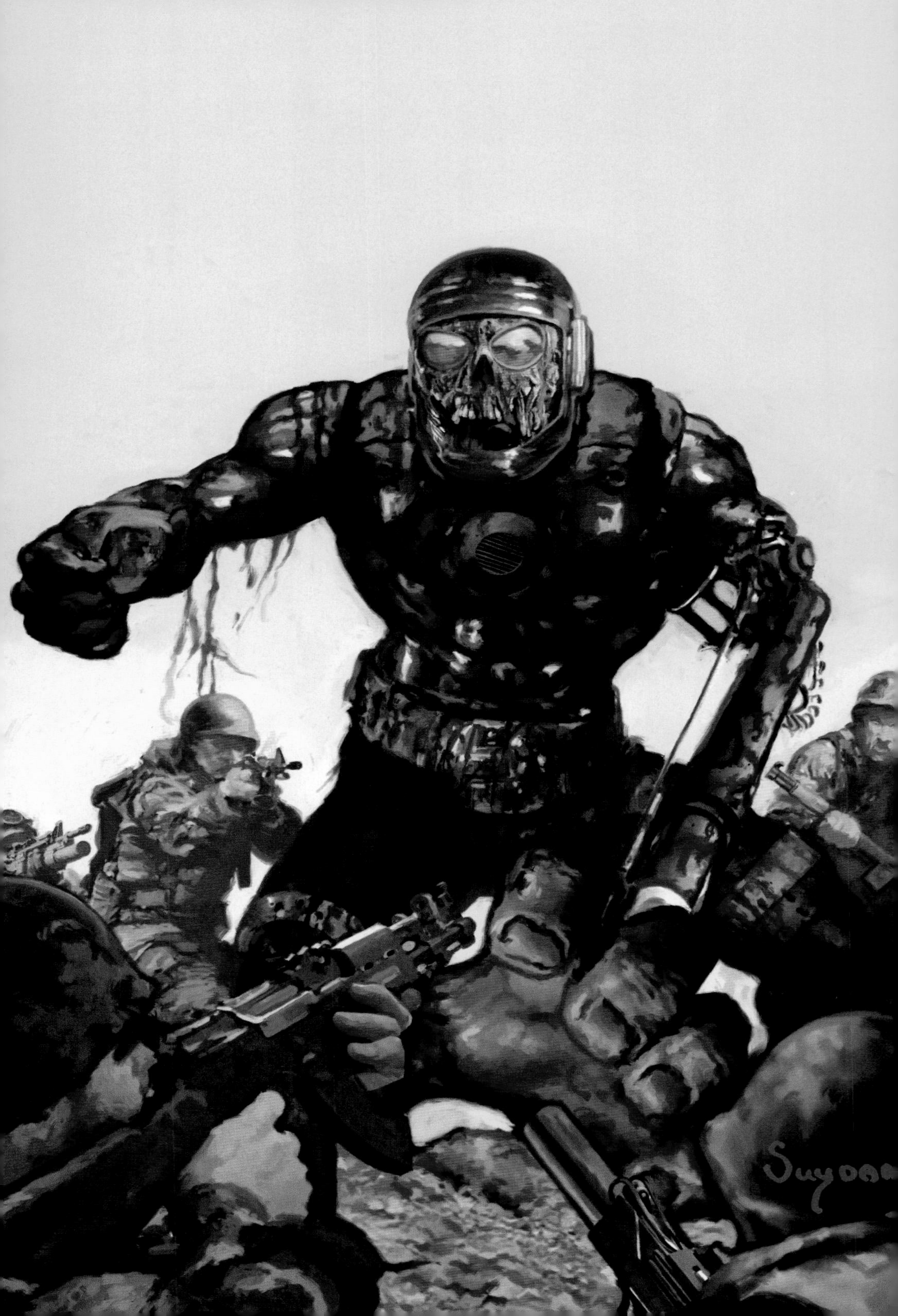
Suydam

MACHINE MAN #1 COVER BY JACK KIRBY & FRANK GIACOIA

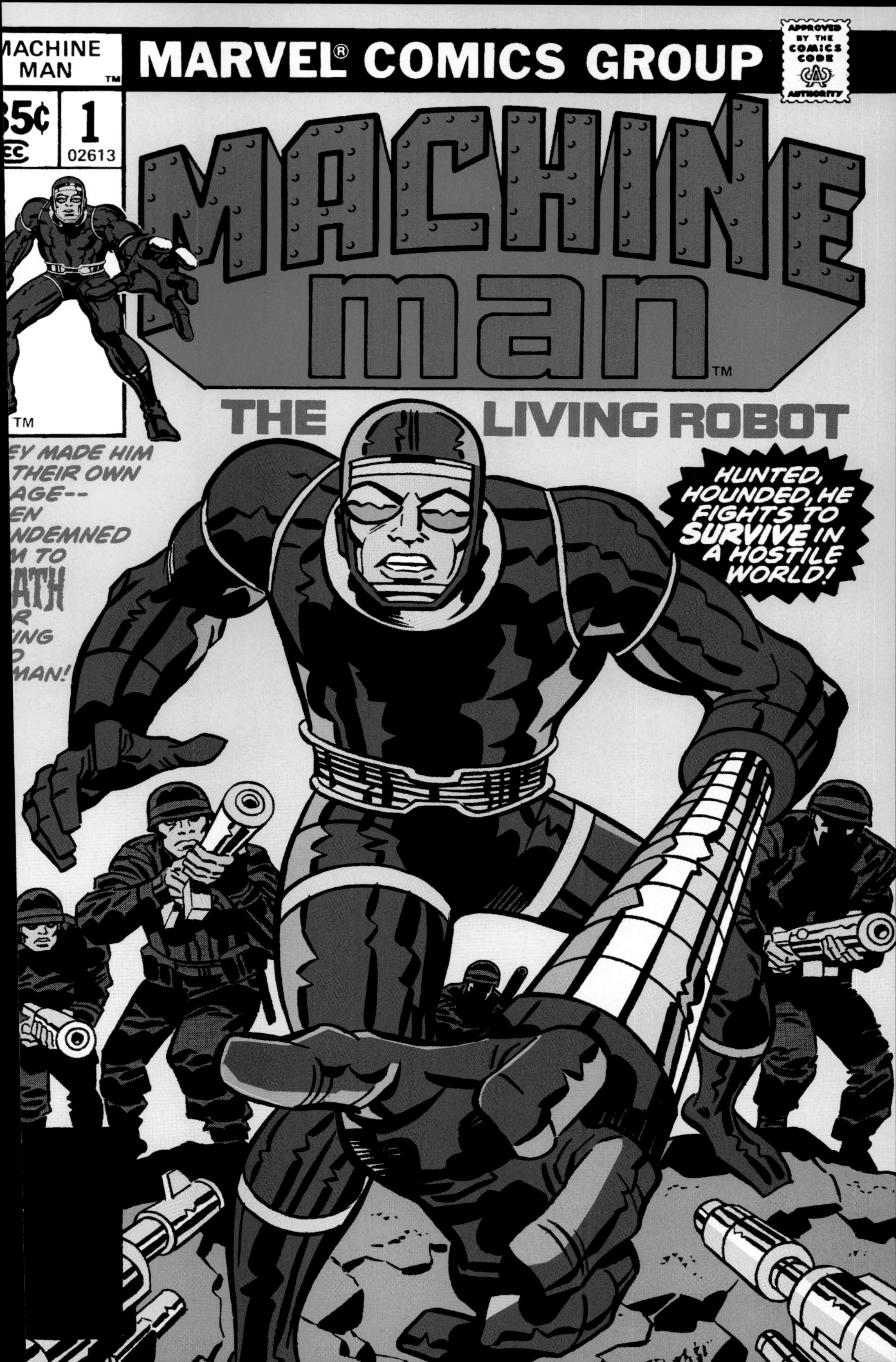
MACHINE MAN
MARVEL® COMICS GROUP
APPROVED BY THE COMICS CODE AUTHORITY
35¢
1
02613
MACHINE MAN
THE LIVING ROBOT
HUNTED, HOUNDED, HE FIGHTS TO SURVIVE IN A HOSTILE WORLD!

#1

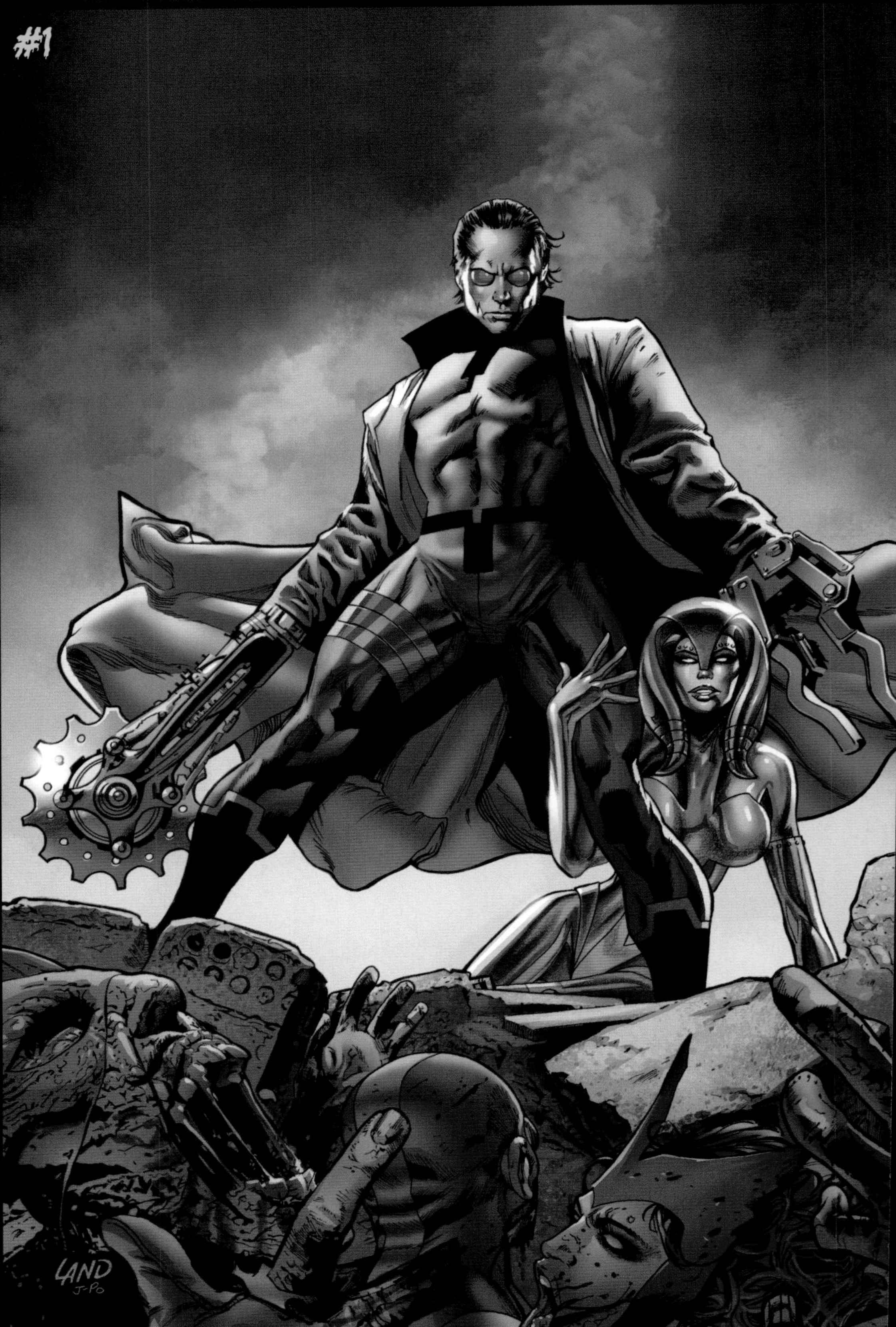
LAND
J-Po

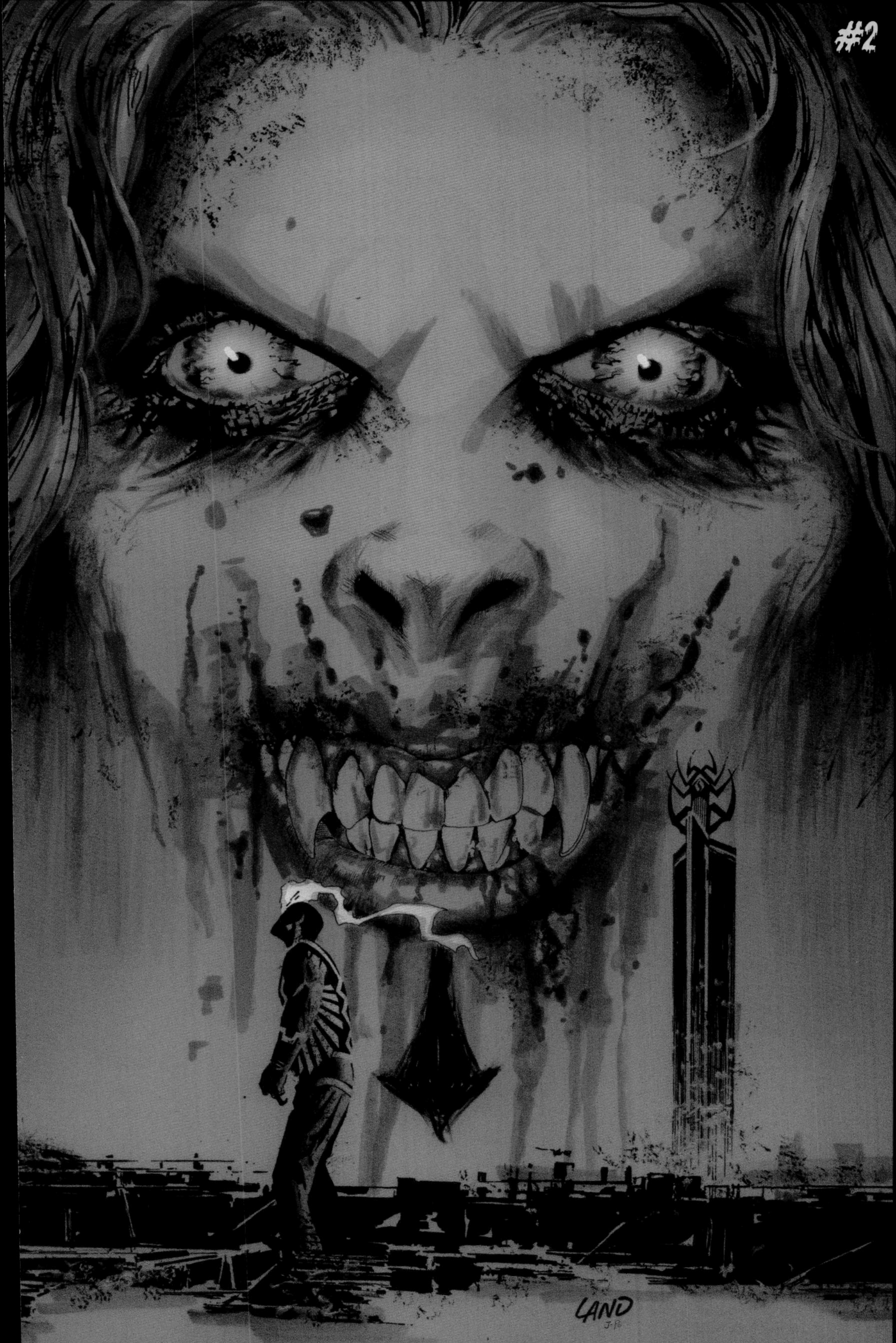
#2
LAND

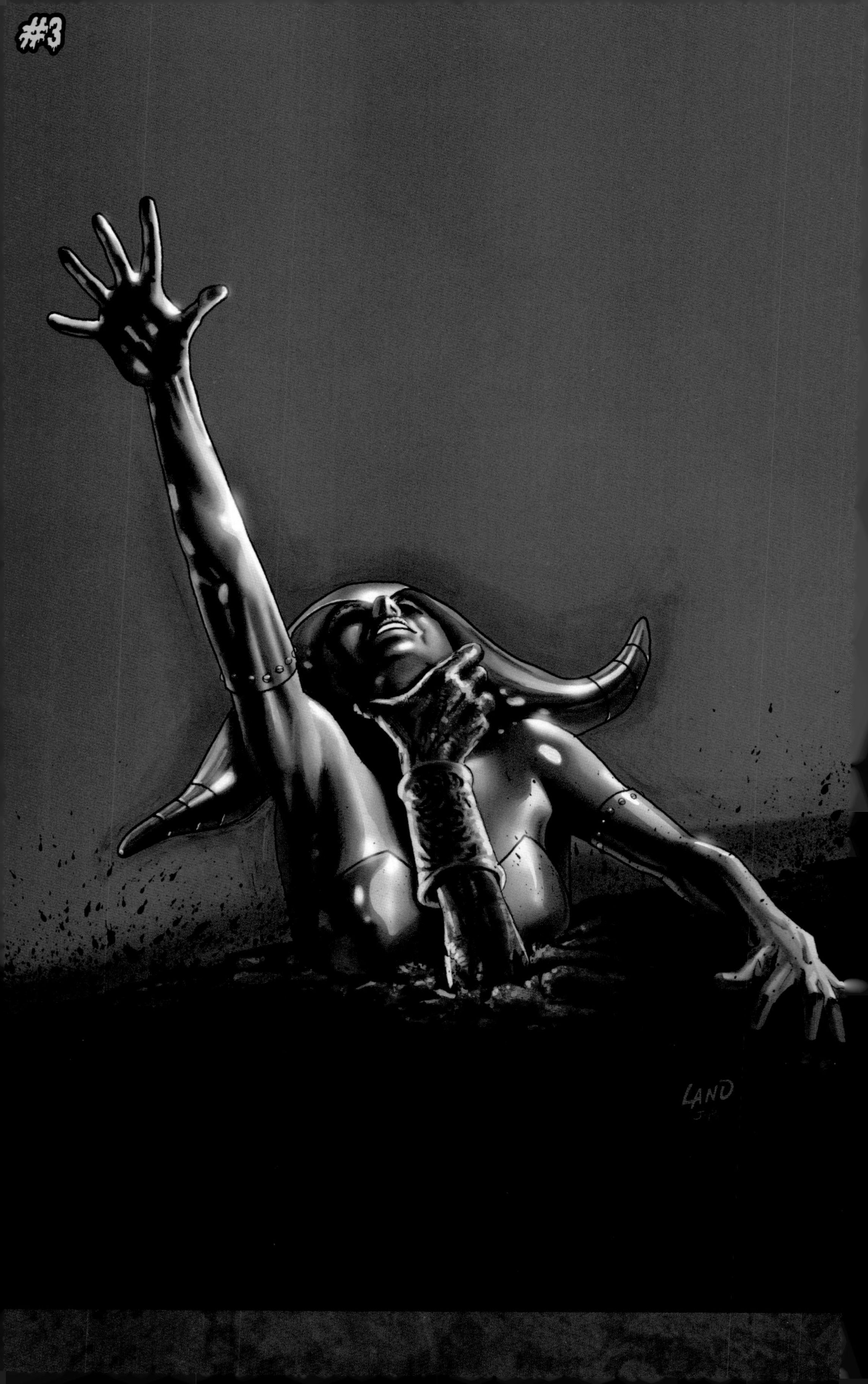
#3
LAND

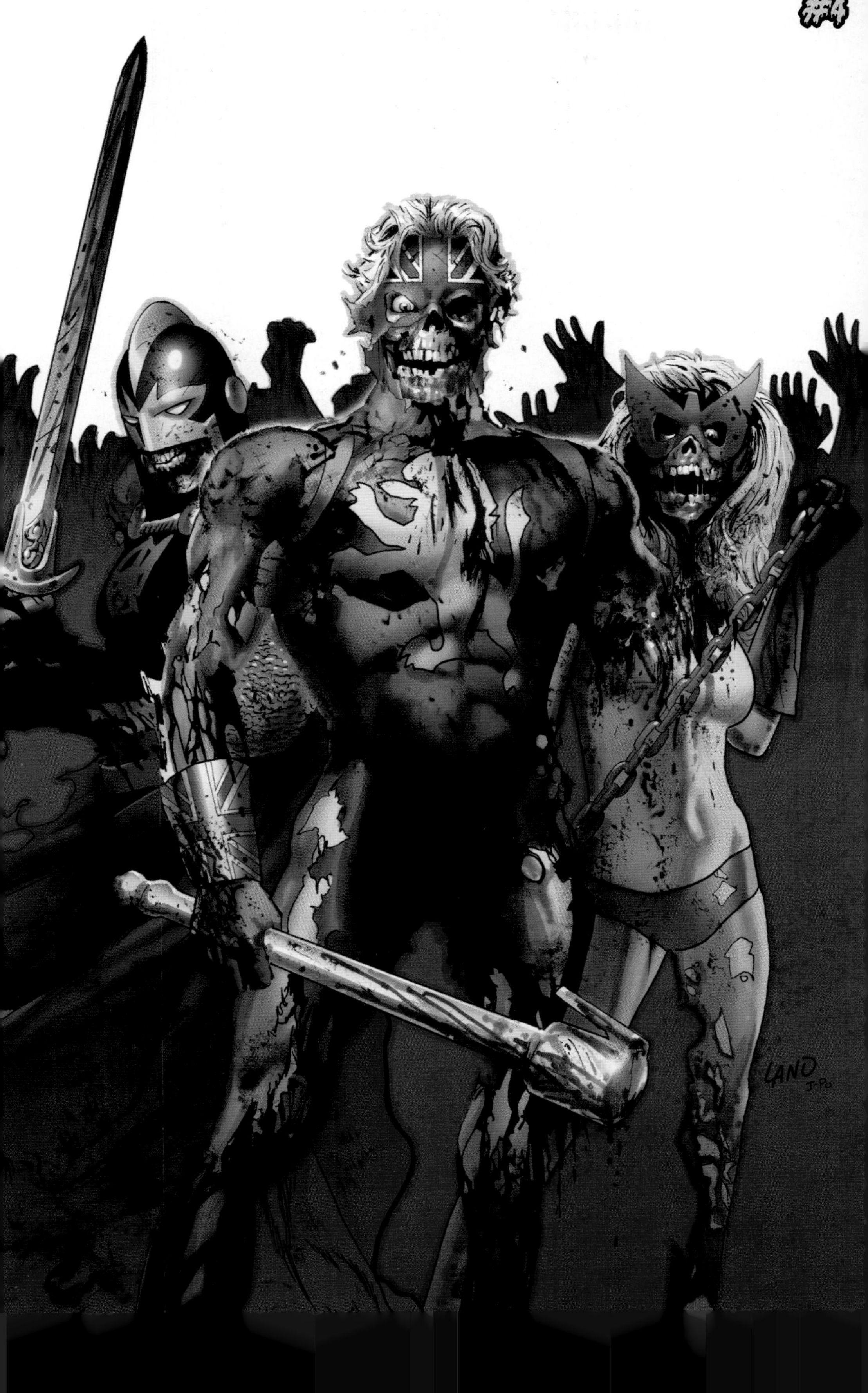
#4
LAND

AMAZING SPIDER-GIRL #25
ZOMBIE VARIANT BY SERGE LAPOINTE & MATT MILLA

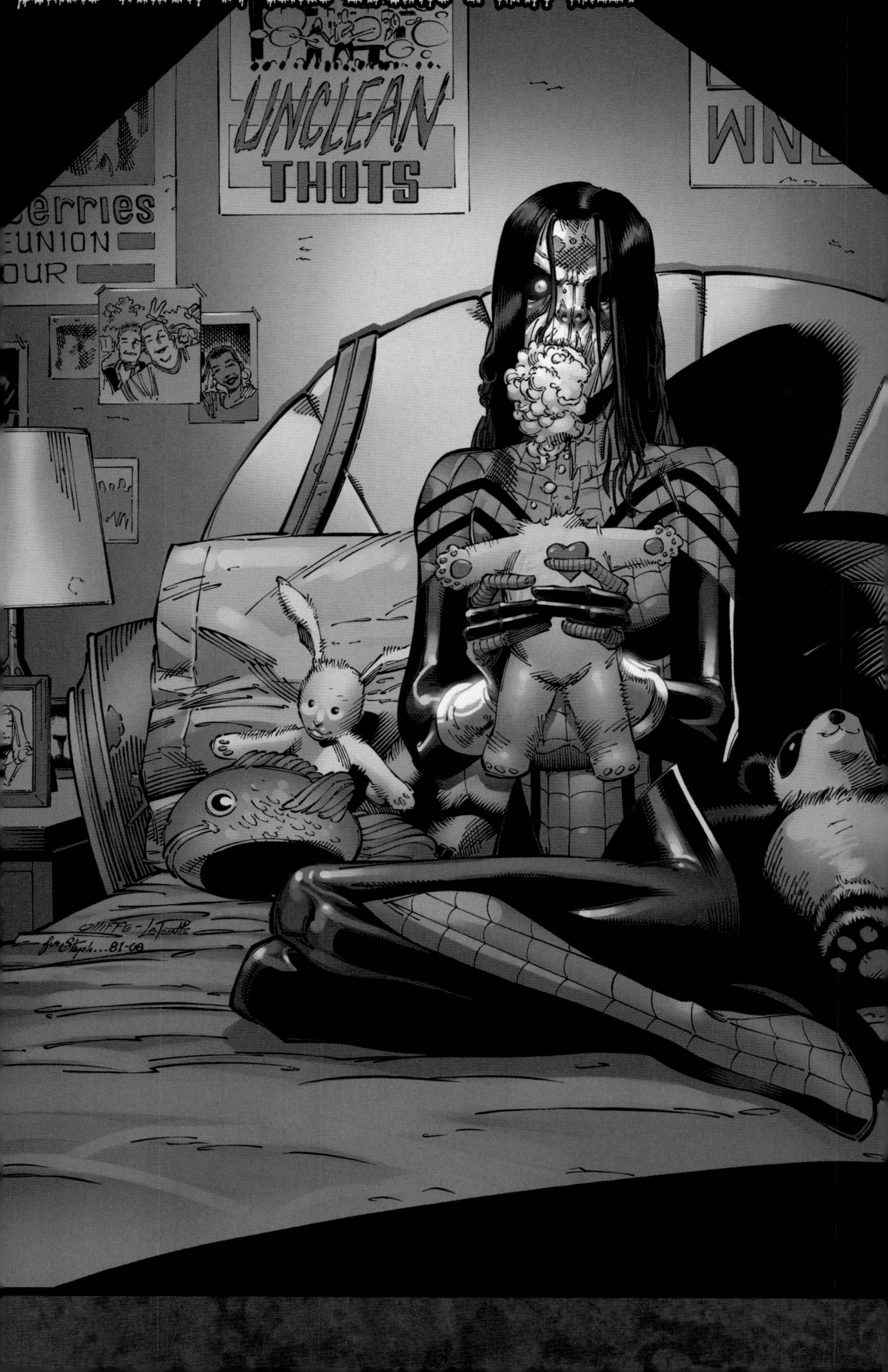
UNCLEAN
THOTS

AMAZING SPIDER-MAN #573 ZOMBIE VARIANT BY MARKO DJURDJEVIC

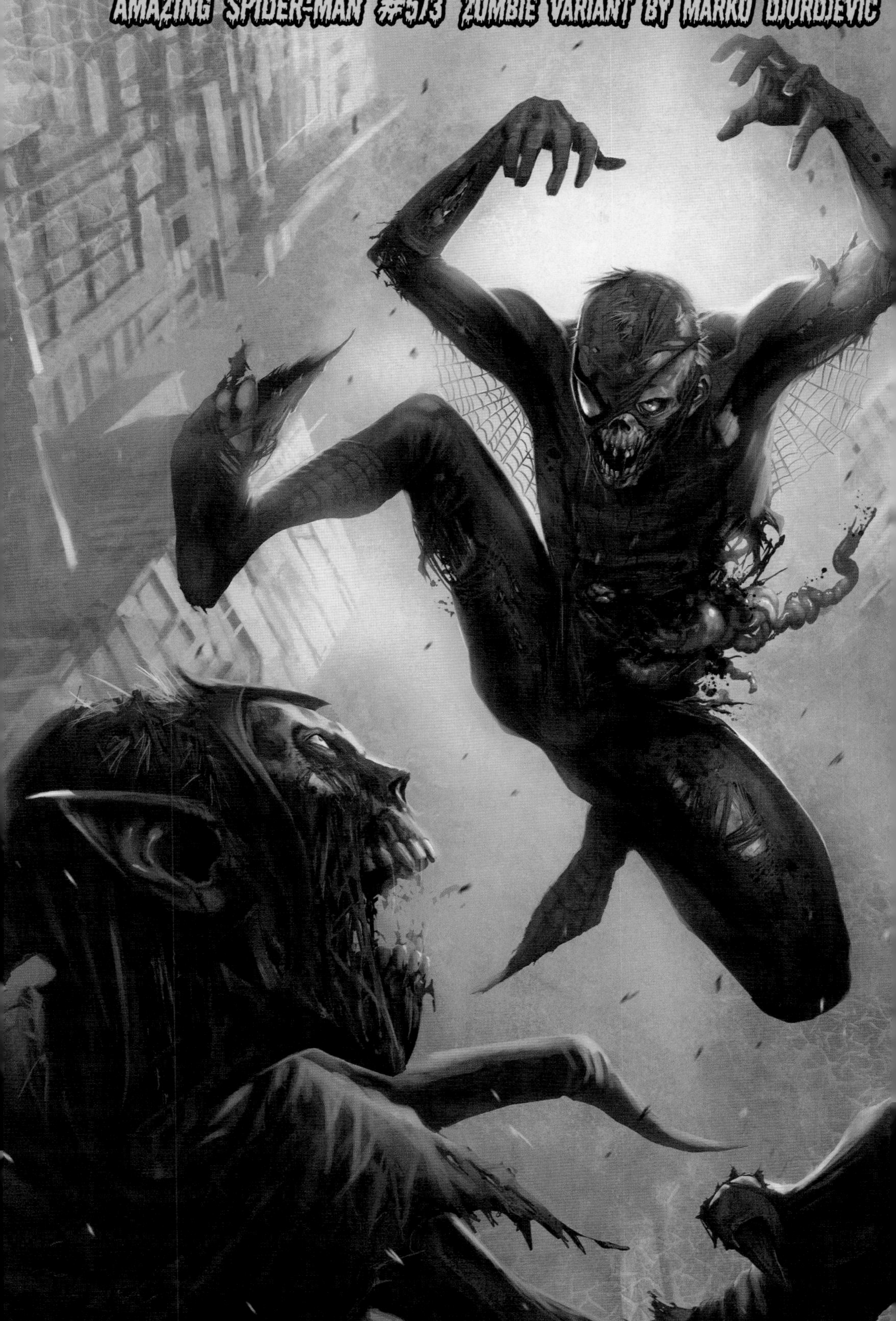

AVENGERS: THE INITIATIVE #18 ZOMBIE VARIANT BY JUAN DOE

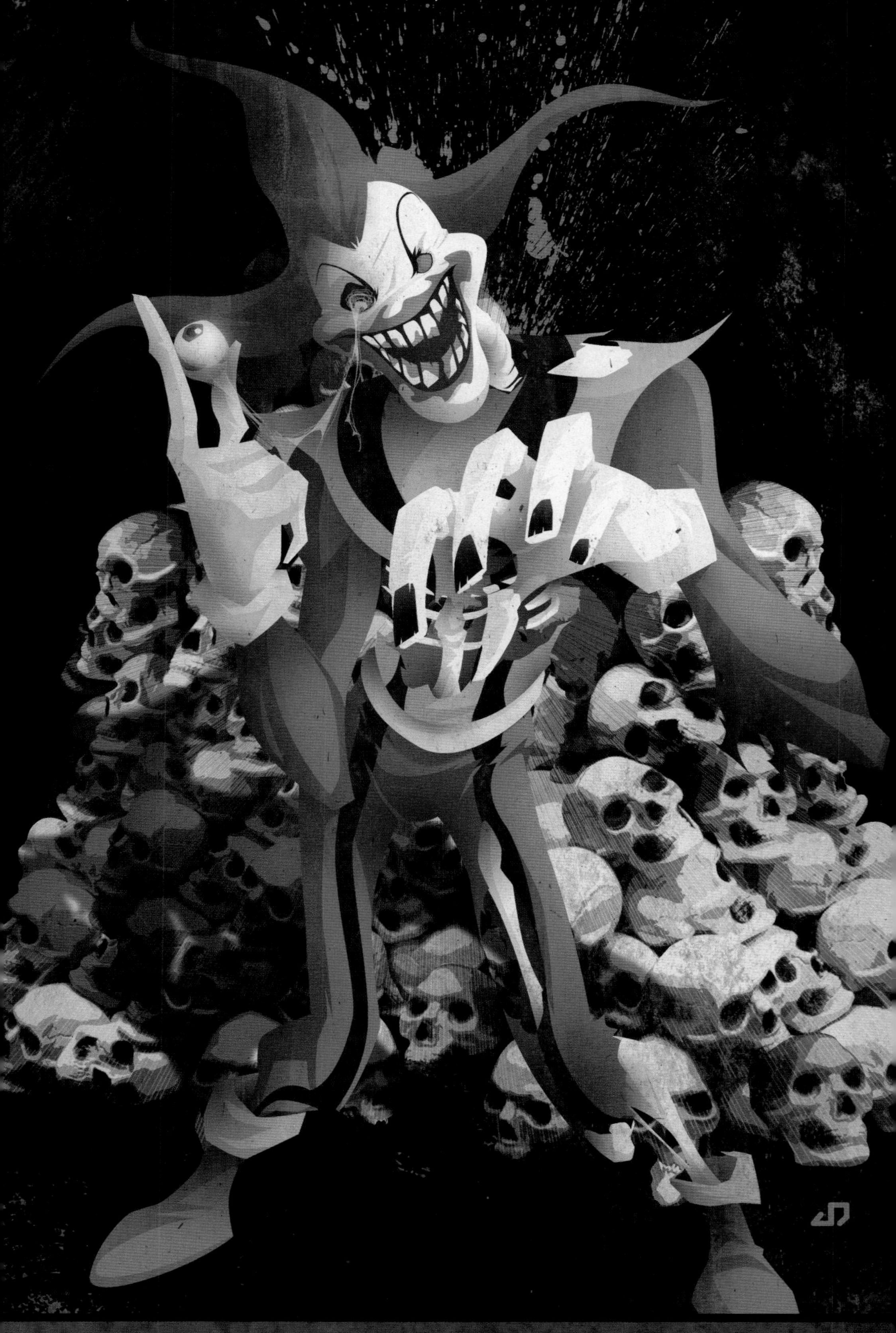

CABLE #7 ZOMBIE VARIANT BY RICHARD CORBEN & JOSE VILLARRUBIA

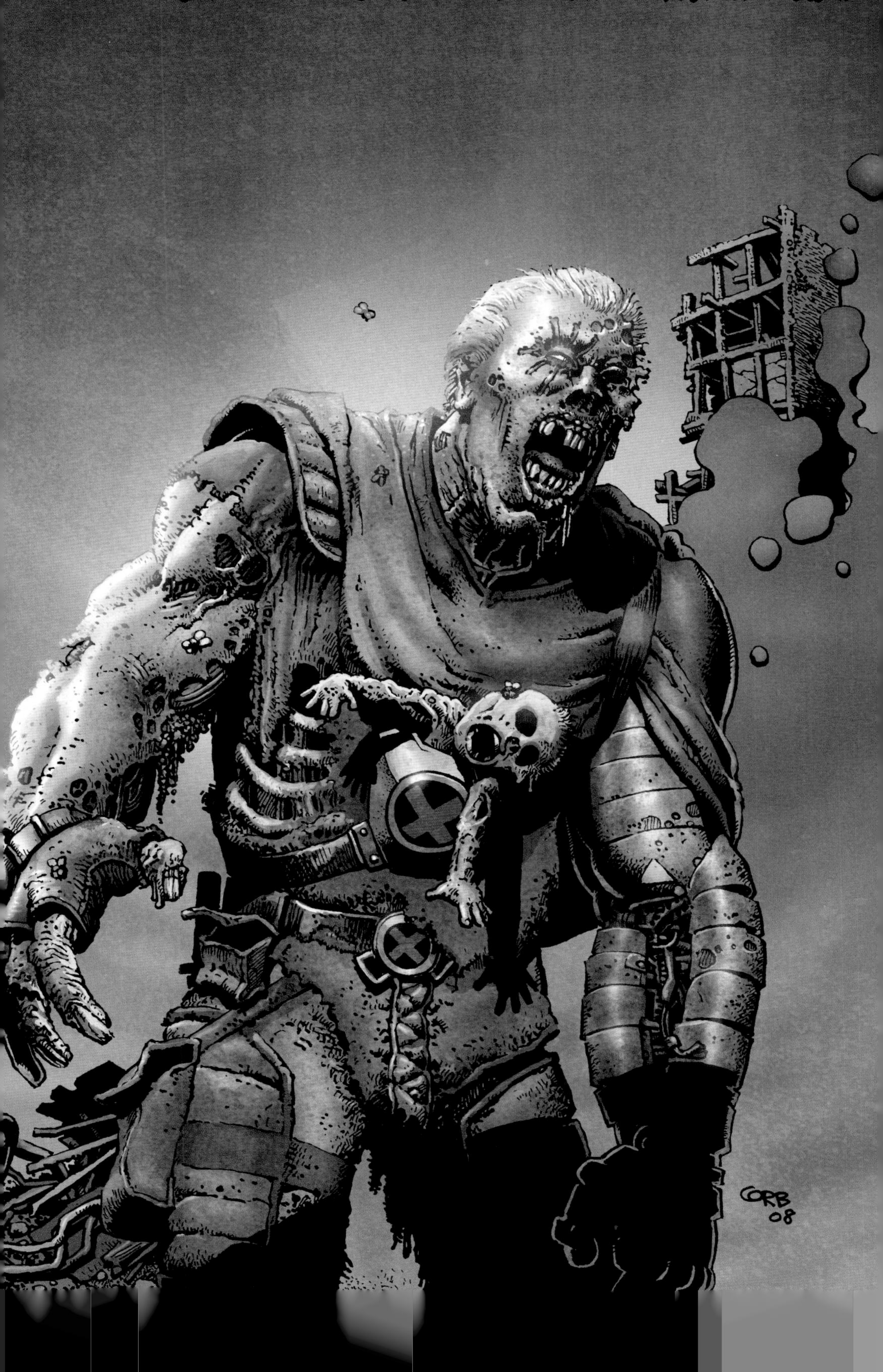
CORB
08

CAPTAIN BRITAIN AND MI:13 #6 BY DAVID YARDIN & MATT MILLA

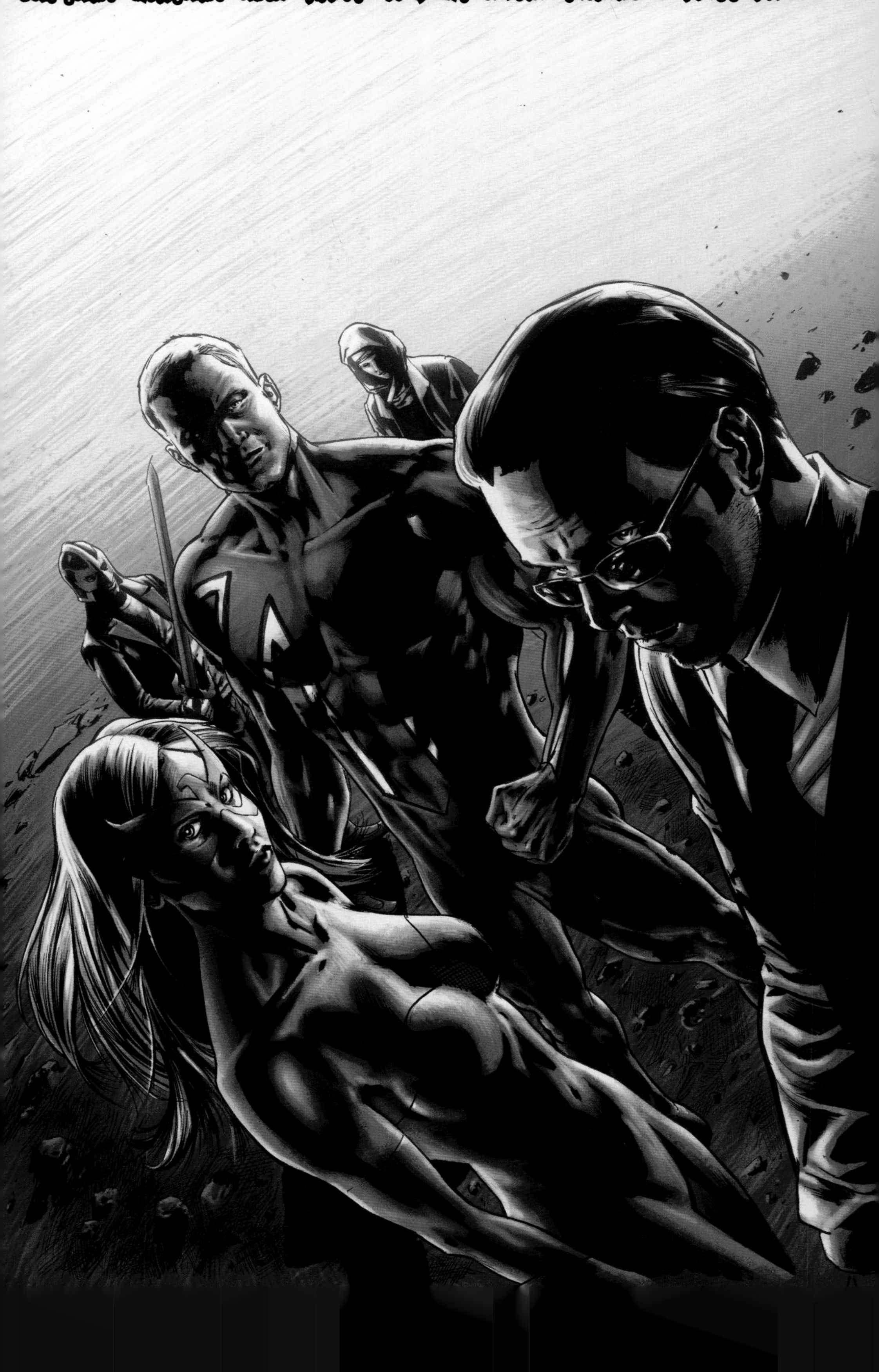

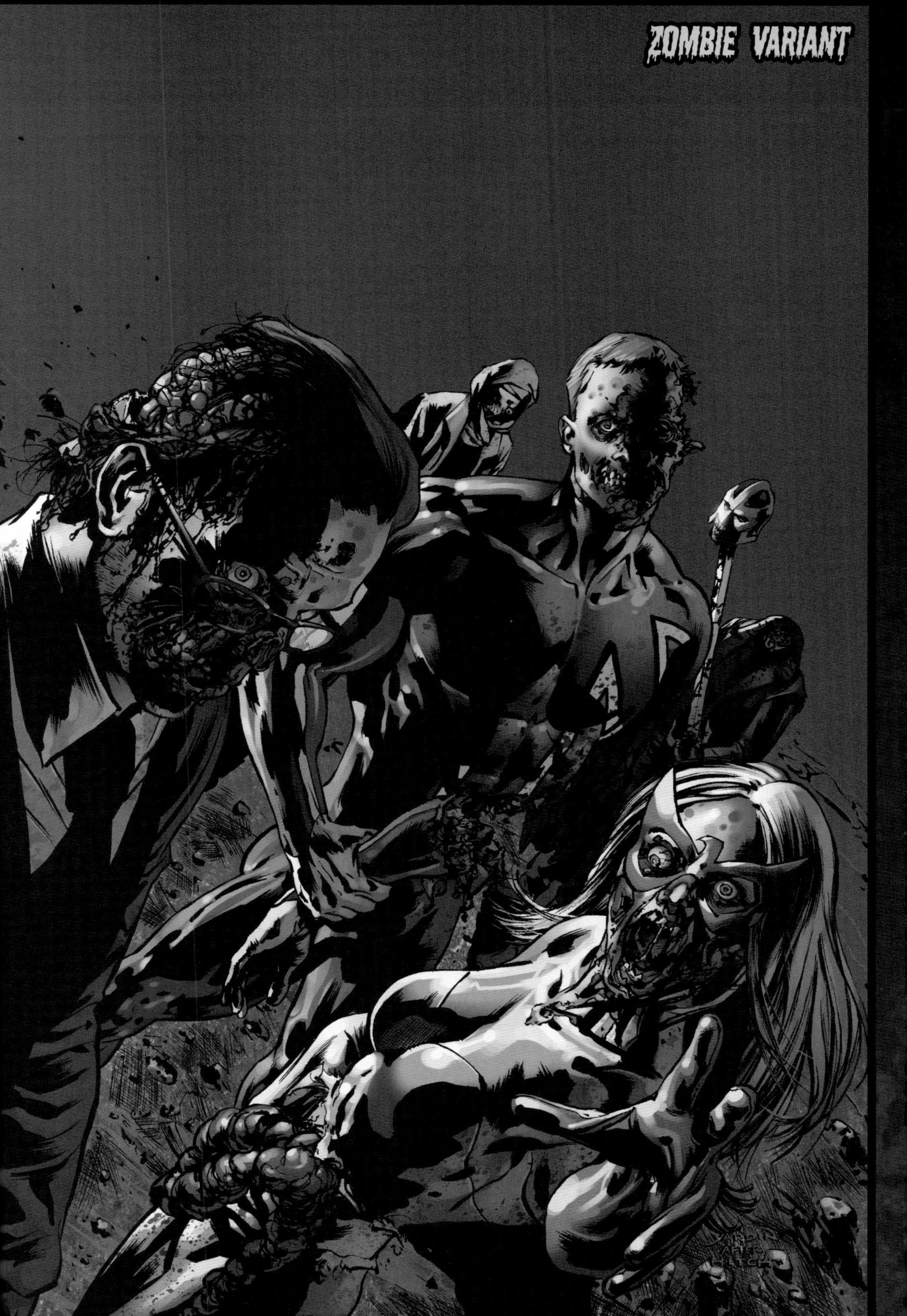
ZOMBIE VARIANT

DAREDEVIL #112 ZOMBIE VARIANT BY TRAVEL FOREMAN & MORRY HOLLOWEL

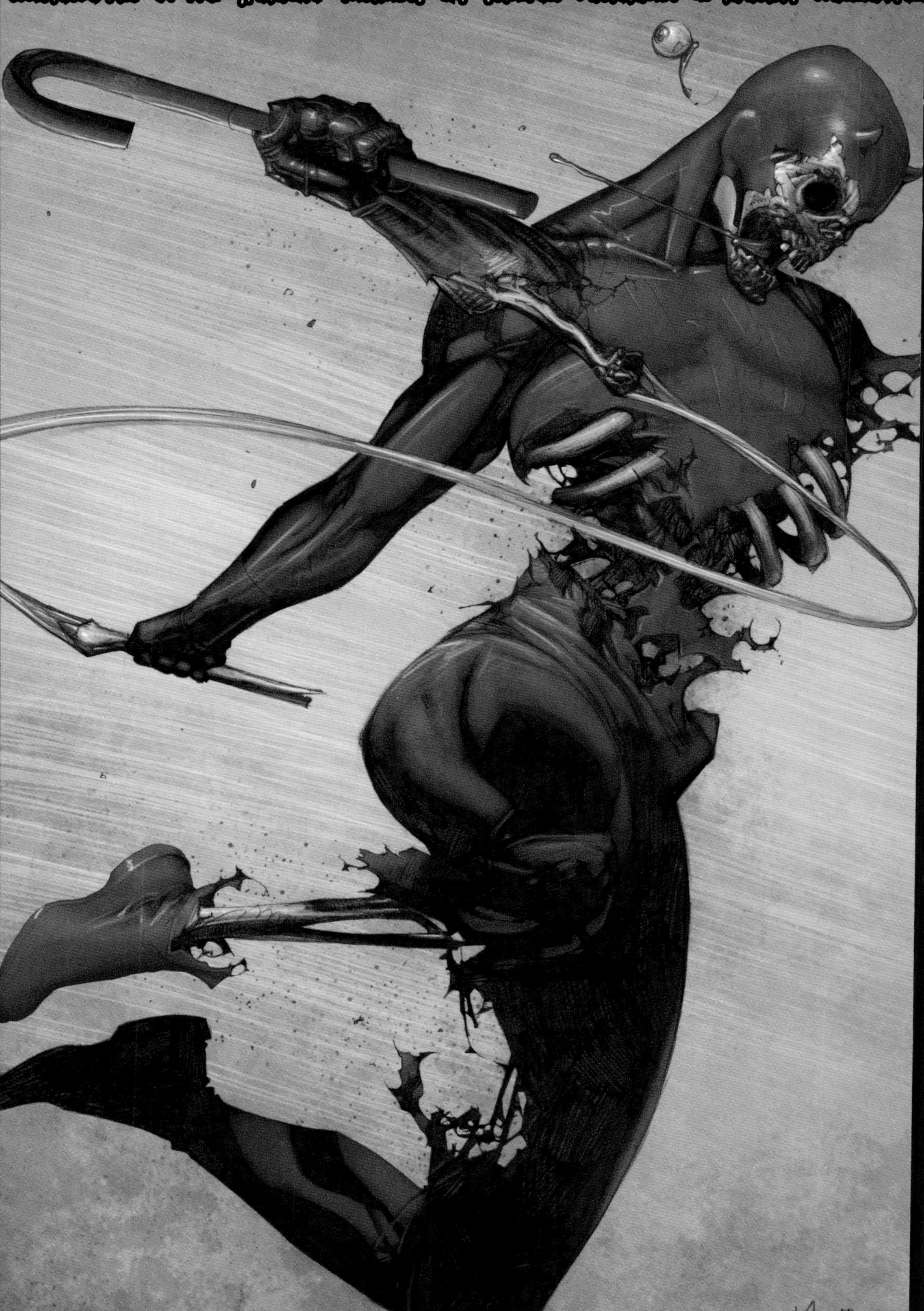

ETERNALS #5 ZOMBIE VARIANT BY ERIC NGUYEN

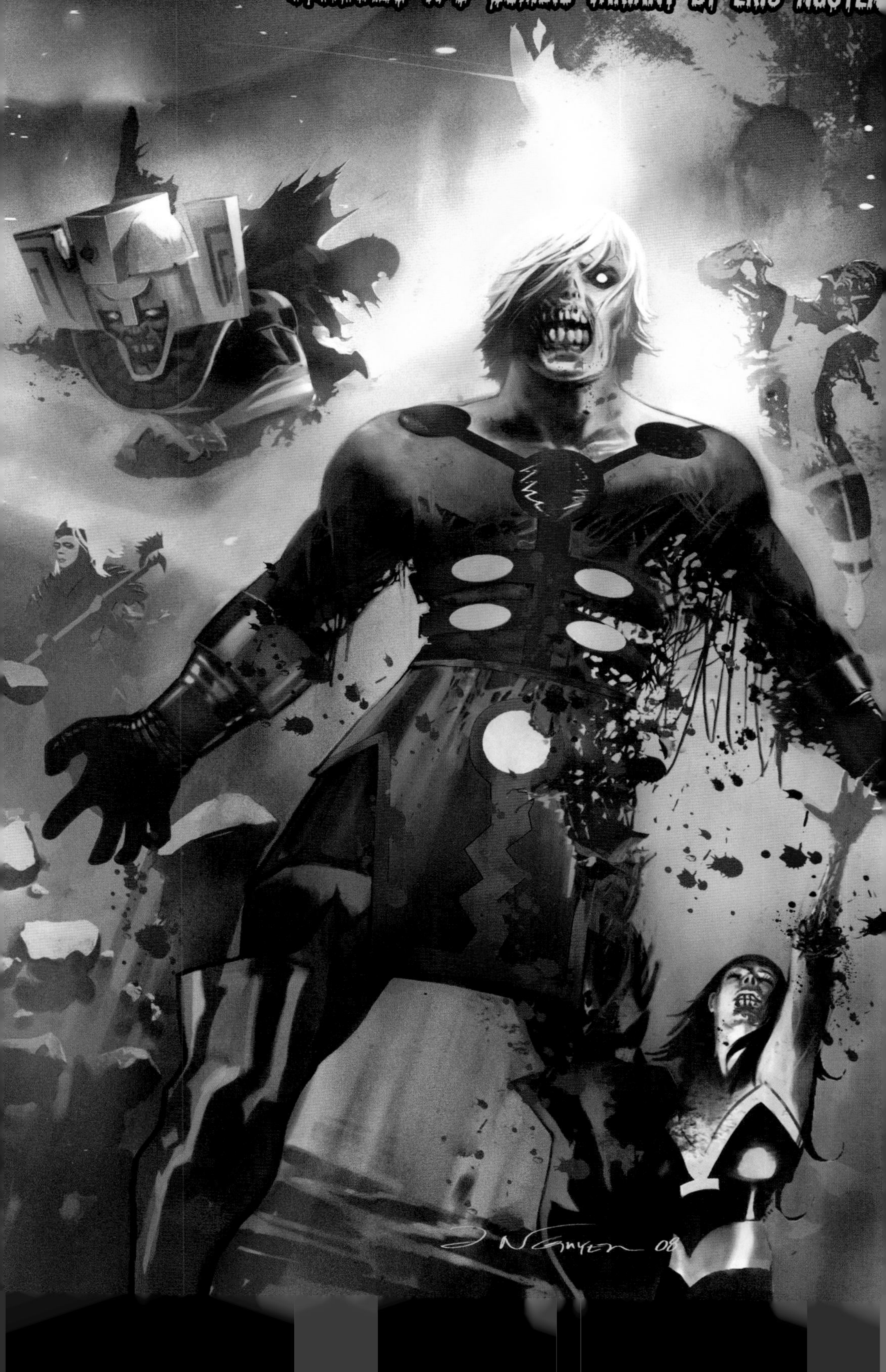

INCREDIBLE HERCULES #122 ZOMBIE VARIANT BY ARTHUR SUYDAM

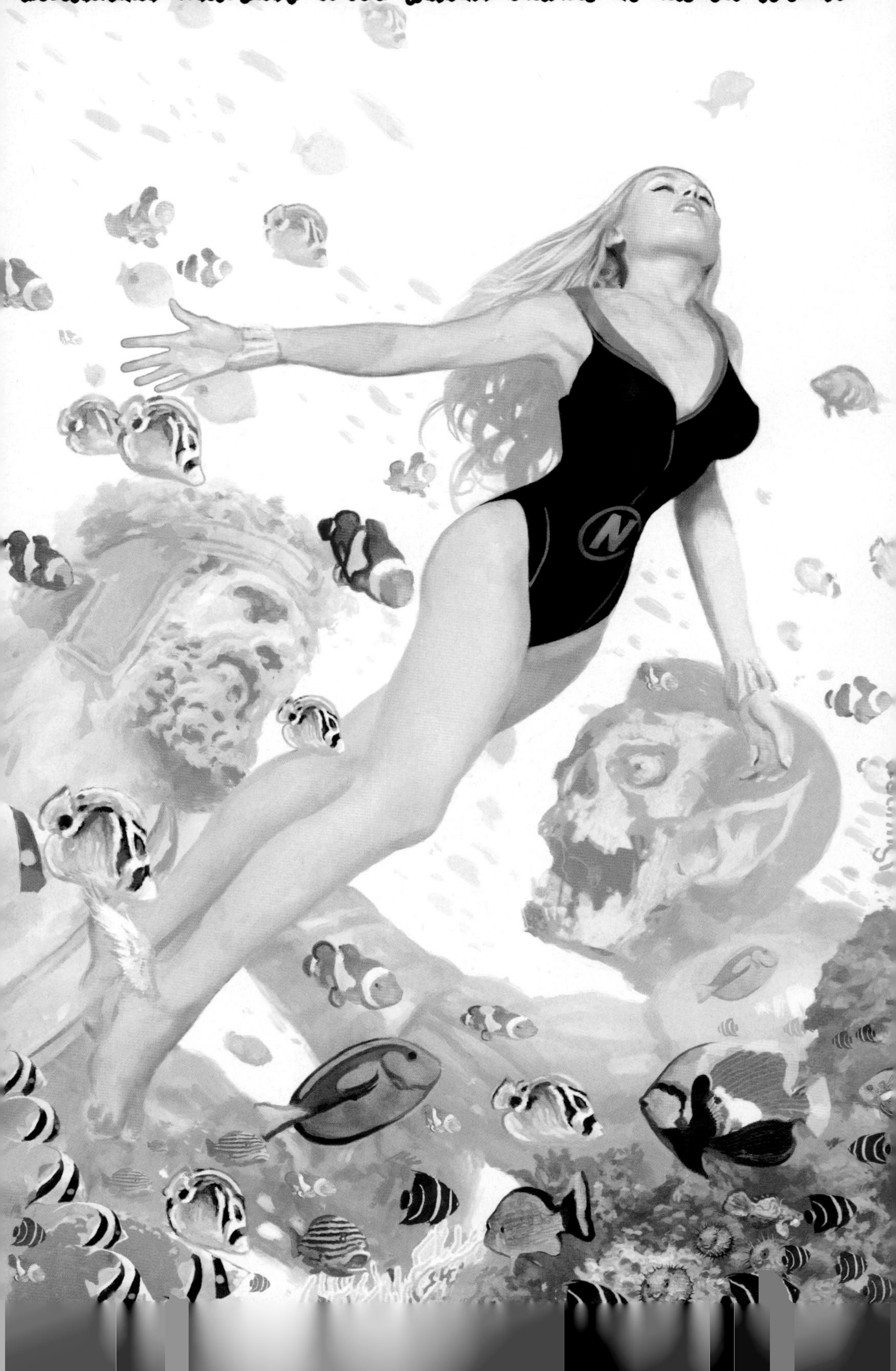

OVA #18 ZOMBIE VARIANT BY WELLINTON ALVES, SCOTT HANNA & GURU-EFX

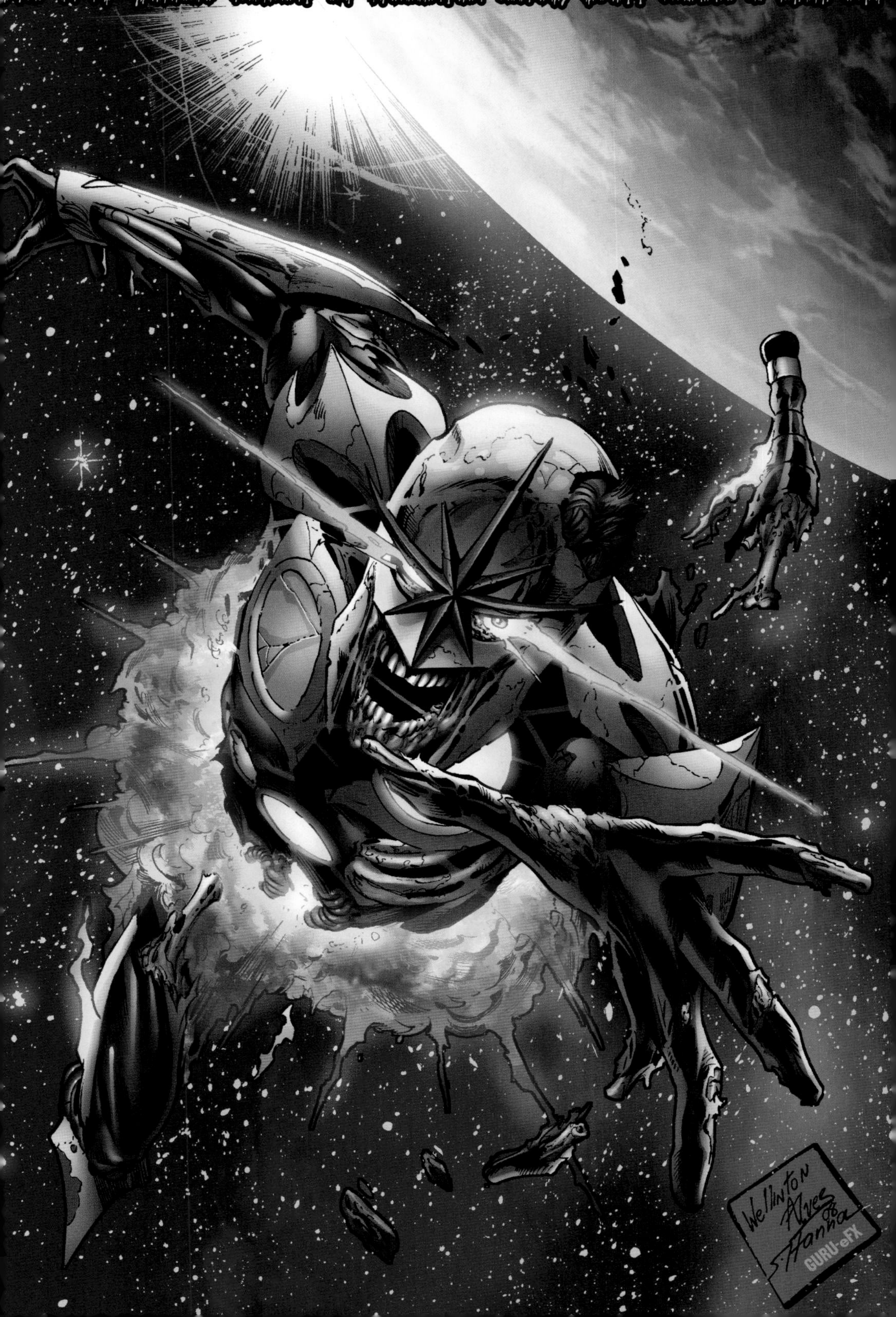
Wellinton Alves 08
S. Hanna
GURU-eFX

SKAAR: SON OF HULK #4
ZOMBIE VARIANT BY DAVID YARDIN & RAUL TREVINO

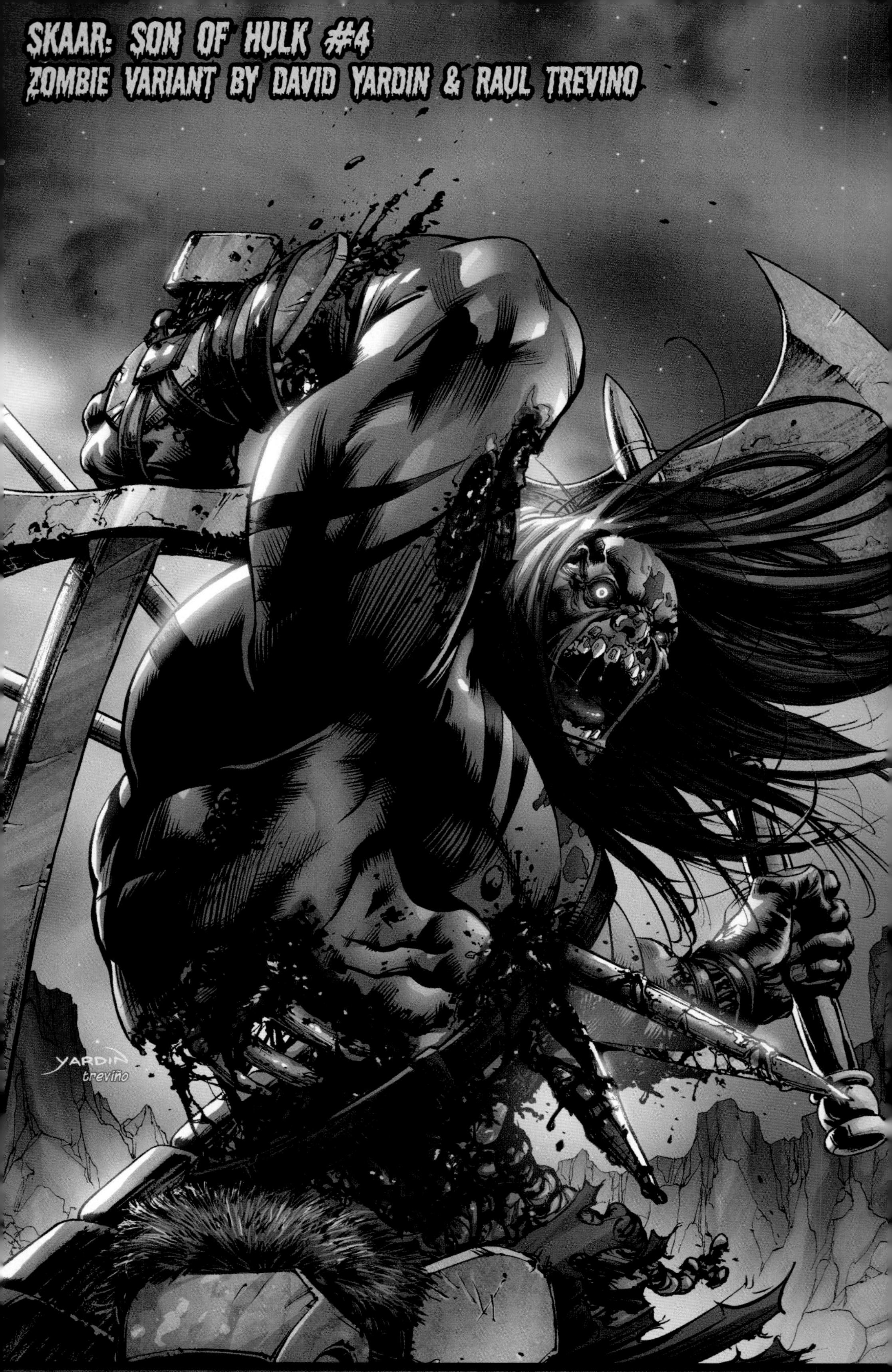
YARDIN
treviño

WOLVERINE: ORIGINS #29

ZOMBIE VARIANT BY MIKE DEODATO & MORRY HOLLOWELL

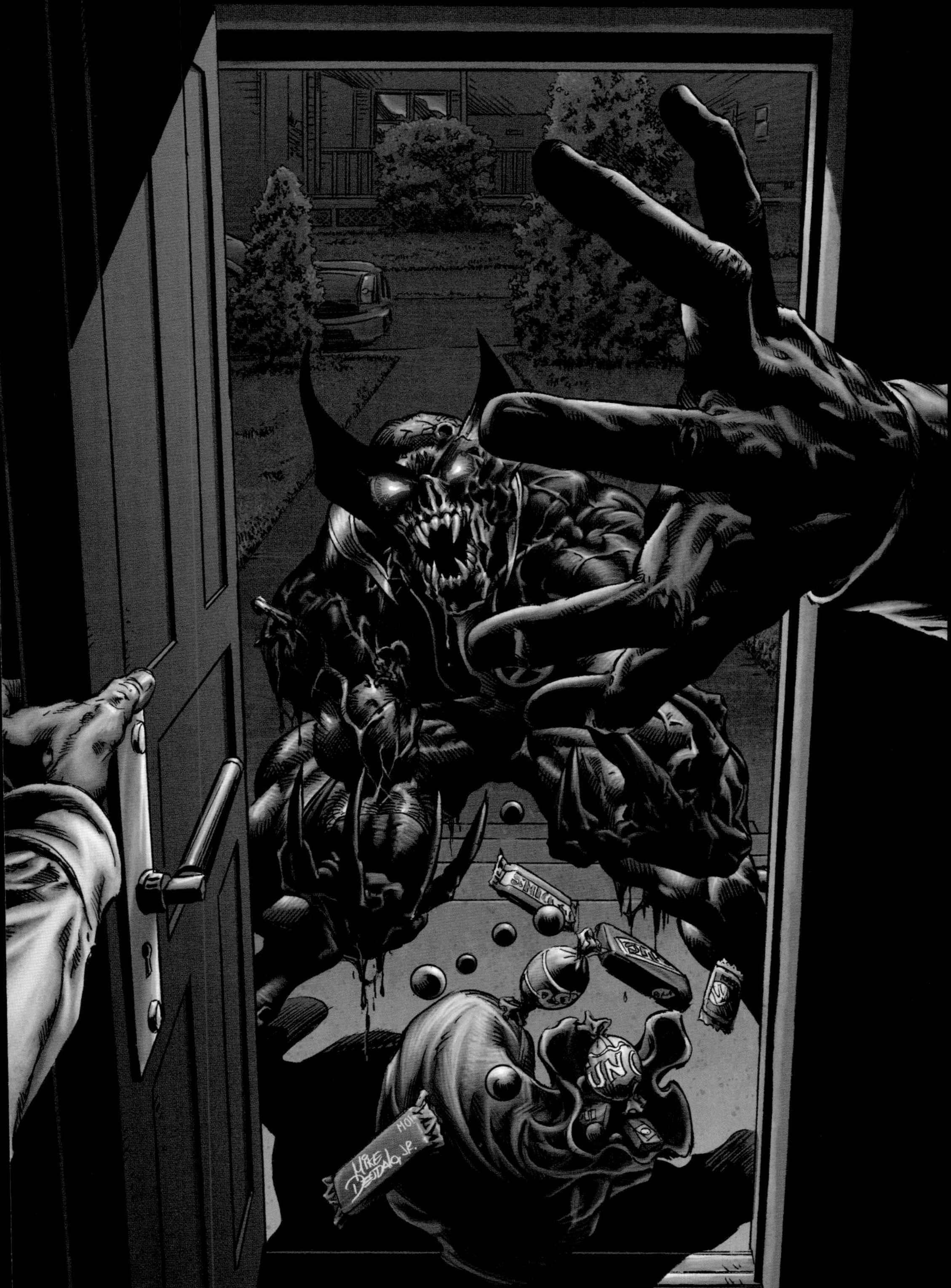

YOUNG X-MEN #7 ZOMBIE VARIANT BY DAVID YARDIN & VAL STAPLES

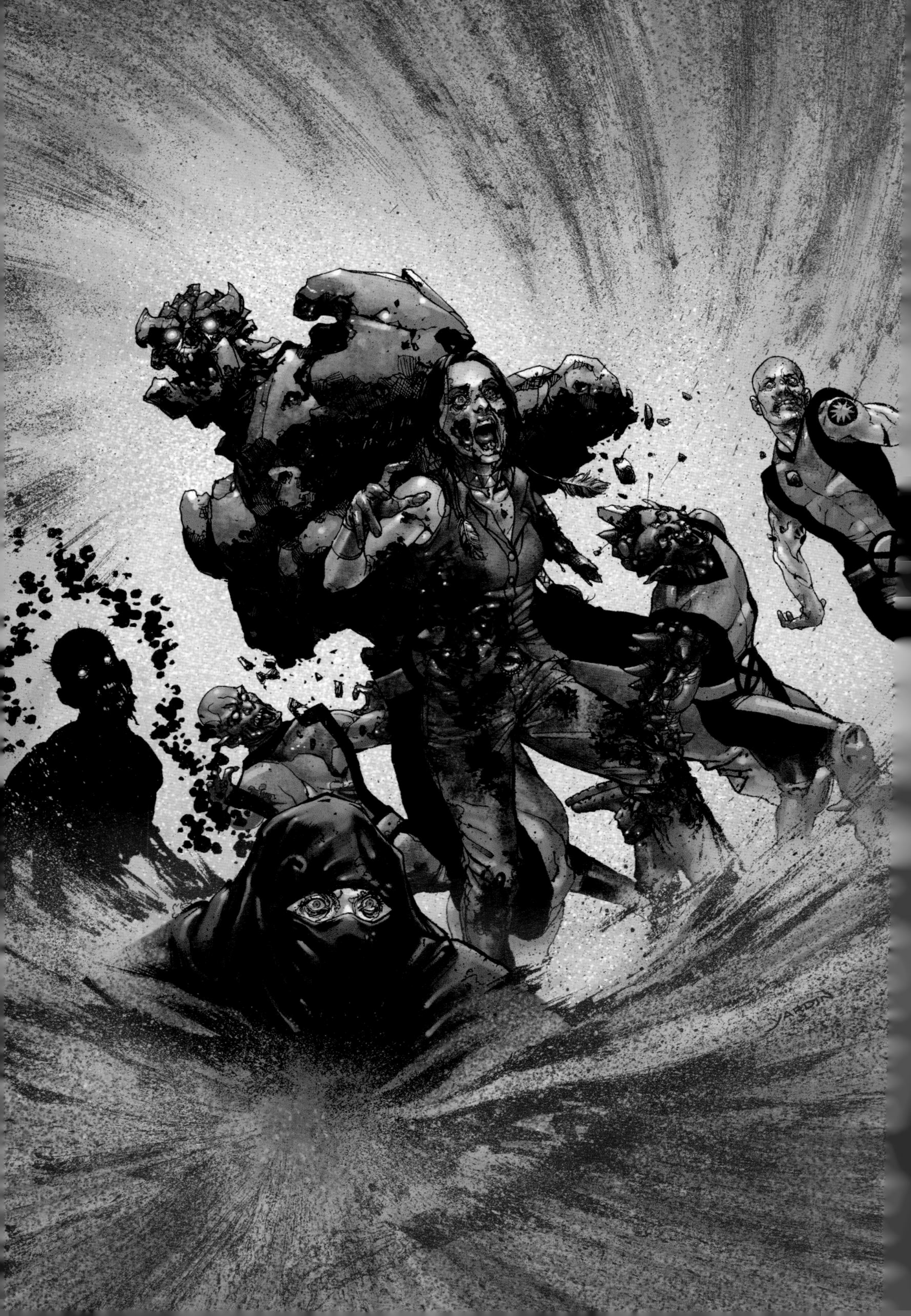
YARDIN

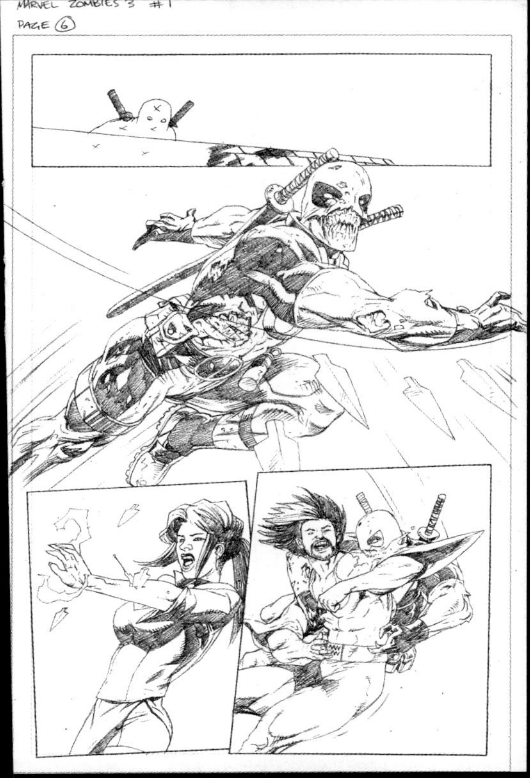
MARVEL ZOMBIES 3 #1
PAGE 6

MARVEL ZOMBIES 3 #1, PAGE 6

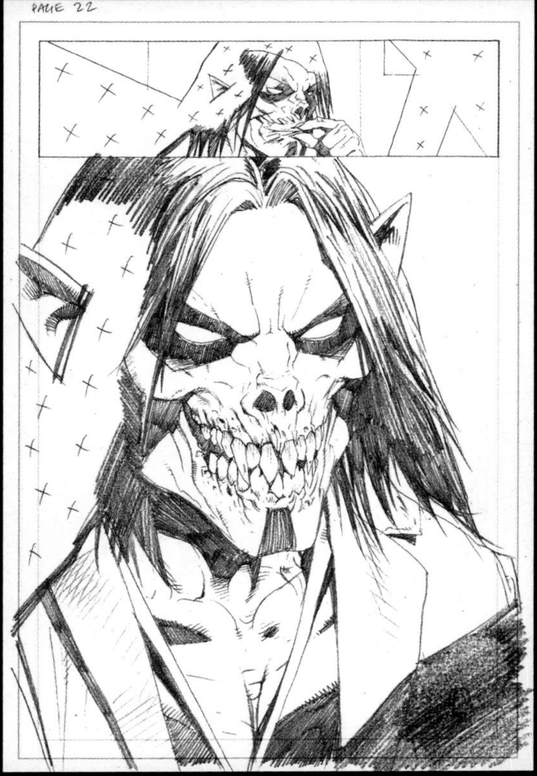
PAGE 22

MARVEL ZOMBIES 3 #1, PAGE 22

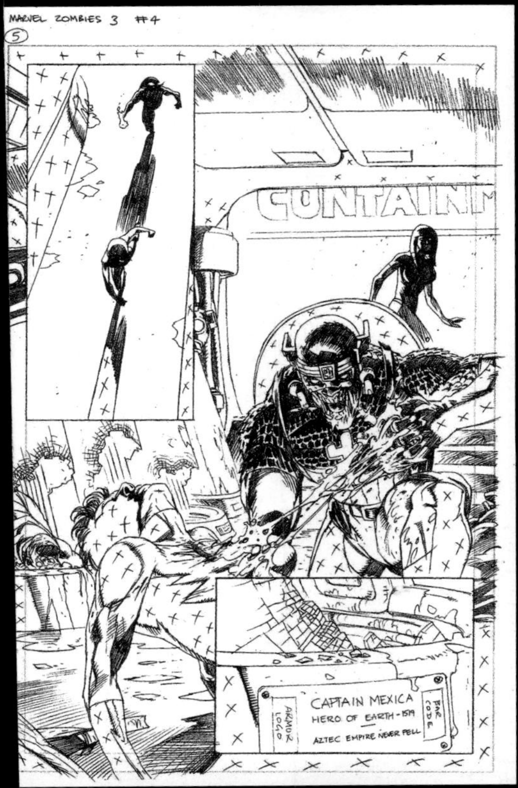
MARVEL ZOMBIES 3 #4
5
CONTAINM
CAPTAIN MEXICA
HERO OF EARTH-1519
AZTEC EMPIRE NEVER FELL
ARMOR LOGO

MARVEL ZOMBIES 3 #4, PAGE 5

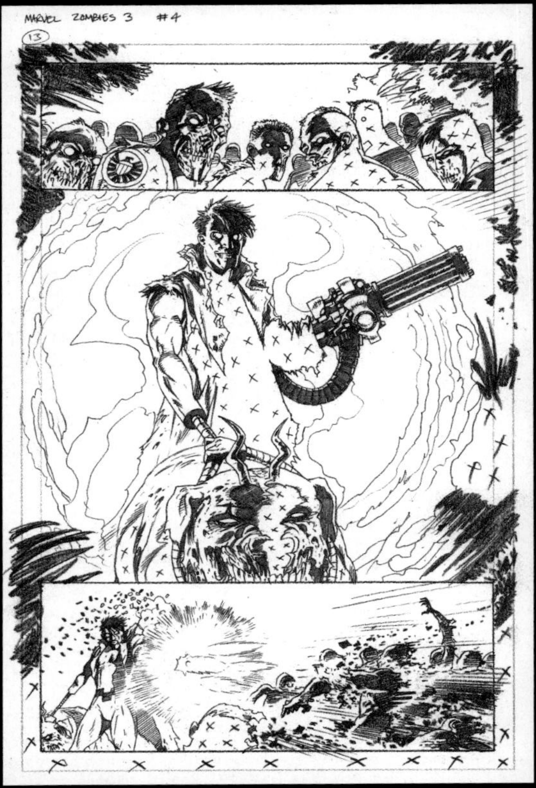
MARVEL ZOMBIES 3 #4
13

MARVEL ZOMBIES 3 #4, PAGE 13

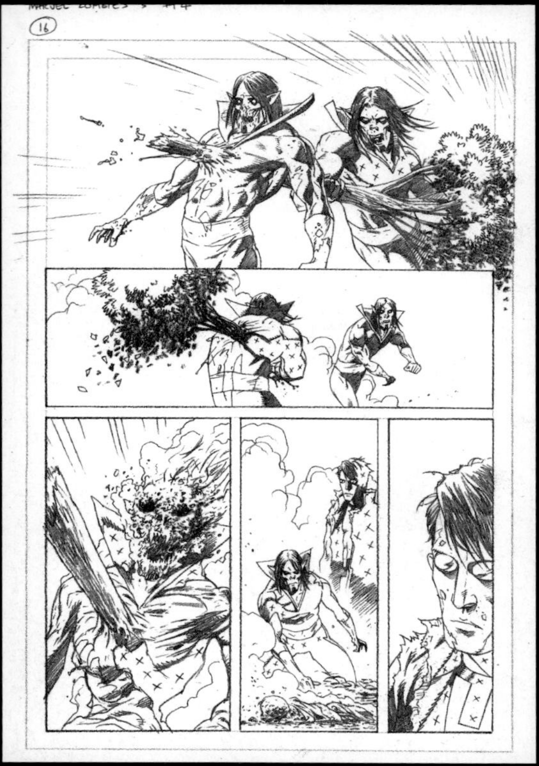
16

MARVEL ZOMBIES 3 #4, PAGE 16

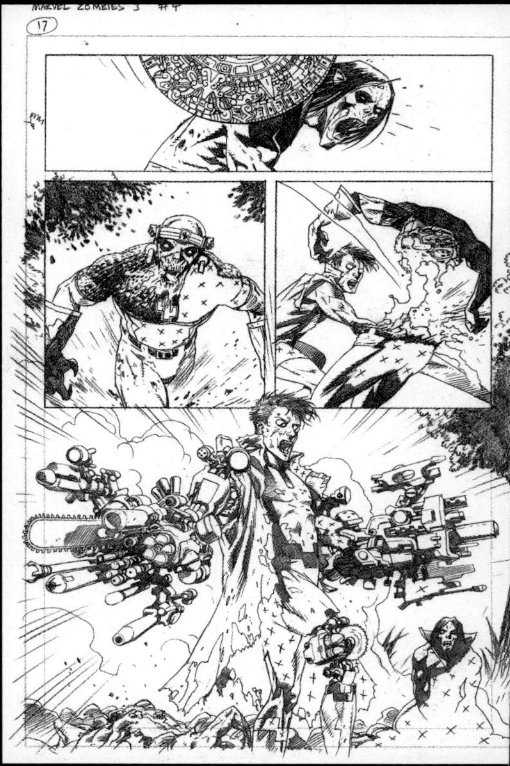
MARVEL ZOMBIES 3 #4
17

MARVEL ZOMBIES 3 #4, PAGE 17

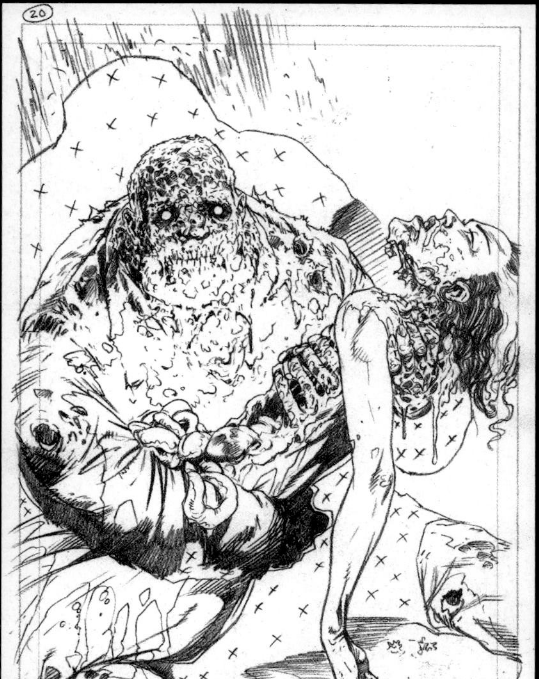
20

MARVEL ZOMBIES 3 #4, PAGE 20

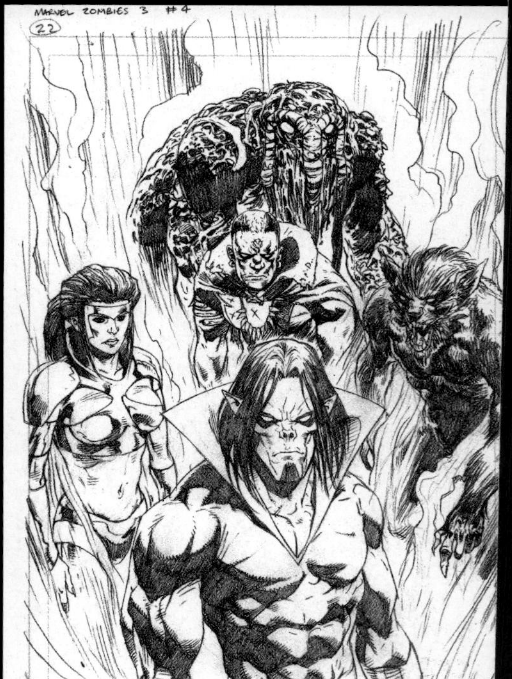
MARVEL ZOMBIES 3 #4
22

MARVEL ZOMBIES 3 #4, PAGE 22